Find a Job

Through

Social Networking

Use LinkedIn, Twitter, Facebook, Blogs, and More to Advance Your Career

Second Edition

Diane Crompton and Ellen Sautter

JIST *Works*
America's Career Publisher®

Find a Job Through Social Networking, Second Edition

© 2011 by Diane Crompton and Ellen Sautter

First edition was titled *Seven Days to Online Networking*.

Published by JIST Works, an imprint of JIST Publishing
7321 Shadeland Station, Suite 200
Indianapolis, IN 46256-3923
Phone: 800-648-JIST   Fax: 877-454-7839   E-mail: info@jist.com

Visit our Web site at **www.jist.com** for information on JIST, free job search information, tables of contents, sample pages, and ordering instructions for our many products!

Quantity discounts are available for JIST books. Please call our Sales Department at 800-648-5478 for a free catalog and more information.

Trade Product Manager: Lori Cates Hand
Development Editor: Michelle Tullier
Project Editor: Heather Stith
Interior Designer and Page Layout: Aleata Halbig
Cover Designer: Alan Evans
Proofreaders: Chuck Hutchinson, Jeanne Clark
Indexer: Jeanne Clark

Printed in the United States of America
15 14 13 12 11 10   9 8 7 6 5 4 3 2 1

Library of Congress Cataloging-in-Publication Data
Crompton, Diane, 1956-
Find a job through social networking : use LinkedIn, Twitter,
Facebook, blogs, and more to advance your career / Diane Crompton And
Ellen Sautter. -- 2nd ed.
    p. cm.
Includes index.
Rev. ed. of: Seven days to online networking : make connections to
advance your career and business quickly / Ellen Sautter and Diane
Crompton. 2008.
ISBN 978-1-59357-817-6 (alk. paper)
1. Business enterprises--Computer network resources. 2. Online social
networks. 3. Business networks. 4. Job hunting--Computer network
resources. I. Sautter, Ellen, 1943- Seven days to online networking.
II. Title.
HF54.56.S28 2011
650.140285'4678--dc22
                              2010036634

ISBN 978-1-59357-817-6

About This Book

If you want to land a new job or advance in your career, social networking should be a key element of your job search or career management strategy. When used for professional purposes, social networking is the process of using social media (Web-based tools) to connect with people and develop relationships in order to reach your career goals and help others reach their goals.

This hands-on, practical guide takes you from understanding what social networking is and why you should do it, to preparing you to work the virtual room, to actually using the various social media. You'll find all the information you need to jump-start your social networking quickly for your immediate goals and to keep it up for the long-term.

As career coaches and frequent speakers at conferences and networking events, we've witnessed firsthand the amazing benefits social networking can have. Whether through virtual communities such as LinkedIn or through Twitter, blogging, discussion groups, or other social media, people are getting interviews, learning about prospective employers, being found by recruiters, enhancing their personal brands, staying on top of developments in their fields, and, yes, landing jobs.

Whether you're a beginner with social networking or already in the thick of it and want to advance your skills, this book is for you. Social networking is a "must do" for effective career management in our global marketplace, and through this book we can guide you through the process. Now, let's get to work together!

—Ellen Sautter and Diane Crompton

Acknowledgments

We have so many people to thank for their support and assistance in the development of this book.

Our colleague and editorial consultant Michelle Tullier, a published author many times over, made the initial introduction for us to JIST and helped us tremendously with *Seven Days to Online Networking* in 2008. She once again encouraged us to write this second book and stood by us, devoting many hours outside of her busy role at Right Management to skillfully guide and support us through the process. Lori Cates Hand, Heather Stith, and Selena Dehne, our publishing friends at JIST, epitomize patience, enthusiasm, and collaboration. We thank them for this opportunity.

Walter Akana, our colleague, is an expert on personal branding and social media in general (Twitter in particular). Miriam Salpeter of Keppie Careers is, like Walter, an expert on Twitter, Facebook, and job search strategies. They helped tremendously with content, advice, and examples. Dan Greenfield, corporate communications and social media consultant, shared his up-to-date information on blogging, Twitter, and corporate social media strategies. Thanks also to Keith Warrick who embraced LinkedIn in a big way and continues to be an ambassador for social networking. We count Walter, Miriam, Dan, and Keith as great friends...and not just on Facebook!

We also graciously thank our clients at Right Management, from whom we learn so much, as well as the hundreds of recruiters, job seekers, business owners, career coaches, and others in our traditional and online networks in various locations around the world who shared experiences, responded to our surveys, and asked us questions that further stimulated our research. We value your friendship and insight: Alison Allen, Amanda S. Ambrose, Angie Amon, Rudy Augsburger, Michelle Barbeau, Katie Bonta, Debbie Brown, Dulin W. Clark, Lori Cleymans, Trudy Cox, Jane Edgar, Greg Hollod, Kate Hutchinson, Alice K. Jorgensen, Scott Kelly, Beth Benatti Kennedy, Elythia Lewis, Barbara Limmer, Mike Muzik, Ellen O. McCarty, Elaine Metzger, Connie Morris, Joy Nakfoor, Tom Oder, Camille C. Roberts, Sonja Robinson, Hamid Rouchdi, Bill Schwartz, Sherri Segari, Vicki Sherry, Ed Springer, George Stecyk, Bill Temple, Judy Tipton, Tania-Rene Valdespino, Tracey Ward, Thomas Wiesneth, Ruth Winden, Mark Winn, and Tonja Zeigler.

We owe our appreciation as well to the many networking groups and industry associations that have invited us to present on this topic, giving us access to hundreds of individuals who shared their experiences with us.

We want to give a special "shout out" to subject-matter experts and busy professionals who shared their time and expertise to provide thoughtful input: Bert DuMars, vice president of e-business and interactive marketing, Newell Rubbermaid; Geoff Peterson, recruiting leader and sourcing consultant; Jenny Blake, blogger for "Life After College"; and Carrie Davis, director of staffing for ADP Canada.

We also wish to express appreciation to our global community of colleagues at Right Management. In particular, our "family" in the Atlanta office has been a pillar of strength and support.

Finally, we thank our family and friends, who encouraged us, read drafts, and endured many conversations on our topic. Mark Crompton was a patient, behind-the-scenes supporter as Diane conducted research, interviewed people, and read blog posts. Carl Sautter tapped into his knowledge and network of Facebook friends to contribute valuable data. And Carol Sautter Williams devoted many hours to helping us with outreach, research, editing, and anything else that was needed.

Contents

Introduction xii

Chapter 1 Connecting Social Networking to Your Career Goals 1

What Is Social Networking? 2

    The Strategy That Never Sleeps 2

    Relationship Development 3

Do I Really Have Time to Network with Millions of People (and Should I Even Want To?) 3

    Much More Than Your 15 Minutes of Fame 5

    Everybody Wins 6

Where in the Virtual World Will You Network? 9

    1. Social Networks 10

    2. Blogs 11

    3. Microblogs 12

    4. Identity-Management Sites 14

    5. Discussion Groups 15

    6. Online Publishing 16

    7. Online Public Speaking 17

Key Points: Chapter 1 18

Chapter 2 Understanding the Benefits of Social Networking 19

Why Job Seekers Must Get Online (and We Don't Just Mean Posting Your Resume on Monster!) 20

    Get Information and Advice 21

    Identify Potential Employers to Target 21

    Find Specific People Within Your Targeted Organizations 21

    Be More Visible to Recruiters and Employers 22

    Feel Supported Through the Ups and Downs 25

How Salespeople, Entrepreneurs, Freelancers, and Other Professionals Can Benefit from Social Networking 25

    Attracting Customers or Clients 26

    Identifying Partners for Collaboration 27

    Generating Referrals 28

    Identifying Targets 28

    Staying Current with Trends 28

    Selling Strategically 29

    Finding Money! 29

Why Everyone with a Career Needs to Network Online 30

Make Better Career Decisions 32

See What's Out There 32

Position Yourself for Raises and Promotions 33

Attract Opportunities Like a Magnet...33

Enhance and Share Your Knowledge Base 33

Key Points: Chapter 2 34

Chapter 3   Standing Out in the Cyberspace Crowd.....................................35

Your Online Identity: What It Is and Why You Need One.....................................36

If There's No Evidence of You Online, Do You Exist?...37

What If Too Many People with Your Name Exist Online? 37

Following Your Digital Footprints 38

Go Google Yourself 38

Assess Your Online Appearance 39

Cleaning Up Your Digital Dirt..40

What Digital Dirt Is 40

How to Clean Up Your Digital Dirt 41

Defining and Conveying Your Personal Brand Through Your Online Identity 43

Tout the Benefits, Not the Features...45

Be Clear and Concise 45

Be Unique...46

Show Your Personality 47

Be Consistent and Persistent 48

Developing a Self-Marketing Sound Bite 48

Putting Yourself on the Map...49

Pitching Your Strengths 49

Backing Up Your Claims 51

Stating What You Want 53

Creating a Sound Bite When You're Searching for a Job.....................................54

Creating Sound Bites When You're Not Actively Job Searching 55

Identifying Your Social Networking Goals 57

Finding a Job 58

Managing Your Career 60

*Enhancing Your Work as a Marketer, Salesperson, Entrepreneur, or
Business Developer*...62

Developing a Full-Service Network...64

Key Points: Chapter 3 66

Chapter 4 Harnessing the Power of Social Networks..**67**

The Language of Social Networks..67

What Are Social Networks?...68

The Benefits of Social Networks 69

How Social Network Sites Work 71

The Ever-Changing Landscape of Social Networks 72

XING *73*

Ecademy..*74*

Ryze *74*

Viadeo...*74*

Social Network Protocol...75

Do *75*

Don't...*76*

The Future of Social Networking 76

Key Points: Chapter 4 78

Chapter 5 Leveraging LinkedIn's Power **79**

Who's Networking on LinkedIn? 79

Join LinkedIn..81

Develop Your Profile 83

Enhancing the Basic Information *84*

Highlighting Your Skills in the Summary and Specialties Sections *86*

Adding Your Experience and Education *86*

Providing Additional Information..*87*

Completing Your Profile *88*

Changing Your Profile and Privacy Settings *90*

Grow Your Network 92

Customizing Invitations..*94*

Choosing an Approach to Growing Your Network: Quality Versus Quantity *97*

Give and Get Recommendations...99

Search for Jobs...103

Research Companies 106

Search for Contacts 108

Connect with Others 111

Join Groups 114

Ask and Answer Questions..117

Tell What You're Working On (Network Activity Update)..................................120

Use Applications...121

Make LinkedIn a Key Part of Your Networking Strategy 124

Key Points: Chapter 5 125

Chapter 6 Using Facebook for Professional Purposes 127

Who's on Facebook? 128

The Facebook Dilemma: Business or Personal? 129

Sticking with Strictly Personal Networking 130

Using Facebook for Professional Networking Only 130

Walking the Fine Personal-Professional Line 131

Joining Facebook 133

Creating a Professional Profile 134

Understanding Privacy and Facebook 138

Building Your Network of "Friends" 139

Searching for Friends 140

Contacting Friends 142

Communicating with Your Network 143

Searching for Jobs...145

Joining Groups 145

Using Career-Focused Applications 146

Making Facebook a Key Part of Your Networking Strategy 147

Key Points: Chapter 6 149

Chapter 7 Building a Following with Microblogging and Twitter 151

What Is Twitter?..152

Benefits of Twitter 153

Your Kind of "Tweeps" 154

Get Started..155

Set Your Objectives..155

Develop Your Profile 157

Go Tweet! 159

Learn the Art of the Tweet 160

Pay It Forward with Retweeting...163

Search for People and Information in the Twitterverse...............................164

Follow and Be Followed 166

Develop a Following...168

Understand the Value of Lists 170

Use Advanced Twitter Features and Applications 171

Make Twitter a Key Part of Your Networking Strategy 174

Key Points: Chapter 7 174

Chapter 8 Building Your Brand in the Blogosphere 175

The Basics of Blogging 175

Blogs Are Dynamic 176

Blogs Are Interactive 176

Blogs Can Be Beneficial 177

The Language of Blogging Defined 178

Deciding Whether to Blog or Just Comment 181

The Writing Factor 182

The Passion Factor 182

The Time Factor 183

The You Factor 183

Commenting on OPBs (Other People's Blogs) 183

Step 1: Scope Out the Blogging Landscape 184

Step 2: Write a Comment 185

Step 3: Submit Your Comment 185

Starting Your Own Blog 188

Step 1: Get to Know Your Blog "Neighbors" 188

Step 2: Choose a Name 189

Step 3: Choose a Blog Platform 190

Step 4: Register a Domain Name (Optional) 194

Step 5: Generate Content 195

Step 6: Decide How You Will Manage Comments 198

Step 7: Go Live! 200

Getting People to Your Blog 200

Links 202

Keywords or Tags 202

Blogroll 203

Categories 204

Trackbacks 204

Visual Elements 205

What Lies Ahead in the Blogosphere? 205

Key Points: Chapter 8 206

Chapter 9 Posting, Publishing, and Podcasting: More Ways to Connect Online 207

Identity-Management Sites 208

Naymz 208

Ziggs 210

Discussion Groups 211
    What Exactly Is a Discussion Group? 211
    Why Use a Discussion Group and Not a Targeted Email List? 212
    Where Can I Find Discussion Groups? 212
    What Are the Benefits of Being a Group Member Versus Being a Moderator? 214
    How Do You Start Your Own Discussion Group? 215
Electronic Publishing 215
    E-newsletters 216
    Articles, Wikis, and Lists 217
Internet-Based Public Speaking 220
    Where to Find Speaking Opportunities 220
    How Podcasts Work 221
    How Webinars Work 223
Key Points: Chapter 9 224

Chapter 10 Growing Your Social Networks **225**
Make a Place for Social Networking in Your Job Search 226
Overcome Your Social Networking Reluctance 228
Re-energize Your Job Search 230
    Take Care of Yourself 230
    Get Out! 231
    Make the Most of the Job Search 232
    Paying It Forward 233
Consider Future Trends 234
    The Growth of Social Media 234
    Homogeneity and Portability of Social Media 235
    Managing the Flow of Information 236
    Organizations' Entry into Social Media 236
    Personal Branding and Social Networking 238
    Social Causes in Social Media 239
Closing Thoughts 239
Key Points: Chapter 10 240

Appendix A Recommended Resources **241**

Appendix B Social Networking Success Stories **249**

Index **253**

Introduction

Networking online is a great time-saver over the more laborious process of traditional, offline networking, but it can also be a huge time-eater. With hundreds of millions of blogs, millions of members on social networking sites, and literally billions of posts to message boards and discussion groups, you could easily spend every waking moment connecting with people online and still only scratch the surface. This book is organized in a way that will help you cut through the online clutter to focus on the social networking avenues that are the best use of your time and best for reaching your goals.

Not Just for Job Seekers

Although this book is primarily geared to job seekers, the advice contained on these pages is just as useful for anyone with a career who is not actively job searching. Managing your own career development is the responsibility of no one but you. Ongoing networking to expand and maintain your professional relationships is key to career success, as is staying abreast of developments in your field and on top of the competition. Social networking is an easy way to network while employed because it does not require that you take time out of your work day to attend meetings or make networking phone calls.

Social networking is also critically important for anyone with sales or business development responsibility, whether you are employed by an organization or are an entrepreneur. You, too, will find that the advice offered in this book is a great fit for you.

From Beginner to Advanced

This book is designed to help you start networking online from scratch if you're a complete beginner. Or if you've already been dabbling in it—maybe you've set up a profile on LinkedIn and accepted a few invitations, or perhaps you've been reading and commenting on some blogs occasionally—you will now be able to take your social networking to the next level.

Where to Find the Information You Need

In chapter 1, you'll learn more about what social networking is. Chapter 2 focuses on why social networking is important for your job search, career, or business. In chapter 3, we help you get your ducks in a row with some important preparatory steps to take (don't even think about skipping those!). In chapter 4, we give an overview of popular social networking sites and some dos and don'ts regarding social networking.

Then, in chapters 5 through 9 we dig in to more specifics of various social media—what they're all about and how to use them. Chapter 5 focuses on the most popular professional networking site, LinkedIn, including how to get started and details on how to leverage various aspects of the site.

We change gears in the next two chapters with tips and guidance on using Facebook in chapter 6 and microblogging and Twitter in chapter 7. In chapter 8, we discuss blogging—both having your own and commenting on other people's blogs—and in chapter 9 we roll up our sleeves and walk you through the process of networking through discussion groups, identity-management sites, podcasts, and other emerging forms of social networking.

Finally, in chapter 10, you'll find practical advice for making social networking a routine part of your life. You'll also find advice for continuing to expand and build both the quantity and quality of your network moving forward.

Getting Up to Speed

You may choose to read a chapter a day for 10 days or skim through the whole book quickly in an afternoon. That's your choice. Whichever pace you choose, keep in mind that this isn't just a book to read: It's a book to work. You'll find exercises to complete, steps to follow, and online resources to check out. Don't have time for that, you say? We understand. That's why we've made it all quick and painless. All you have to do is set aside a little bit of time now to save a lot of time down the road.

Think of Us as Your Social Networking Coaches

We know your time is valuable. We also know how overwhelming it can be to navigate your way through the world of social networking. You need a practical handbook to help you start or to redirect your efforts if you've already been networking online but lacking focus. We wanted to bring you simple but powerful advice that you can put into action right away.

As career coaches, we draw on more than 12 years of combined experience with social networking as well as the experiences of thousands of clients. We also pull from our backgrounds in recruiting, training, marketing, business development, and entrepreneurship. In addition, we surveyed hundreds of career coaches and job seekers, plus social media experts and professionals in a broad range of roles and locations who willingly shared tips and advice. The resulting book is based on the collective experiences of many people. And the information will benefit not just job seekers but also anyone who needs to expand a customer or client base for business success.

The scope of this book is not to cover every detail of blogging, Twitter, or the most advanced features of LinkedIn or other business-oriented social networks. The topics in each chapter of this book could fill a lengthy book in their own rights, and we know that you probably don't have time to read a multitude of books right now. You need to start moving with social networking as quickly as possible without sacrificing quality so that you can land a great job or advance in your career or business. In short, you need the help this handbook can provide. We're happy to be your social networking coaches and provide you with that help. Now, let's get started!

CHAPTER 1

Connecting Social Networking to Your Career Goals

Who would have thought that a former educator and recruiter with a passion for coaching people face-to-face and no formal background in technology would become an advocate of networking online? And who would've thought that a career consultant known for her painstaking process of connecting clients individually with just the right hand-picked person would amass her own network of millions of contacts using entirely electronic means? It's true. And if we can do it—and enjoy the process—so can you!

We wrote this book because we are believers in the amazing power of social networking for job seekers, entrepreneurs, and anyone looking to get ahead in a career or business. We've seen countless success stories from our clients and colleagues who have climbed aboard the social networking bandwagon, and we've benefited from it ourselves as well. We share many of these stories throughout the book.

And we are not alone. Millions of people are connecting with each other around the globe as members of professionally oriented social networks such as LinkedIn, Ecademy, Viadeo, XING, and more. On the microblogging site Twitter, millions of people are sharing their tips, thoughts, and activities. A whopping 126 million blogs also have people around the world talking (and the number will probably be higher by the time this book gets from our keyboards to your hands). Google has archived more than one billion posts to message boards and discussion groups. Any way you look at it, a lot of people are doing a lot of multinational mingling.

Not looking for a job or client halfway around the world? That's okay. Social networking has proven to be equally useful for connecting with people down the street and around the corner. The beauty is that you don't have to pound the pavement or work the phones to get to them.

Enough of this build-up. It's time for you to find out exactly what social networking is and how it's going to enhance your life.

In This Chapter
- *Learn what social networking is.*
- *Identify which social networking avenues are best for reaching your goals.*

What Is Social Networking?

Social networking is the process of using Web-based tools to connect with people for the purpose of reaching your career and business goals and, in turn, helping others reach their goals. Like traditional offline networking (meeting with people in person or speaking by telephone), networking online is an important part of any job search, personal career management plan, sales strategy, or marketing plan. Whether you call someone on the phone or write a comment on someone's blog, you're making a human-to-human connection. Whether you attend a business mixer in a hotel ballroom across town or join the conversation on Twitter from your home office in the basement, you're networking. It's essentially all the same thing.

The Strategy That Never Sleeps

One big difference between social networking and traditional networking, however, is that social networking is a tool that works for you 24 hours a day, 365 days a year, regardless of whether you're making an effort or are even awake. Another difference is that it gives you a reach like you've never had before. In a short period of time, you can dramatically enlarge the scope, depth, and quality of your network in ways that traditional networking would take months, if not years, to achieve.

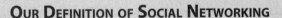

OUR DEFINITION OF SOCIAL NETWORKING

Social networking is the process of using Web-based social media tools to build relationships with people for the purpose of sharing knowledge, ideas, leads, contacts, and support. These social media tools include social networks (a.k.a. virtual communities), microblogs, blogs, discussion groups, and Internet-based publishing and public speaking.

Relationship Development

As with traditional networking, effective social networking is based on relationships. It's about getting to know people to exchange information and ideas, pass along leads and contacts, and support one another. The relationships might be somewhat short term to meet immediate objectives and goals, such as landing a job or finding a candidate to fill an open position, or they can develop into lifelong professional friendships. Either way, the key is to think in terms of mutually beneficial relationships that develop over time, not simply amassing lots of contacts in LinkedIn or posts on your blog.

TIP

Although social networking has its time-saving aspects, you cannot expect the people you meet online to jump through hoops to help you right away. Building trust with the people you meet online takes time. In order to earn this trust, you have to ease into the relationship slowly, start a dialogue, and show that you're willing to give as much as you want to get.

Social networking, like any kind of networking, is as much about quality as it is quantity. It's not a numbers game or a flash-in-the-pan activity. You are developing a large network of people who know you—your talents, expertise, goals, and personality—and you, in turn, know theirs. In other words, your network has substance, not just a list of names.

Do I Really Have Time to Network with Millions of People (and Should I Even Want To?)

Yes, you do. Yes, you should. With a minimal investment of upfront time to set yourself up online, and with a manageable investment of time to maintain your online presence, you can save huge amounts of time connecting with other people more efficiently. Do you have to get to know millions of people on a first-name basis? Of course not. But if you have access to millions of people through common networks and shared online activities, are you more likely to be able to find just the one person you're targeting when a need arises? Of course you are.

FINDING THE NEEDLE IN THE HAYSTACK

Consider the example of Gary P., a senior executive searching for a new job due to a restructuring at his previous company. He heard about opportunities at a global consulting firm, a logical target for his background. Unfortunately, he didn't know anyone there, and neither did members of his immediate traditional network. So he approached his career coach at one of Right Management's offices in Virginia. That person emailed his colleagues in other Right Management offices to enlist their help.

Ellen, in the Atlanta office, received the email. Although she couldn't think of anyone she knew personally at that company off the top of her head, she checked her LinkedIn network and instantly identified 126 people currently with that firm! These were people who knew people that she knew.

The contacts were located in 11 different U.S. cities and in 10 other countries on 3 continents. Gary wanted high-level contacts in the organization, and the 126 people included 8 associate directors, 3 principals, 4 directors, 18 vice presidents, 13 managing directors, a human resources manager, the chief technology officer, and the cofounder and owner! Gary was able to select the contacts he deemed most appropriate based on their job levels, locations, and biographical information in their profiles and get introduced to them through the LinkedIn network.

With social networking, you experience greatly enhanced efficiencies in your job search or business development efforts. You reach more people more quickly—and not just more people, but the right people. Social networking is a networking accelerator that puts you on the fast track toward your goals. Imagine how long it would have taken Gary or his consultant in the "Finding the Needle in the Haystack" example to find the contacts he needed at his target company. They would have had to search databases or directories to find the names of people who work for that company and then call or send email messages to hundreds of people to hit upon someone who knew any of the names they had targeted. This process could have taken days or weeks unless they happened to get lucky and make a connection more quickly.

With social networking, you don't have to rely on luck. You rely on the six degrees of separation idea, although with sites such as LinkedIn, it's really more about two to three degrees of separation. All it took was the consultant in Virginia emailing other consultants to request the inside track to this particular company. All Ellen had to do was spend a few seconds doing a keyword search in her LinkedIn network to come up with 126 names of people at that company who know people that she knows.

Much More Than Your 15 Minutes of Fame

Social networking also saves time and opens you up to a wider array of career or business opportunities because it lets you network passively. You are more visible to the world, and the world is more visible to you.

Think about how a business with a website reaches a much broader audience of potential customers than one that has to rely on putting up signs in the neighborhood or mailing out brochures and flyers (paid attention to much junk mail lately?). The website serves as an online brochure that advertises the business 24/7 and that isn't tossed into the recycling bin with the junk mail.

Whether you have a business to advertise or simply want to be visible as an individual to attract opportunities, you can achieve similar results with your own Twitter presence, blog, or online profile posted on a networking site. You can also do so by participating in online discussion groups and commenting on other people's blogs.

When you take 15 minutes to post your thought for the day—not your thoughts on what you had for breakfast, but some relevant piece of information for people in your field—you reap the benefits of hours and hours and hours of people getting to know you by reading that post in the days or weeks that follow. Or if you've written a whole article for a website or a short comment on a blog that has staying power, your archived information might be read for months and years to come.

TIP

Wondering just how visible you are online? You probably already know that websites and blogs can have a built-in ticker that counts the number of visitors, but did you know that there are also ways to track your visibility even if you don't want to have your own website or blog? Sites such as Naymz.com and Ziggs.com let you post a profile to establish your online identity and then alert you by email each time your profile is viewed.

Everybody Wins

In chapter 2, we cover the benefits that specific groups of people may enjoy through social networking. Although the focus of our career coaching and the primary focus of this book is job search, you will benefit from a broader perspective. If you are searching for a job, you may also be considering entrepreneurship as a full-time or part-time option. Chapter 2 explains how small business owners can reap rewards from social networking.

And when your job search ends and you land that great new role, you still need to manage your career effectively and efficiently because you might need to take your skills to market at some point in the future. That means continuing to network and build your personal brand. In chapter 3, you'll learn about building and protecting your personal brand, or online identity.

QUOTE

The acronym *YOYO* captures where we have evolved from a professional and career development standpoint. It boils down to this: "You're On Your Own" when it comes to responsibility for your education, training, and professional development as a productive adult in our business society.

It's not up to your employer's HR department—employers recognize that long-term tenure is a fleeting concept and have drawn the purse strings tighter on professional development training. It's not up to your manager—managers often have their hands tied in terms of budgets for their team members' professional development. It's not up to your coach or mentor—if you have one. They can play a supportive role, but execution, motivation, and the time commitment are up to you.

But we do have help in a very big way. We have an amazing resource at our disposal—a resource full of information, ready to help us when we need it, and always present. That resource is our network of connections. And in today's world, it is social media that provide the "distribution channel" for developing, cultivating, expanding, and communicating with our network.

Our network is the most productive asset we have, and it produces the highest return on investment if we utilize it to its fullest. It is the single best career management resource that we have.

—Andy Robinson, executive career coach

Job seekers, the self-employed, employment recruiters, salespeople, and any career-oriented individual looking to be more successful will find specific reasons for networking online. But some reasons to do it are common to everyone:

- **It's 24/7 networking.** Your profile and other content that you create online work for you day and night. The Internet never closes!

- **It's a screening tool.** You can learn a lot about a person through his or her online identity before investing the time in building a relationship. By reading someone's profile or by viewing the quality of that person's contributions to blogs or discussion groups, you can evaluate whether someone's knowledge, experience, and style are compatible with the goals you have for your network.

- **It gives unprecedented access with the utmost convenience.** You can participate in multiple networking "meetings" in the same day or evening from your computer, putting you in touch with hundreds or thousands of people you would not otherwise have been able to meet, or at least could not have met so quickly.

- **It's less threatening and intimidating.** Many people, especially introverts, find face-to-face or phone networking challenging. Networking from the comfort of your own computer screen can be much less intimidating. Social networking isn't a substitute for picking up the phone or showing up at a networking event, but it can be a less scary way to meet people and start to build professional relationships that can then be moved offline.

- **It lets you show off your technical skills and appear tech savvy.** Social networking requires such basic technical skills that even a computer novice or technophobe can do it successfully and appear to be in-the-know.

- **It gives you a wide platform for communicating who you are.** Your talents, expertise, and unique selling points— all the things that make up "brand you"—can be conveyed to a broad yet targeted audience.

- **It's a way to build your credibility.** All social networking venues offer an opportunity to share your knowledge with others, whether through blogging, microblogging, Question & Answer areas of social networks, or participation in discussion groups.

- **It levels the playing field.** If you have a physical disability, or if your outward appearance or speaking voice is not your best asset, networking from behind a computer screen is ideal. You can build relationships without other people's personal biases getting in the way. And if you have mobility issues, you can enjoy connecting with people from the convenience of home.

- **It's a springboard to offline meetings, appointments, and relationships.** Social networking is not a substitute for traditional face-to-face networking; it's a catalyst for those relationships.

 TIP

Worried about privacy, personal security, and spam issues that might arise from making yourself so visible in cyberspace? Although it's prudent to have some concern and be careful, most social networking venues allow you to control how people get your contact information. You can choose the level of anonymity you want.

Clearly, the benefits are many, and the downsides are few. What is the downside to social networking? For starters, you have to watch how you spend your time. If you're already someone who spends time browsing or researching on the Internet, you know how the time can fly by before you realize it. Social networking is the same. You could spend all day blogging, tweaking the content in your profile, and poking around in social networks to see who's who. Social networking can be a major time-eater, so you have to set limits on how much time you spend doing it on a daily or weekly basis.

You also have to be careful not to focus all your energy on social networking and not spend enough time connecting with people offline. Social networking is not a substitute for getting out of the house or office and attending networking events, meeting people for lunch or coffee, or picking up the phone to have a live conversation.

QUOTE

Social media have transformed the Web and our lives—both personal and professional. Every day I witness the predictions from *The Cluetrain Manifesto* materializing with and through the connectedness [that] the Web provides. I am active with my own blogs, on Twitter, Facebook, and a few other sites. The challenge is to balance social media interaction with the many other demands for my time and focus.

—T. Shea Ellison, creator of *The Success Principles Plus* workshop

Where in the Virtual World Will You Network?

You probably know by now that accomplishing anything on the Internet means being a wise consumer and making good choices. If you've ever planned a vacation or booked a business flight online, you probably had to choose between using Expedia, Orbitz, or Travelocity. Or maybe you went straight to an airline's own site or through a travel agency with an online presence. The bottom line is that you had more than enough choices to get the information you needed and make the transaction.

The process of social networking is not all that different. Most Web-based networking options fall into a handful of main categories, such as social networks, microblogs, blogs, and discussion forums. But there are usually several popular choices in each category, as well as many lesser-known choices.

In this section, we briefly define each of the main social networking technologies to help you start thinking about which ones are the best fit for you and your goals and needs. Then, in chapters 4 through 9, we elaborate on these networking avenues to deepen your understanding of them, explore the pros and cons, and walk you through the how-tos.

This book groups social networking technologies into these seven main categories:

1. Social networks

2. Blogs

3. Microblogs

4. Identity management sites

5. Discussion groups

6. Online publishing

7. Online public speaking

There are many ways to slice the social networking pie into categories, so we don't claim that our way is the only way. For example, microblogs and social networks often overlap, and blogging is a form of publishing. But looking at the options as seven distinct categories will help you start to navigate your way through the options to focus on the ones that will work best for you.

1. Social Networks

Picture yourself in a large convention hall with thousands of business cards flying through the air like confetti. Imagine yourself struggling to make your way through the crowds and the "confetti" to meet the right people. Suddenly, you come upon a trusted business colleague or former classmate who takes you by the hand and introduces you to someone who, in turn, leads you to a person you need to meet. With online, business-oriented social networks, this scenario is more reality than dream.

How Social Networks Work

Social networks such as LinkedIn, Ecademy, XING, Ryze, Viadeo, and many others help people connect with each other to do business, make career moves, and advance professionally. In chapter 4, we go into much more detail about social networks—how they operate and how to use them—but here we want to introduce you to the concept and help you start to see whether social networks are for you.

On these sites, you build a network by first posting a profile—basically a bio and other information about yourself and your professional interests—and then invite other people to join your network. You can also accept invitations from other members, thereby linking their networks to yours. Membership in these networks is typically free, or you can pay a nominal fee for an upgraded membership that offers added benefits—namely, greater access to the membership at-large.

Who Social Networks Are For

Just about anyone can benefit from joining a business-oriented social network. Job seekers secure interviews and land jobs through them, recruiters find qualified candidates, and business owners or business developers broaden their referral bases and find key players in their targeted customer organizations.

Membership in a social network requires minimal technical and writing skills. This membership is easy to maintain.

2. Blogs

Blogs—shorthand for *web logs*—are one of the most significant developments in the history of the Internet. A blog is a type of website that consists primarily of short comments or essays entered frequently (often daily) by the blog owner(s) to form a chronological log. It's like an online journal of one's thoughts. Readers of the blog can then post their comments about what they think of the entries. Blogs helped the Web morph from a purveyor of fairly static online content to a forum for interaction and dialogue. The Internet became not just a place to read about stuff, but a place to have a conversation—or more likely, many conversations.

How Blogs Work

If you're already familiar with blogs—maybe you have your own or have commented on other people's—then you know that blogs come in all shapes and sizes. Some have been active for years and are rich in content. Many posts and comments have been archived over time, so you can catch up on past discussions. Some are frequently updated with fresh postings on a daily or at least weekly basis. Others have less activity. Maybe they are newer or just have fewer, less frequent postings and a smaller audience.

Whichever shape and size a blog takes, it is an excellent vehicle for expression of a personal brand and establishment of a digital trail. If you write a comment on a popular blog, you will make a mark that will be picked up by the major search engines. If you have your own blog and post on it regularly, you will see references to your blog come up when anyone googles your name. Chapter 8 has more information on blogs.

A Few of Our Favorite Blogs

- **Force of Good by Lance Weatherby:** http://blog.weatherby.net
- **JibberJobber by Jason Alba:** www.jibberjobber.com/blog
- **Threshold Consulting by Walter Akana:** www.threshold-consulting.com/
- **Keppie Careers by Miriam Salpeter:** www.keppiecareers.com

Who Can Benefit from Blogging

Just about anyone can benefit from blogging. Commenting on other people's blogs is free, and setting up your own is quick, easy, and inexpensive. Of course, you do need to have some degree of writing skill and like to write, but if you comment on others' blogs rather than having your own, minimal skill is needed.

Commenting on blogs is especially helpful for job seekers. Your blog comments are likely to turn up high in a list of Google hits for your name, and it's a great way to show off your expertise and thought process. Having your own blog might be worth the effort if you are an entrepreneur who needs the visibility for marketing purposes or if you're a professional looking to make a mark in his or her professional world.

3. Microblogs

Microblogging got its start in 2006 with Twitter, and the popularity of this site and participation on this site have grown by leaps and bounds. Microblogging, like blogging, is a way to share your ideas, showcase your expertise, meet like-minded people, and have conversations. Twitter isn't the only microblogging tool, but it is currently the most popular one, which is why it is the primary focus of chapter 7.

One of the biggest benefits of Twitter is its ability to foster easy connections with others and create conversation and community. Also, the feel of Twitter is more casual than the formal social networking protocols associated with sites such as LinkedIn. Instead of long articles and white papers, communications on Twitter, known as *tweets*, are limited to 140 characters each. The 140 characters can include links to blog posts, articles, websites, and white papers. So there is certainly the opportunity to share longer content.

How Microblogging Works

You sign up on Twitter—a free site—and complete a profile similar to the social networks. You can watch the conversation initially or jump right in with a few tweets of your own. You search for and start following people in your field who typically will follow you back. That's how conversation gets going. If you are new to Twitter, chapter 7 will tell you all you need to know to network on the site. If you are already tweeting, you'll find lots of helpful tips there to make your Twitter networking experiences even more productive.

Who Can Benefit from Microblogging

As with blogging, Twitter is an excellent vehicle for expression of a personal brand and establishing a digital trail. Tweets are picked up by the major search engines. Others will see references to your tweets when they Google your name. So the additional exposure for job seekers can be very helpful in getting your name and online identity out there.

Beyond the added visibility, job seekers can greatly expand their networks, stay updated on trends, and easily connect to thought leaders in their field. One of the unique benefits of microblogging is the ready accessibility to top minds and industry leaders.

If you can write and communicate in concise phrases and short sentences, Twitter might be a great social networking vehicle for you and a good alternative to writing lengthy blog posts. In fact, several bloggers we surveyed indicated that the discipline of writing short, concise tweets has made their blog posts better.

4. Identity-Management Sites

Across a blurry line from the business-oriented social networks are the sites that we call identity management sites. They're also known as profile management sites and even as reputation builders. On these sites, you post your profile as a way for people to find information about you when they do a keyword search for you online. Some of these sites also offer ways for you to connect with other members, so they are similar to social networks, thus the blurry line.

How Identity-Management Sites Work

Most sites offer profile placement free, but on some you can upgrade your membership for a nominal fee. This upgrade gives you premium placement status, meaning that when someone searches for you on major search engines such as Google, your profile will come up at the top of the page.

The profile you post is much like one you would put on LinkedIn or Ecademy. It's basically a bio with an overview of your professional background, with the option to include some bells and whistles such as a photo or links to your own blog or website.

Two of the most popular sites in this category are Naymz and Ziggs. Naymz describes itself as "focused on reputation, personal branding, and identity verification," an innovative reputation network that lets you establish and promote your name online. Ziggs calls itself a "one-stop source for building your online brand, marketing yourself on the Web, and simplifying communications with people."

The benefit of both sites is that you can gain some control over your digital identity by ensuring that at least one Google hit for your name (or two, if you join both sites) will have accurate, up-to-date information about you. Of course, you have to manage your profile to keep it up-to-date and accurate.

 TIP

Sites like Ziggs and Naymz are especially helpful if your name is not unique and you want to establish your identity online under a variation of your name, such as by including your middle initial, middle name, or full maiden name. You can start to build up a digital footprint under that name by using it when you join these sites.

Who Can Benefit from Identity-Management Sites

Identity-management sites are easy to use, quick to join and set up, and free (or inexpensive for upgraded membership) and require minimal ongoing maintenance, so they are good for just about everyone. They also require minimal writing and technology skills. (Just be sure to get some help writing and proofreading your profile if you're not a good writer.) These sites are especially useful for anyone who has little to no online presence and needs to start developing a digital footprint.

There's very little downside to these sites because they require minimal output of effort, skill, or money.

5. Discussion Groups

Long before blogging technology came into existence, people were communicating on the Internet through various forums. Like a virtual water cooler, discussion groups and other online forums have enabled people with common interests to form communities for sharing ideas, opinions, advice, and best practices in their fields.

Yahoo! and Google are credited with having some of the most extensive offerings of special-interest discussion groups online, although many lesser-known organizations have them as well. In these discussion groups, participants post comments or questions in a sort of virtual bulletin board or message board format, and others post replies or rebuttals.

With discussion groups, unlike chat rooms and instant messaging, you can log on at any time to post or read others' posts; the exchanges are not live in real time. This format can be quite convenient. As with reading email, you can do it whenever you feel like it. And even without real-time, live exchanges, you can form surprisingly strong bonds with fellow group members. Discussion groups can be a great way to express your brand because you are able to demonstrate your knowledge and expertise.

TIP

Some discussion groups might have people who meet locally offline, that is, in person. Check to see whether any discussion group you participate in has live meetings somewhere convenient so that you can transition from social networking to offline.

6. Online Publishing

When you think of the networking process, writing for publication probably isn't the first thing that comes to mind. It doesn't seem as interactive as meeting someone for coffee or mingling at a professional conference. But, in fact, writing for professional publications has always been one of the best-kept secrets of networking.

Writing articles, editorials, and book or product reviews for professional newsletters and journals, trade publications, and popular media is an excellent way to express your personal brand and gain visibility. Remember that networking isn't just about going out and meeting other people; it's also about attracting people to you through activities you become involved with, leadership you exhibit, and good works you do.

The Internet has opened the door for just about everyone to get published. If you can't get your writing accepted in prestigious journals, you can start your own blog or e-newsletter (an electronic newsletter that you email to subscribers) and become an instant author.

TIP

Writing reviews of books relevant to your business or profession for Amazon (www.amazon.com) is a great way to become known. Amazon reviews tend to come up high in Google searches, so you'll enhance your digital footprint as well. Just be sure that you've actually bought and read the book you're reviewing!

Of course, in order for this to be a viable social networking avenue for you, you need to be a decent writer and have some interest in it. Writing is not for everyone, so don't feel you have to pursue this form of networking. But if you do have a knack for writing, consider adding online publishing to your networking repertoire.

Online publishing is also priced right in that usually no cost is associated with it at all. There's also little ongoing maintenance, because after an article you write or comment you submit goes live on the Web, your work is done.

7. *Online Public Speaking*

Public speaking is another frequently overlooked networking method. You don't have to make a living as a full-time motivational speaker or expert lecturer to make connections and gain visibility; you can speak on an occasional basis as a way to establish your professional identity.

Public speaking online happens primarily through webinars and podcasts. If you work for an organization that uses webinars to train or convey information to employees in various locations, you are already familiar with these processes and know that they are relatively easy to use as either host or participant. If you're not familiar with webinars, you might be surprised at how much they feel like the experience of a live presentation. If you are the featured speaker for a webinar, you will upload a presentation, such as PowerPoint slides, using an online meeting platform such as WebEx, GoToMeeting, or Live Meeting. You will speak about your visual presentation using traditional telephone conference calling or using Voice Over Internet Protocol (VoIP) technology, which is the routing of voice conversations over the Internet rather than through phone lines. You can encourage audience interaction through online polls or surveys and with questions texted in or asked over the voice line.

In a podcast, you are essentially broadcasting as if on the radio, but the audio feed is through computer technology instead of airwaves.

Whether you're speaking in a webinar or podcast, you'll enhance your professional stature and visibility significantly. And both webinars and podcasts can be recorded to provide ongoing access and a longer shelf life. In chapter 9, we go into more detail on how to use webinars or podcasting as a social networking tool.

Key Points: Chapter 1

- Social networking is the process of using social media (Web-based tools) to connect with people for the purpose of reaching your career and business goals and, in turn, helping others reach their goals.

- Even if you're not actively trying to find or fill a job or develop new business, you can enhance your professional stature, security, and performance by connecting with people online.

- Social networking is a convenient complement to traditional networking in that it gives unprecedented access to more people more easily.

- Before determining which social media you'll use for networking, you need to identify your career or business goals so that you can choose the right avenues for reaching those goals.

- Social networking is a complement to, not a replacement for, traditional "offline" networking conducted in person or by telephone.

- The seven main categories of social networking are social networks, microblogs, blogs, identity management sites, discussion groups, online publishing, and online public speaking.

CHAPTER 2

Understanding the Benefits
of Social Networking

When the first edition of this book was published in 2008, there were 17 million people on the five-year-old LinkedIn. As of this writing, more than 70 million people are on LinkedIn. Facebook had 80 million active users in 2008. More than 400 million "friends" are on the site today. Twitter was brand new in 2006 and now boasts more than 100 million people sending tweets to their friends and followers. This rapid growth in the popularity of social networking is driven by the almost overwhelming amount of potential benefits such networking offers.

The huge amount of information shared, contacts made, jobs found, and business transacted through social networking is activity that may not be available or accessible through other means. You need to participate or be left behind. To stay in the game, all people with a career to manage need to be connecting, communicating, and collaborating via social networking.

In This Chapter
- *Discover how social networking helps job seekers land jobs.*
- *Learn how salespeople, freelancers, and business owners can benefit.*
- *Understand why everyone needs to be doing it.*

Why Job Seekers Must Get Online (and We Don't Just Mean Posting Your Resume on Monster!)

As career consultants for a global human resources solutions firm, we coach all kinds of job seekers, and we see what works and what doesn't in a job search. And although some people (especially those with clearly defined, tangible skills such as IT or accounting professionals) do land jobs through online job boards such as Monster, CareerBuilder, and the many other employment sites out there, networking is still the way most job seekers find their next position.

Networking has typically consisted of calling, emailing, and meeting with people you know, or people they know, to let them know you're looking for a job, as well as attending networking events to meet new people. This form of networking will always be a critical element of a job search. There's no substitute for traditional, offline networking as a way to build meaningful professional relationships. But with social networking, you can propel your networking efforts into a whole new dimension. Next, we describe some of the ways you might use social networking in your job search.

QUOTE

What a shock it was when this suddenly unemployed (through no fault of my own) baby boomer discovered the only way to find employment in the 21st century was networking. I scurried from one career course to the next, talked to career coaches, read recommended books, took webinars, and learned how to create an Internet presence using LinkedIn. I did people searches in LinkedIn and was able to reconnect with business professionals I had lost touch with over the years who gave me recommendations and connected me with other individuals and companies that might be hiring. I joined LinkedIn professional groups, gave recommendations to others, and searched for information on companies where I'd like to work. I must admit this new way to professionally network and job search is somewhat refreshing and has saved me a lot of money because I don't have to pay membership fees, buy several "interview" suits, [spend more on] gasoline, wear out my shoe heels, or buy Epsom salts to soak my feet that are tired and aching from "pounding the pavement," looking for a job.

—Gwendolyn Chaffin, forms and graphic design professional

Get Information and Advice

As you attempt to define your career goals and job objectives, you can find people online who might help with your decision-making and focusing process. These connections are particularly important if you are considering changing career fields—your functional role or industry—but they are also helpful for staying up on trends and developments in your existing field to help identify new areas of opportunity.

Identify Potential Employers to Target

After you define an employment objective, you need to come up with a "hit list" of employers that you would like to work for based on the criteria you've identified as important to you. Databases, directories, chamber of commerce listings, and magazines and journals for your field are all tried-and-true methods for finding organizations you might want to work for, but social networking adds another source. You can search the memberships of social networks to see where people work, can read company blogs to get a feel for various corporate cultures, and can ask people in your social networks which organizations they recommend for your list.

Find Specific People Within Your Targeted Organizations

When you have your "hit list" developed, your next step is to approach someone within the organization by phone or email to let that person know about your interest in working there or to request an informational interview to explore the possible fit between your skills and the organization's needs. You need to identify the right person to connect with and not just send a "To Whom It May Concern" type of inquiry to the human resources department. You might also see job listings online or in other sources and want to find someone specific to talk to instead of applying somewhat anonymously.

Consider Deborah G., a marketing communications manager who found an ideal position on a major job board and submitted her resume online. Not content with simply firing off her resume into a black hole and sitting back to wait for a reply that might never come, she set out to find a contact inside the company. After determining that none of her personal acquaintances worked at the company, she searched her LinkedIn network. However, she was a relatively new member of LinkedIn with a small network on that site, and her search yielded no connections.

Fortunately, Deborah knew someone with a large LinkedIn network. That person found 32 contacts at the company. In reviewing the list, Deborah was surprised and pleased to discover the name of a former colleague. She emailed him and found him happy to hear from her and glad to help out. He presented Deborah to the hiring manager and also coached her on interviewing strategy given his knowledge of the organization. She landed the job!

Just like Deborah G., you can leverage your membership in virtual communities to find the best person to talk with.

TIP

To easily connect job postings with people in your network, consider taking advantage of sites that aggregate job listings from a variety of Web sources. SimplyHired, for example, is an aggregator site that is connected with both LinkedIn and Facebook. By activating the features that help you use these types of sites in tandem, you can gather job postings from all over the Web and your connections at those companies all in one place and save yourself some time.

Be More Visible to Recruiters and Employers

Executive search consultants, recruiters in staffing agencies, and internal recruiters in companies are flocking to the Internet in droves to find candidates to fill positions. By having a well-written profile on LinkedIn or other virtual communities and by being active on blogs to show off your knowledge or on Twitter to stay visible, you will attract recruiters and hiring managers.

QUOTE

I believe the saying "If you're not out there [on social networking sites], you don't exist."

—Carrie Davis, director of staffing, ADP Canada

For example, Michelle A., a job seeker client of ours, was recently hired by a recruiting firm for an administrative role. The firm found her on LinkedIn, which indicates that recruiters are using it to fill positions internally as well as to find candidates for their client companies. She happily accepted the recruiting firm's offer but was delighted to report that three other prospective employers had also contacted her based on her LinkedIn profile! She's a LinkedIn member for life.

NOTE

Through social networks, recruiters and employers can do "unofficial" background checks. On LinkedIn, recruiters and employers can view recommendations that bosses, colleagues, subordinates, vendors, and customers can post for an individual. But beyond that, recruiters and employers can identify and approach individuals not on an official reference list to hear about their candidates. Or they can do a search on Google or another search engine to check out a candidate's electronic footprint.

Ray L., an IT executive, decided to start a blog to showcase his skills and build a personal brand for his executive-level job search. Within two months of launching his blog, he counted more than 1,300 views of his online bio and resume. Eight opportunities had been presented and had yielded four interviews. And he had scheduled five speaking engagements! Clearly, the blog was an effective marketing vehicle for his job search.

Don't misunderstand us; we don't mean that if you join LinkedIn or set up a blog, the job offers will start pouring in. (They might, but we're not making any promises!) Just as with traditional networking, you have to be strategic about how you use social networking to get to a job offer or even just to find the opportunities and reach the interview stage.

RECRUITERS ON LINKEDIN

As the largest exclusively professional social network, LinkedIn is a favorite tool of recruiters. One statistic from a recruitment blog (www.booleanblackbelt.com) cited that 1 out of every 20 LinkedIn profiles belongs to a sourcing, recruiter, or human resources professional. This could equate to over a million recruiting and HR professionals on this site, and that number is growing every day. Many recruiters have very large networks on LinkedIn, indicating that they see great value in this form of social networking and have chosen to invest time in building and maintaining their networks.

We conducted some informal surveys of recruiters to ask about their usage of and reactions to LinkedIn. We heard the following:

- LinkedIn is a great professional tool.

- Candidates should use LinkedIn extensively. They should be using LinkedIn before they are out of a job!

- LinkedIn is a great tool for business development, candidate sourcing, and job posting.

- We use LinkedIn to find people with specific qualifications and experience, and it works really well.

- Two years ago, we were using four major job boards to find candidates. We've now dropped three job boards and purchased the corporate solution from LinkedIn.

These comments were representative of the larger pool of survey responses. No respondent expressed negative comments about LinkedIn, and all suggested that it is now a key part of their business process.

In addition to using LinkedIn to search for just the right candidate, recruiters post jobs on LinkedIn and other social networks to draw a broad candidate response, possibly from people who didn't have a profile on the site. (You can see jobs posted on LinkedIn regardless of whether you have a profile on the site.)

Note that although LinkedIn has become known as a favorite site for recruiters, it's by no means the only social network out there. In chapter 4, we tell you more about additional sites, such as Ecademy, XING, Ryze, and Viadeo, and help you see which ones might be the best fit for you.

Feel Supported Through the Ups and Downs

A job search can be a long, arduous process. As part of online communities, you can receive valuable advice, support, and encouragement to help you through the rough patches.

TIP

Remember that everything you say and do online leaves a digital trail that reflects either positively or negatively on your reputation and character. It's natural for job seekers to want to vent their frustrations, but be careful what, where, and to whom you do that online. You don't want prospective employers to see you as a whiner or to read about your personal or social activities that might detract from—rather than promote—your professional brand!

With the average tenure on a job in the United States currently at about four years, establishing the long-term relationships that are critical to developing a solid network is becoming more and more difficult. When you need to look for a job, you might find that you and all your colleagues have moved around so much that you don't have much of a grounded network. By incorporating social networking techniques, you can find and reconnect with former contacts and make new connections, too. With social media tools, you can greatly enhance the size and quality of your network and make your job search go much more smoothly.

How Salespeople, Entrepreneurs, Freelancers, and Other Professionals Can Benefit from Social Networking

Cultivating business relationships face-to-face, or at least through frequent phone contact, is a critical element of business development. We don't deny that in the least. You have to get out there and call on your customers and clients as well as knock on the doors of your prospects. You also have to show up at networking meetings, conferences, and any events that are relevant to your targets; that is, go to the places where your customers congregate or where the people who could refer business to you congregate. You also have to do some wining and dining, bonding with your clients over meals, on the golf

course, and at any sporting, arts, or social events that your client would enjoy being treated to. None of that has changed or is likely ever to change.

There's no substitute for face time, but what if you could use the Internet to get a foot in the door so you can get that face time? Or what if you could use it to have the inside track that gives you an edge in writing a proposal or making a sales presentation? That's what social networking can do.

If you skipped over the sections of this chapter that described social networking for job seekers, please go back and read them. Job seekers market themselves to potential employers. As a salesperson, freelancer, or business owner, you market yourself to potential customers who could use your product, service, or expertise. So the benefits of social networking for job seekers are much the same as those for salespeople and entrepreneurs. You can be more strategic in how you go after business, can be more visible so that the business comes to you, and can get ideas from others that might enhance your own success. The following sections expand on these points.

Attracting Customers or Clients

To win business, you need to market your services effectively. But when you are visible online, whether through membership in a social network or by blogging, you don't always have to be pounding the pavement to find people to buy your product or service or to find your next gig if you're self-employed. Social networking strategies can greatly enhance your business development efforts by making it easier to find prospective clients.

- **Networking opportunities:** Just as most new jobs come from networking, so do most new clients. So the enhanced networking opportunities on sites like LinkedIn can give you greater access to more people and more prospects.

- **Communicating brand:** And just as job seekers need to have a complete and enticing profile on the social networks, freelancers and business owners need to communicate their brand and promote themselves through their profile data, data that works 24/7 to attract new business.

Identifying Partners for Collaboration

Social networks such as LinkedIn can provide additional resources to identify potential alliance partners and create new revenue opportunities.

For example, Will M., an independent consultant, was an early adopter of Twitter. By following people with a similar consulting focus and building a strong following there, he has greatly expanded his network and effectively promoted his personal and professional brand. He's even taken some of these relationships offline. Recently he collaborated with another consultant on a major project, and they now have new projects on the horizon. This new business partner lives several thousand miles away from Will. They would likely never have met were it not for Twitter.

SOCIAL NETWORKING CHALLENGES FOR RELATIONSHIP-BASED BUSINESSES

Although the use of social networks can have an overwhelmingly beneficial impact on relationship-based (or just about any) businesses, it's not all positive. The open nature of social networks works on the model of sharing contacts and information without expectation of a fee. This model can be problematic if your business is based on providing services that connect people or provide information.

There is no one right way to handle a request that involves this sort of conflict. You may decide to share a limited number of contacts or amount of information in the hopes that it might lead to increased business in the future, or you might decide to use such requests as an opportunity to pitch your services.

Another challenge is that access to social networks is not exclusive. Your competitors can use information from this huge global database, too. For example, if you are a freelancer, other freelancers in your field can gather leads on potential clients by reading your profile and seeing whom you have worked for. Yet this transparency can also work to your advantage, with social networks providing opportunities to check out your competition and get intelligence on other vendors.

(continued)

(continued)

Social networks also can make it easier for clients and vendors to connect directly to avoid third-party fees. This can be a problem if your business is to provide some type of third-party services, such as employment or recruiting services. Of course, these issues existed before social networking; social networking has just made the conflicts more intense in some ways. Yet experienced and effective professionals and businesses will continue to be able to offer convincing cost-benefit justifications for their services. Overall, the benefits to establishing an online presence far outweigh the potential challenges.

Generating Referrals

LinkedIn and other comparable sites provide an opportunity for you and your organization to build credibility. When you participate in blogs or discussion groups, people get to know you as a representative of your organization and will turn to you when they hear of someone who needs to do business with someone in your space. Because they see you online and read what you have to say, and because your communications there sound more genuine and less like marketing collateral or website content, they come to feel like they know and trust you and will feel comfortable telling other people about you. Approaching a prospective client through a common connection, showing that you are well networked and someone good to know, can help to gain that client's trust.

Identifying Targets

Scouring the membership of online social networks and checking out blogs and discussion groups to see who's talking are great ways to identify people who might need to know about you and your products or services.

Staying Current with Trends

Staying current and relevant is a challenge for all professionals. New information and developments happen at a rapid rate. With social networking, you can ask questions of the masses on LinkedIn, read blog posts of thought leaders in your industry, and follow relevant conversations on Twitter.

Selling Strategically

You do your due diligence on a prospect before you make your first call or design that first PowerPoint slide for a sales presentation. You probably ask around among people you know to see if anyone has the inside scoop on the individual or organization. You probably do some research online to see what you can find. With social networking, you can be more focused in your strategizing. You can view profiles of leaders in these prospect organizations to learn about their background and identify areas of common interest. You can also find people in your virtual communities who have the insights and inside track you need to get the competitive advantage.

Finding Money!

As an entrepreneur, you might need to secure venture-capital funds or find angel investors. Sure, traditional research methods work well, and face-to-face meetings are critical. But by also turning to virtual communities where investors might be members, you can reach your hand much deeper into the honey pot.

USING A BLOG TO FIND NEW CLIENTS

An entrepreneur that we know in the career coaching business is an avid blogger, using that low-cost vehicle combined with equally cost-effective traditional networking to market her services. In her pre-blog era, her clients came to her largely from word-of-mouth advertising. Today she attributes 90 percent of her business to the Internet, her blog, and her Twitter presence. In her blog postings, she showcases her skills and services in a credible and subtle manner instead of having to resort to hard-sell strategies, thereby winning the trust and confidence of prospective clients. Not all of her new clients read her blog. In fact, Twitter has served as a great catalyst to build her visibility and direct people to her blog.

We've experienced the revenue-generating benefits of social networking ourselves. Although business development is not our primary function with our employer, by networking online and being visible to decision makers at companies, we receive inquiries about our company's products and services, often from companies that our business development team has never contacted or from organizations that our sales staff had not been able to penetrate.

So what are you waiting for? Get online and start enjoying the same kinds of successes!

Why Everyone with a Career Needs to Network Online

You're reasonably happy with the job you do and the employer you work for. You stay relatively busy at work most days, maybe even extremely busy. You know that you ought to be networking to stay connected to people in your field and to have people to turn to in case you end up needing to look for a new job in the future. You try to go to your professional association or industry meetings and conferences from time to time, and you try to meet for lunch with acquaintances from other organizations, but you often feel guilty for not doing enough of this—or maybe for not doing it at all. It's just too hard to find the time and the motivation.

Social networking might be your answer. Instead of having to struggle to break away from work, fight traffic, and find the energy to attend an after-hours networking meeting, you can connect with people online through blogging or microblogging, discussion groups, or email exchanges with fellow social network members.

Instead of spending hours writing articles for your field's professional journals or lining up speaking engagements to be visible in your field, you can gain even broader visibility by having your own blog. Sure, you have to make the effort to keep your content current on the blog or website, but you can do that whenever and wherever it's convenient for you.

QUOTE

I have always benefited from knowing good things and great people. In fact, every leadership role I've held, from being an HR manager to being president and CEO of the largest national African American human resources association, has surfaced from networking. With the innovations of social networking technology, the sky is the limit on connecting with people and building credible relationships with others across all borders at no cost. My only investment has been time. How foolish it would be for me to underestimate the power and reach of social networking as I build my professional brand and expand my career options.

—Carl Jefferson, human resources leader and organization
    development strategist

We're not saying that you shouldn't still make an effort to be visible in the traditional ways—writing or speaking in your field, or perhaps taking a leadership role in a professional association that meets face-to-face—but you can use the Internet-based methods to your advantage as well.

TIP

Even if you're not in job search mode currently, don't hesitate to build relationships with recruiters online. You never know when you might need them in the future.

Whether you work in the corporate world or the nonprofit or public sectors, if someone else employs you and cuts your paycheck, you cannot afford to be complacent about your job security. You've probably figured out by now that no one is indispensable. Maybe you've been the victim of job cuts or have witnessed close friends or family members suddenly losing their jobs despite having done great work for their employers. It happens to dedicated factory workers, seemingly indispensable administrative assistants, highly skilled technical workers, and the most senior executives. No one is immune. Organizational restructuring and downsizing, outsourcing and offshoring, economic and political factors, and a host of other catalysts are all constantly churning the job market.

In our career coaching roles, hardly a day goes by that we don't hear one of our clients express regret over the fact that he or she didn't maintain an active network while still employed. "If only I had stayed in touch with people and forced myself to get out to networking events, I wouldn't feel like I'm starting my network from scratch now," they say. Perhaps if they had known how much can be done online, they would have been able to keep up their networks better. You have a golden opportunity not to let yourself get in the same predicament.

Through social networking, you can

- **Ensure online information about you is accurate:** As things change in your professional life, you can provide information easily and immediately to everyone in your network by updating your online profiles or blogs.

- **Make yourself visible, even if you have a lower profile job:** People in nonleadership roles are usually not listed in business directories. But people in all different types of jobs are visible and accessible on social networks. Social networking gives you the opportunity to present your expertise and connect with people at all levels in an organization.

- **Showcase your skills:** Through presenting yourself online, you can illustrate areas of expertise that may not be as evident through traditional self-marketing documents and demonstrate your written communication skills and attention to detail.

The following sections outline some of the other ways you might benefit from social networking now rather than later.

Make Better Career Decisions

By having a huge network of professional colleagues at your fingertips, you can get valuable input on new directions you might want your career to go, whether within your current organization or elsewhere. You can check out new roles, new industries, and new markets. You can also get feedback from others on whether to accept a promotion or relocation opportunity you've been offered.

See What's Out There

As you interact with, or read the profiles of, other people online, you get a bigger-picture view of the employers and roles and professions that exist than you would if you stayed in your own bubble. You'll either find that you've got it pretty good where you are and ought to stay put or that the grass looks greener somewhere else.

Position Yourself for Raises and Promotions

We don't claim that plum jobs and big money will come raining down on you like manna from cyberheaven just because you blog or join a social network. What we do know, however, is that the more you present yourself to the world as a well-connected mover and shaker in your field, the more your own employer will see that your professional stature is an asset to the organization. And, if your boss or boss's boss can't see that, you might need to move on! Your blog can help you do that as well.

QUOTE

In today's business world, your worth is about the value you can create for your organization. What better way to create value than to tap into the combined knowledge of millions of people from all corners of the world?

—Bob Logston, vice president, international; WARN Industries Inc.

Attract Opportunities Like a Magnet

Let's say you aren't actively looking for a new job, but you're always open to exploring opportunities that might bring you more job satisfaction or a fatter paycheck. When you have a profile posted online, or when you share your knowledge by posting on blogs related to your profession or industry or communicating on Twitter, you become what recruiters call a *passive candidate*. They can easily find you to tell you about jobs you didn't even know you were interested in.

Enhance and Share Your Knowledge Base

Believe it or not, successful career management is not all about you! It's not all about getting better jobs, coveted assignments, or more money. It's also about learning, growing, and giving back to others. By connecting with people online, you can share your knowledge and soak up ideas and information from others, all the while enhancing your performance and making your work life more stimulating and interesting.

TIP

Woodrow Wilson is credited with saying "I not only use all the brains that I have, but all that I can borrow." Keep this philosophy in mind as you network. Share knowledge with your professional community and learn from others instead of trying to solve all of your career or work problems yourself.

If you carve out some time from your busy work schedule to get involved online in some way, you, too, can reap the benefits outlined in this section.

But before you dive into social networking, you'll need to take some simple preparatory steps. In chapter 3, we help you get your ducks in a row so that you can start benefiting from social networking as soon as possible.

Key Points: Chapter 2

- Through social networking, job seekers can get advice about their search techniques, identify employers to target, connect with key decision makers, and become visible to recruiters.

- By networking online, freelancers, salespeople, and entrepreneurs can identify and check out prospects, be introduced to potential customers, and find sources of funding.

- Social networking is not just for those who are making a career transition or building a business, it's also essential for anyone with a career who would like to keep the door open to better ideas, better connections, better opportunities, and a better way to build their professional brand.

CHAPTER 3

Standing Out in the Cyberspace Crowd

Now that you've learned what social networking is and why you should be doing it, you might feel ready to dive right in. Maybe you're ready to join social networks, start a blog or write a comment on one, or follow someone on Twitter. Because some of these things are so easy to do, it's tempting to jump the gun a bit. We've had people create a blog or join LinkedIn in less than five minutes while sitting in the audience of our training sessions. (We thought they were hanging on our every word and taking notes on their laptops, but they were already off and running, putting our words into action!)

We appreciate that enthusiasm, but we recommend proceeding carefully. Social networking puts you in front of millions of people with one touch of the Enter key. Almost every piece of content you put on the Internet forges your online identity for years to come, so don't venture into social networking without first reading this chapter to prepare yourself.

In this chapter, we introduce you to the building blocks of creating your online identity. In later chapters, as you learn how to use specific social media, you'll continue to build your presence online with further guidance from us. Our aim is to help you stand out by being carefully, not carelessly, visible. This is a working chapter in which you'll complete some simple exercises to start developing your online identity, so enter your thoughts directly into the worksheets provided later in this chapter or set up electronic versions if you prefer.

> **In This Chapter**
> - *Stand out from your competition on the Internet.*
> - *Determine what sort of identity you have online, if any.*
> - *Deal with negative online information about you.*
> - *Develop your self-marketing sound bite—a key communication tool.*
> - *Identify your social networking goals.*
> - *Complement your traditional (offline) networking efforts.*

Your Online Identity: What It Is and Why You Need One

Just as large companies have images and reputations, known as their brands, you have a brand as well. Your knowledge, skills, contributions, accomplishments, goals, values, communication style, personality, and even physical appearance all make up your brand. A critical element in your personal brand is your online identity. Every move you make online and even some offline moves that are chronicled online create a trail of digital footprints in the sands of cyberspace and become part of your online identity.

 QUOTE

Most of us approach the job search with a "Fire…Aim…Ready" strategy. "Ready…Aim…Fire" is the only approach—figure out what you want to do and save applying for the last stage. Decide what you want to do first, then tell everyone and anyone in all possible ways—face to face, snail mail, email, and all social networking avenues.

—Richard Pfleger, career coach

Having an online identity that reflects positively on your brand is becoming increasingly important for all sorts of professionals. In the past, a business card and nameplate on your office door or a resume and interview suit were all you needed to establish yourself as "real" in the minds of others. Of course, the quality of your work and ethical standards were—and still are—the essential substance behind the window dressing, but your professional image and identity were primarily conveyed through these nonelectronic outer trappings. These days, your presence online is just as important as these offline image-makers.

If There's No Evidence of You Online, Do You Exist?

Recruiters and employers, as well as prospective clients or customers, now expect to find you online. They turn to the Internet to scope out your credentials, opinions, and even appearance. If you have no online presence (a search engine turns up no matches for your name) or, even worse, a negative online presence (a search engine brings up unfavorable or irrelevant information about you), you need to develop or improve your online identity to stay competitive in the job market.

QUOTE

Your name and your identity leave an indelible impression online, making reputation management a new-century skill. Anything that is connected to your name on the Internet can be viewed as a reflection of your character and integrity.

—Dave Opton, CEO and founder of ExecuNet in "Dealing with Your Digital Dirt 2.0," ExecuNet, Inc.

What If Too Many People with Your Name Exist Online?

The opposite problem of not having enough of a presence online is having too many of you present online! If your name is fairly common, you might find that lots of other people who share your name have left a digital trail that is not yours. And sometimes it's a trail you'd rather not be associated with.

This common dilemma has various solutions. You can start to create a unique name for yourself by including an initial rather than only a first and last name when you do anything in public offline or online. You can also more aggressively build up your digital presence so that the first matches for Mary Jones or John Smith point to you and not someone else.

Following Your Digital Footprints

Before establishing yourself online, you need to know what's already out there about you. If prospective employers decide to look you up online, what will they find, if anything? If potential customers want to know more about you as the owner of a business they might deal with, how much will they find online about you? The first thing most people are likely to do when they want to learn more about you is to look you up using a search engine. Google is arguably the most popular search engine, so that's where we'll start.

Go Google Yourself

Your first step in assessing your online identity is to google yourself. Simply type your name into the keyword search field of www.google.com and see what comes up. Use variations of your name, such as with or without a middle initial, or use your formal first name instead of a nickname.

Also, be sure to put quotation marks around your name so that only exact matches will come up. Otherwise, you'll end up pulling up content that includes your first and last name but not necessarily the two names together. If your name is common enough that it's likely to pull up results for many other people, try combining your name with a company you're employed by (or have been employed by in the past) or your business name. Use the plus symbol to add these additional criteria to your search. Example: "Ann Jackson" + "Western Airlines."

TIP

Don't forget about other search engines! Just because Google gets all the attention doesn't mean you should ignore other top search tools such as Yahoo!, Bing, and Ask.

But don't drive yourself crazy feeling that you must check all these all the time. You can limit your regular (weekly or monthly) monitoring to Google and one or two other sites, but keep a full list on hand so that you can check all of them periodically. To find a comprehensive list of search engines beyond those listed here, go to Wikipedia (www.wikipedia.org) and search for "List of Search Engines."

Assess Your Online Appearance

As you browse the results of your search, ask yourself the following three questions to determine how strong and favorable your online identity is:

- **How many?** The *quantity* of results is important. The higher your stature and longer your tenure in your professional or business arena, the more hits you should have.

- **So what?** Asking yourself this question helps you determine the *relevance* of your matches. Do search engines direct people to the most relevant information about you? The Google (or other search engine) results for a search of your name should lead viewers down a digital path lined with hallmarks of your personal brand. It's okay to have some results that reflect nonprofessional areas of your life, such as community service and recreational or social activities, as long as those activities don't reflect negatively on the professional image you want to convey.

TIP

When you google yourself, go beyond the usual Web text search and check also for images, video, news, blogs, and other search options that might bring up matches for your name. On the Google home screen, simply click on one of those choices, usually located near the top of the screen, and then type your name in quotation marks in the search field and see what comes up.

- **What good does it do?** How *positive or negative* are the results of your search? Does the search dig up information from your past that you'd rather someone not see? Or are the results positive—helping to enhance your professional stature or build credibility for your business?

By taking this first step of googling yourself, you get a handle on what your online identity starting point is. Do you have negative information to clean up or not enough information at all? Do you need to create more relevant, positive hits for your name? Next, we look at what you can do to establish the best possible online identity.

TIP

To keep an eye on when, where, and how you appear online, set up a Google Alert (www.google.com/alerts). With a Google Alert, you receive updates by email of new content on the Web that relates to a topic you've requested. That topic should be you, of course. To set it up, enter your name as the search term and select whether you want to receive updates once a day, once a week, or as they happen.

Cleaning Up Your Digital Dirt

The term *digital dirt* was coined in the 2005 ExecuNet report "Dealing with Your Digital Dirt" to describe negative information lurking on the Internet that can damage reputations, cause embarrassment, prevent job seekers from getting hired, and even get people fired. According to a survey of employment recruiters conducted by ExecuNet, 83 percent of recruiters have used search engines to uncover information about candidates, and more than 43 percent have ruled out candidates based on information found online about them. Clearly, your online identity and digital dirt play a significant role in your job search success.

What Digital Dirt Is

Digital dirt comes in all shapes and sizes and varying degrees of lethality. Typical examples of digital dirt are the following:

- Personal information you'd rather not share in the workplace.

- Controversial associations, opinions, or memberships.

- Embarrassing evidence of unprofessional behavior (such as photos of you appearing drunk at a party).

- Public records or references to lawsuits or felonies.

- Information about your credentials that contradicts data on your resume or business marketing materials and therefore suggests you might be lying.

- Evidence of a moonlighting business that could be a conflict of interest with, or distraction from, your primary work.

Digital dirt doesn't have to be disastrous. It can be simply something that is irrelevant to your professional reputation and distracts people from the real message you want to get across about who you are and what you have to offer. Regardless of how dirty your dirt is, it's something you'd rather not have. The next section explains what sort of action you can take against it.

How to Clean Up Your Digital Dirt

If you have negative information or irrelevant information that bugs you, you have three choices for getting rid of it:

- **Wash over it.** Create so much new online content about yourself that the negative or irrelevant information is buried under fresher, more relevant, and more positive content. This method is also useful when you're dealing with digital content that relates to someone else who shares your name. The more positive, relevant content you can create that is truly yours, the more you'll stand out from the pack of Jane Smiths and John Does.

- **Wash it out.** Get rid of it entirely. Having online content deleted is not easy. Unless you or someone you know well created or posted the content in the first place, you might have a difficult time getting the owners of sites to remove the offending content.

- **Wait it out.** Take no active measures to hide or delete the content, but just let nature take its course. Nature, in this case, is the natural sequence of events in most reasonably active, visible professionals' lives. We recommend this approach only if you write, speak, or blog fairly often.

Whichever method you choose to bury or eradicate your digital dirt, be patient because it might take time to achieve your desired results.

TIP

For more help with assessing your online identity and cleaning up your digital dirt, turn to personal branding experts William Arruda and Kirsten Dixson at www.careerdistinction.com.

DISTRACTING, BUT NOT DAMAGING, DIGITAL DIRT

A management consultant we know googled herself and discovered that despite 20-plus years of professional accomplishments—several published books and magazine articles, lots of public speaking, and various bios posted online—her 11-year-old wedding announcement from the *New York Times* was the first search result that came up at the top of a list of 15,600 Google hits about her! She certainly wasn't ashamed of being married, nor was it anything she wanted to keep secret, but an 11-year-old wedding announcement was not exactly the first thing she wanted people to see when going online to get to know her professionally.

Why was this happening? The *New York Times* is such a powerful online media outlet that Google is likely to pull up a name that has appeared in that newspaper before other newer, but less heavily trafficked sites.

Our management consultant friend knew that the *New York Times* was too formidable an institution to be likely to honor a request from her to remove the wedding announcement, so she didn't even try the "wash it out" approach. Her only realistic options were to take active steps online to bury the content under more brand-relevant information (wash over it) or just let it get buried eventually without taking any action—the "wait it out" method.

She decided to take the "wait it out" approach. As a published author and active member of her professional community, she was likely to have more online content developed about her even without her intervention. Plus, the wedding announcement was merely distracting, not damaging, so she wasn't in a huge hurry to bury it. Sure enough, she googled herself again a couple of months later and found that five new search results topped the list over her wedding announcement without her having done anything. (The results were related to some new sites listing her books for sale.)

Another option is to call in professionals to clean up your digital dirt. Just as there are services you can hire to monitor the security of your financial credit in order to protect against identity theft or other inappropriate credit uses, there are also businesses that will keep an eye on your online reputation and help you keep it clean.

One of the pioneers in this field, ReputationDefender (www.reputationdefender.com), goes on a search-and-destroy mission. This organization (see figure 3.1) scours the Internet to dig up every bit of information on you and then sets out to destroy (at your request) any negative information by getting it corrected or removed, whenever possible.

Figure 3.1: *ReputationDefender helps clean up your digital dirt.*

Defining and Conveying Your Personal Brand Through Your Online Identity

Our local chapter of the national organization ExecuNet holds networking meetings twice a month that attract six-figure job seekers, recruiters, and entrepreneurs, as well as executives who simply like to stay connected even when they're not in job search mode. Each meeting features an informative speaker and some mingling time over hors d'oeuvres and soft drinks, as well as a block of time for every attendee to stand at the front of the room and give his or her "elevator speech."

The term *elevator speech* is based on the notion that if you find yourself riding on an elevator with someone who could be valuable to your career or business, you should be able to communicate your selling points by the time that person gets off the elevator. Borrowing a

term coined by author Michelle Tullier in *Networking for Job Search and Career Success* (JIST Publishing, 2004), we call this your *self-marketing sound bite*—a quick synopsis of who you are, what you've done, what you have to offer, and what you're looking for.

We've been speakers and participants at these meetings and always find that only a handful of the participants' self-marketing sound bites stand out as memorable. The rest tend to sound too much like everyone else's. They're usually a recitation of work history chronology and some vague comments about goals—nothing disastrous, just not very distinctive.

 QUOTE

From time to time, I read blog posts or comments that state or imply that cultivating a personal brand is about shameless self-promotion. Arguably, if you look at the very strong brands of some of the executives and celebrities of our time, it sure can seem that way. And yet having, cultivating, and even promoting a personal brand is anything but a shameless ego trip. It is really about using your strengths and your passions to make a difference for other people.

—from the blog of Walter Akana, www.threshold-consulting.com

Whether you're a six-figure executive or someone just looking for a paycheck that'll cover the rent, you have to develop the habit of speaking about yourself in a way that will make you stand out from the pack and will establish your personal brand in the minds of others. Making an effort to be visible and memorable is even more important when you're networking online. In this case, you have to rely on the written word to get your message across rather than body language, tone of voice, or attire. Your words must pack a punch.

What makes your message memorable? We recommend five strategies:

1. Tout the benefits, not the features.

2. Be clear and concise.

3. Be unique.

4. Show your personality.

5. Be consistent and persistent.

Tout the Benefits, Not the Features

Take a tip from tried-and-true advertising strategies and don't give the details of your work history or a laundry list of degrees and credentials. Instead, give a few key highlights of your experience, accomplishments, and contributions. It's like a cereal box telling consumers that the contents will help lower their cholesterol without getting into the food chemistry behind why that will happen. People who are going to hire, network with, or do business with you don't need to know every detail of your history. They just need to know what you've done for others and what you can do for them. If they really do want or need the details, they can always read your resume or bio later.

 TIP

Not sure how to articulate the benefits you offer? Take stock of your skills and positive personal qualities by completing quick, self-directed assessment exercises or formal testing through a career coach. Links to sites that offer do-it-yourself assessments and information on the coach-led ones are provided in appendix A.

Be Clear and Concise

When you network with someone, you're not only telling that person about yourself, but also hoping that this contact will spread the word to others about who you are and what you have to offer. Whether you meet with individuals one-on-one or in a group setting, offline or online, you are in essence training those people to be your sales force. They are going to go out and spread the word about you and your needs, goals, talents, or services.

Of course, when networking online, you reach a larger number of people more quickly, so if each of those connections tells a friend, who tells a friend, who tells a friend…well, you get the picture. The viral marketing quality of networking has the power to do great things for you, but only if the message that is being spread about you is the one that you want spread. It is critical, therefore, that every message you share about yourself be clear, concise, and easy to understand. Networking this way is like training that sales force to go out and market a product. They won't be successful if they don't have a solid understanding of the product and some language to use when talking about it.

TIP

When you're networking online, your self-marketing sound bite will typically be delivered in writing rather than being spoken. To make sure it is clear, easily understood, and quick to read, ask some friends and colleagues to test-drive it for you. Have them read your self-marketing sound bite and give you feedback on what they glean from it and how long they took to read it. A concise, effective self-marketing sound bite should take someone anywhere from 15 to 30 seconds to read.

Be Unique

Michelle Tullier, our editor for this book and a longtime career counselor, has an interesting tidbit of information that she almost always includes when speaking about her background. A few years ago, she was invited jointly by the United States Department of State and the King of Jordan to spend a few weeks in Jordan helping that country's universities establish or improve their career counseling departments. Since then, when she has to give a brief overview of her experience and credentials, she often mentions that experience, even though it is not directly relevant to her current career emphasis and goals. (She operates more in corporate than academic arenas now.) It's unique and interesting, though, so it makes her self-marketing sound bite stick in people's minds. And it establishes her brand as a subject matter expert with an international flair.

Think about what makes you unique or different. What adds color and interest to your pitch? It doesn't have to involve high levels of government or royalty! Anything that is a little out of the ordinary will work, whether it's a special project, an especially impressive accomplishment, or anything else that is likely to make you more memorable.

QUOTE

Branding myself simply helped me positively grab companies' attention by creating a unique, unforgettable image for myself and my services. Personal branding, by definition, is the process by which we market ourselves to others. It is about "self packaging." It's identifying the unique qualities, marketable skills, and institutional knowledge that someone possesses and building a reputation that captures the attention of others (clients, managers, prospects, or future employers). No matter how old we are, what titles we hold, what business we are in, we all need to understand the importance of self-branding. We all own "Me, LLC"; we need to be unique in who we are and what we do to stand out from the crowd.

—Sahar Andrade, social media strategist, global marketing/diversity consultant

Show Your Personality

Let your personality show through in all you do when connecting with others online. Unless you're interacting with people live through a podcast (a live audio broadcast like a radio program but via the Internet) or other voice connection, your message will be delivered online in a fairly static, one-dimensional fashion. People will get to know you through your profile statement on a social network, through your tweets on Twitter, or through comments on blogs or discussion groups.

In social networking, people have to get to know you through your written words. They won't see your confident body language or animated facial expressions. They won't feel your firm handshake or sense the energy in your voice. You have to find a way to let your personality, energy, and enthusiasm shine through. This can be done by writing as if you were speaking directly to the reader, using humor where appropriate, and expressing opinions (as long as they are relevant to the topic at hand and won't get you into trouble!).

Be Consistent and Persistent

A message heard once is not likely to be remembered or acted upon. If you know anything about advertising, you know that placing an advertisement once is usually not sufficient. Media campaigns involve repeated placements of ads over time and often in multiple media sources, such as newspapers, magazines, websites, and maybe even television or radio.

If you are marketing yourself for a job or for career advancement or business development, you need to have a multipronged approach to getting out the word about you and what you have to offer. In chapter 1, you learned about the various online avenues for gaining professional visibility. As you read the remaining chapters and get more details on how each of those works, you can start to select the best ones for you.

QUOTE

What makes you unique—makes you successful! In any social media venue be prepared to communicate how you distinguish yourself differently from others. What makes you unique? Capturing that quality is key to your career success. What makes you unique is the cornerstone of your legacy and what makes you memorable in the selection process.

—Walt Gansser, executive coach and former human resource executive with a Fortune 100 firm

Developing a Self-Marketing Sound Bite

You'll use your self-marketing sound bite as the foundation for the profiles you'll post online as well as when emailing people or chatting in online communities. A good self-marketing sound bite hits the highlights of who you are, what you've done, and what you or your business has to offer. It conveys your personal brand and online identity. Your sound bite should do four main things:

- Put yourself on the map.
- Pitch your strengths.
- Back up your claims.
- State what you want.

Putting Yourself on the Map

Putting yourself on the map means establishing who you are in terms of your work or educational status, situation, and roles. That might include your job title, career area, functional role(s), and an overview of your experience or your business offerings and background.

Examples:

I have 15 years of experience in software sales, including 5 years in sales management roles.

I'm a physical therapist specializing in sports injuries.

I'm a junior at Georgia Tech majoring in civil engineering and have held internships with Garrett Construction and in city government.

As an independent consultant for the past several years, I've helped more than 50 small businesses gain market share and grow their revenues through cost-effective local marketing efforts.

TIP

Remember that your self-marketing sound bite is a building block for profiles you post on social networks or for your bio on a blog or microblogging site like Twitter, so it will be out there for all the world to see—literally. Protect your privacy by not including personal data such as your address, Social Security number, or tax ID number.

Pitching Your Strengths

When pitching your strengths, mention the positive points that will help you reach your goals. These points may cover the categories described next.

Skills

Don't give a laundry list of skills, but cite two or three examples. Remember that the assessment sites listed in appendix A can help you come up with your top skills if you don't already know them off the top of your head.

Examples:

I am fluent in Mandarin and Russian, both written and spoken.

I am highly proficient in Excel and PowerPoint.

My particular talent is in turnaround situations, winning back business from dissatisfied clients and driving growth and revenue.

Areas of Expertise

Think about what you have to know to do your job or be successful in your business. This is your content knowledge or subject matter expertise.

Examples:

I'm a human resources generalist with in-depth knowledge of compensation and benefits.

My interdisciplinary major exposed me to many current issues in education and public policy.

Personal Qualities

What distinguishes you from others you've worked with or other businesses in your market?

Examples:

My managers have always commented on my initiative and strong work ethic.

I'm known as a resourceful problem-solver.

My clients appreciate my ability as a consultant to get at the heart of their needs quickly and develop cost-effective solutions.

Backing Up Your Claims

Making claims about what you can do is one thing. It's another to provide evidence of what you have done. You therefore should include a very brief mention of one of your achievements as part of your self-marketing sound bite. Remember, be brief. You can always elaborate later if someone is interested in hearing the whole story. Note that the best achievement statements include both the actions or effort taken as well as the positive outcome. In other words, don't just say what you achieved; tell how you did it.

Examples:

I reduced accident incidents on the plant floor by 32 percent in a 12-month period by developing and implementing new safety procedures.

After taking over a call center that was getting too many customer complaints and had been operating over budget for the past year, I streamlined operations to reduce expenses by 40 percent and enhanced training programs to improve customer feedback ratings by 20 percent.

As president of my homeowner's association, I spearheaded improvements that led to an equity increase of $1.5 million across the 120 homes, a much higher rate of increase than that of surrounding subdivisions.

My consulting firm recently helped a client identify $6,000 per month in operating cost savings opportunities as a result of hiring us for a process re-engineering engagement.

To help you develop your achievement statements, pull out past performance reviews; logs you may have kept of successes at work; project files; letters of praise from bosses, colleagues, or customers; and anything else that will help you remember what you've contributed to your employers or clients. You might also have included examples of accomplishments in your resume, so refer to your current or past resumes for ideas as well.

What Have You Done for Us Lately?

To develop your achievement statements, ask yourself the following questions to jog your memory about noteworthy things you've done. Don't worry if not all apply to you; just try to find a few that help you come up with achievements you can talk about in your networking. Write examples on the lines that follow each question.

Did I save an employer or client money?

_____

Did I help an employer or client make more money?

_____

Have I done something in a new and better way? Developed a new system or process? Been innovative and creative?

_____

Have I received any awards or special recognition?

_____

Am I known for being particularly good at something that distinguishes me from my peers? Am I relied upon as the go-to person for something?

_____

Have there been particularly challenging situations in which I've excelled?

_____

Did I ever take on extra work or a special project that wasn't part of my regular role?

_____

What am I the most proud of in my professional and/or civic life?

_____

Stating What You Want

A final component of your sound bite is to clarify what you want or need. If you're looking for a job, you would briefly state why you are in the market and what jobs you're targeting. If you're seeking career management or advancement advice, give a concise description of where you are in your career and why you're seeking help. If you have your own business, indicate the types of customers, clients, or referrals that are appropriate for you.

Examples:

I'm hoping to expand my eldercare business into the southwestern United States and would like to learn more about the assisted-living market in that region.

My position with XYZ Company was eliminated as part of a major reduction-in-force, and I'm now looking for a position as a marketing manager in a midsized company in the banking or finance industry.

 TIP

Your self-marketing sound bite is all about you, you, you! Don't forget, though, that genuine networking is about giving to others as much as you ask them to give to you. Talking about what you need is okay, but also make sure that you ask others how you can help them.

If you're not currently looking for a new job or actively seeking to develop new business, you don't have to include the "tell them what you want" section of your sound bite. You might instead offer simply a value contribution statement that tells people what you can do for them. A financial advisor, for example, might say something like

I help my clients shave years off their retirement target date.

A software salesperson might say

I make money by helping you save money. I offer cost-effective software solutions that will improve your operating efficiencies and cut costs.

Creating a Sound Bite When You're Searching for a Job

To make it easy for you to construct a self-marketing sound bite, we've provided the following template. All you have to do is fill in the blanks to customize a sound bite for yourself. Keep in mind, though, that using a template like this doesn't allow much room for originality. Feel free to mix up the order, jazz up the wording, and make the message your own. This template should serve only as a basic guide to help you start; then you can be creative and let the real you show through.

Job Seeker's Sound Bite Template

With _____ years of experience in the _____ industry, I've developed expertise in _____ and _____ . I've held roles in/as _____ [your functional areas or titles] and most recently have been [or currently am] a _____ [current or most recent functional role or title goes here] with _____ [current or most recent employer name].

Within _____ [overall functional area, for example, marketing, sales, public administration], I have special expertise in _____ and _____ . Recently, for example, I _____ [accomplishment example].

Throughout my career, I've gained a reputation for_____ _____ [skills and personal qualities]. My work experience is complemented by _____ [educational degree, certifications/licenses, or other relevant credentials].

I'm seeking a _____ [type of position sought] in _____ [target industry or type of employer].

Following is a sample self-marketing sound bite for a job seeker looking for a high-level management job in the banking industry:

With more than 20 years of experience in banking, I've demonstrated a consistent track record of growing market share and generating revenue. I've held a variety of progressively responsible roles in marketing and client relations and most recently was vice president of client services with Regional Bank.

I have special expertise in using Web-based solutions for customer acquisition and retention. Recently, for example, I was recognized with our Chairman's Award for the most outstanding contribution to the organization last year for leading my team to develop Internet marketing strategies that broke the mold.

Throughout my career, I've been known for my innovative but practical solutions to challenging business retention and development issues.

I'm now seeking a leadership role in a community bank with an entrepreneurial environment where I can contribute my talents and experience for rapid growth and profitability.

Creating Sound Bites When You're Not Actively Job Searching

If you're not actively looking for a job but simply want to enhance how you do business, whether you're employed in an organization or self-employed, you still need a self-marketing sound bite. It will enable you to convey to people who you are and what you have to offer so that you can attract the right kinds of people to network with—people with whom you can share ideas, knowledge, leads, and referrals.

You can use many components of the job seeker's sound bite, including the overview of your experience, skills or personal qualities, and contribution highlights, but you don't have to get into what you're looking for.

Here's a sample all-purpose self-marketing sound bite:

Over the past 12 years I've developed a solid track record in sales management, consistently leading teams that exceed revenue plans and expand market share. I've become known as "the turnaround guy"—someone who can win back accounts that are on the rocks and get business units back to profitability.

(continued)

(continued)

I began my career with XYZ Corporation, where I was an outside sales rep for three years before promotion into management. From there, I held sales leadership roles with increasingly larger territories and responsibilities in the chemical and pharmaceutical industries.

I'm currently vice president of a nine-state region for QRS Corporation and serve on the board of directors for IJK Foundation.

Now that you have a sense of how important your online steps are to projecting your professional brand to the world and how to start going about doing so, you're ready to develop a plan for exactly where to go online and how much time to spend there.

MANAGING YOUR TIME ONLINE

So many choices, so little time. That's a common lament of social networkers. Like any activity on the Internet, connecting with people virtually and maintaining an online identity can be major time-eaters. You therefore need to be focused in your efforts and realistic about what you can accomplish on a daily or weekly basis. That means having a solid handle on what's involved in the various social media and understanding which ones are the best fit for your particular situation. Chapters 4 through 9 in this book survey the various categories of social networking tools so that you can start to decide where to devote your time (and sometimes your money) to yield the best return on investment.

You have to know what you're getting into when you network online. You can think of this as the old "look before you leap" advice. Some social media require significant start-up time and some expense but minimal ongoing maintenance, whereas others are easy and cheap to dive into but require constant care and feeding.

You might start out in some of the more high-maintenance networking activities with the best of intentions, but like dieting, exercising, and cleaning out the garage, unless you commit to keeping up your efforts long term, you won't achieve much success. Developing a LinkedIn profile and not doing anything with it, for example, is worse for your professional image than not having one at all. Similarly, developing a Twitter profile is a good first step, but unless you take the time to create conversation, develop a following, and connect with other people, you're not actively participating.

Identifying Your Social Networking Goals

Networking should be a part of every professional's or business owner's life on an ongoing, "don't-even-have-to-think-about-it" basis. Having a large network of quality people to turn to for assistance at a moment's notice is critical for success. And having a range of people who can turn to you for support as they strive to reach their goals is highly rewarding. So in some sense, your networking goal should be very broad: Just do it! You never know when you'll need to call upon a contact to help you out or when you will have the opportunity to get satisfaction out of helping someone else.

Nevertheless, there are times in the life of a career or business when networking—both offline and online—needs to be a more concentrated effort. You might need a new job or advice on getting a raise or promotion. Or maybe you need to lift your business out of the doldrums and generate more sales and revenue. Whatever the reason, there is a social networking avenue that can help you solve your problems and achieve your objectives. The following sections examine some of the specific goals you might have, depending on your situation.

QUOTE

LinkedIn has greatly enhanced and positively impacted my job search and career social networking activities. I began two and a half years ago to build my LinkedIn network and add to my profile. I realized that my profile was the single most powerful tool I had to get my personal "brand" out there in the U.S. and abroad. As a result, I have had both a headhunter and a potential employer at a Fortune 100 company contact me directly.

—Katie Bonta, sales and marketing executive

DON'T DO IT JUST BECAUSE WE SAID SO!

If you're a job seeker, don't network online simply because a career coach told you to. Do it because you have specific employment goals in mind and know that networking on the Internet will help you reach your targets. If you are networking online to develop business or make sales, don't do it just to jump on the bandwagon. Do it because you know that online tools can help you drum up leads and intelligence on your prospects.

Finding a Job

Depending on whose survey results you believe—and many such surveys are conducted every year—75 to 85 percent of jobs typically are found through networking. Connecting with people who can lead you to potential employers—or attracting the right people through your professional visibility—is usually the most effective job search method for most people. With social networking avenues to complement your in-person, offline networking efforts, you have more chances than ever of landing a position through connections you make.

IT'S ABOUT PEOPLE, NOT POSTINGS

Don't confuse social networking with using online job boards. Sites such as Monster, CareerBuilder, and many more still play a role in identifying employment opportunities through the job postings they offer. But uploading your resume to a job site or applying for positions through those sites is not social networking. It's simply applying for jobs and might not yield the positive return on investment—time investment, that is—that you can get from social networking. The process of getting to know real people or making yourself visible so that real people get to know you is always going to be the better strategy.

Through social media, you, as a job hunter, can accomplish everything that you would in offline networking. Social networking helps at all phases of your search. Some specific things you might be looking for include the following:

- Advice on determining your specific career or job objective.

- Information about industries, fields, and occupations you are targeting in your search or considering targeting.

- Strategic advice about your self-marketing plan and approach to your search.

- Input on the tools of your search, such as feedback on your resume, cover letters, self-marketing sound bite, and more.

- Suggestions of general types of employers or recruiters to target, as well as names of specific organizations or search firms to approach.

- Insight into the culture, strengths and weaknesses, hiring methods, or other characteristics of organizations you are targeting for employment, as well as industry-specific information.

- Names of people to contact to learn about actual employment opportunities.

- Direct leads to job openings.

- Advice on evaluating and negotiating job offers.

- Emotional support through the ups and downs of your search.

- A way to job search when your time is limited or a way to be visible and search passively yet still effectively.

 QUOTE

I have clients using LinkedIn to research the profiles of individuals with whom they have interviews scheduled. This allows them to get a "feel" for the person and adopt interviewing strategies accordingly.

—George Stecyk, executive consultant, Stewart, Cooper & Coon

No matter which social networking path you choose to follow, the important thing is simply to do it. Make it a part of your search as you would attending a live networking event, working with recruiters, sending out resumes and cover letters, attending job fairs, and applying to positions online.

SOCIAL NETWORKING REALLY IS WORTH THE TIME

As career coaches, we often find that it's a struggle to convince job seekers that networking is worth the time and effort. We know it's so much easier to sit at your computer and fire off resumes in reply to job postings. But would you rather do that for months on end or cut down your job search time considerably by networking your way to a job? With social networking, you now have the best of both worlds. You can do it from the convenience of your office or plopped on the couch with your laptop, and it still counts as networking! So there really are no excuses for not networking in a job search.

Managing Your Career

Even if you're not actively searching for a new job, you ought to network anyway. Staying visible in your professional community and maintaining a solid network of business relationships are key to career satisfaction and success. Think of networking as "taking a village to raise a career." Sure, you—and only you—are ultimately responsible for steering your career where you want it to go, but having an army of allies at your disposal doesn't hurt.

QUOTE

There's been a huge paradigm shift. The days of mutual loyalty and trust between companies and employees has changed forever. The relationship with your company can end at any moment. We have all become "at-will" workers and constantly need to be renewing our value to the organization, enhancing our skills and experience, and understanding the value of what we deliver. We need to keep resumes up to date, immerse ourselves in social media tools, and network with others. Adopting this new paradigm in your career allows you to focus on adding value that benefits both you and your employer.

—Bert DuMars, vice president of e-business and interactive marketing, Newell Rubbermaid

Networking online can be an asset throughout the entire life cycle of your career, from becoming established, to advancing or changing roles in your organization or career field, to deciding when to scale back toward retirement. Some specific goals you might have for your social networking include the following:

- Enhance your job performance and productivity by learning best practices for innovation, creativity, and efficiency. This knowledge can come from people in your field as well as those in other industries or professions who might have a fresh perspective for you.

- Position yourself for promotions, advancement, and raises by being more savvy about your field and your role and by getting strategic negotiating advice from people in your network.

- Keep an eye on the competition—know what other organizations in your market are up to.

- Get more familiar with your customer or client base, vendors, suppliers, or any other constituencies that you and your employer buy from, sell to, or serve.

- Be on the lookout for opportunities for a career change or job change, just in case the grass might be greener somewhere else.

- Position yourself as a passive job candidate, someone who is not actively searching but can be found online by recruiters and employers if the perfect opportunity comes up.

- Feel connected to your professional community at-large and gain a sense of collegiality.

- Get ideas for semi-retirement career options and ways to start to phase out your full-time career.

Whether you're at the entry level of your career or well established, social networking can enhance your satisfaction and success. It helps you make sure that where you are is where you want to be. And if you're not where you want to be, it helps you get there.

QUOTE

Because I had my identity stolen many years ago, online networking, Facebook, etc. were not very appealing options. Reluctantly, I put a profile on LinkedIn but still did not put a photo, address, or phone number in my profile. As long as LinkedIn protects the massive database it is accumulating, I will remain on LinkedIn because it was helpful in making new contacts, getting back in touch with old coworkers and college friends, and making connections with recruiters and HR staff.

—Mike M, engineer

Enhancing Your Work as a Marketer, Salesperson, Entrepreneur, or Business Developer

Developing business for your own entrepreneurial endeavor or as a sales or marketing professional is more than placing ads and making cold calls. People like to do business with people they know, so networking is critical for business owners and salespeople.

Networking online helps with all aspects of running and growing a business or making sales, such as the following:

- Help with making the decision to go into business for yourself.
- Strategic advice about structuring and launching your business or a particular product, including writing the business plan or marketing materials and hiring staff.
- Referral sources of customers or clients.
- Connections to actual customers or clients.
- Getting advance information about a business prospect to make this a "warm" connection.
- Sourcing strategic alliance partners or employees.
- A sense of connection to a larger community—a sort of virtual team of coworkers for a small or solo business.
- Information on possible vendors or suppliers for the business.
- The ability to keep an eye on the competition.

- Insight into the needs, culture, quirks, and other characteristics of your target customers or clients.

- Virtual marketing options for launching or expanding the business or product lines.

- Emotional support through the ups and downs of starting and running a business or closing deals.

Entrepreneurs and salespeople often feel too busy for social networking—or so they think. Salespeople are usually on the go, calling on clients, wining and dining prospective clients, or attending in-person networking events. Rarely are they found sitting in front of a computer, at least not by choice. Similarly, entrepreneurs are usually not tied to a desk. They're pulled in many different directions to run all aspects of the business.

We're not saying that any of those things should stop. We simply recommend adding social networking to your business development arsenal. You might find that you save time because of the shortcuts it offers for reaching more people, more quickly.

Your Social Networking Goals

Now that you have a sense of the many possible goals that you can attain through networking online, it's time to put on paper the specific goals you want to reach. You can do so by answering the following questions, either here in the book or by creating your own form on paper or electronically.

What is your top-priority goal? This is the big-picture goal. It might be long term or fairly near term. For example, "I want to land a job in an organization that is more family-friendly." Or "I want to develop new business among midsized companies in the pharmaceutical industry." Write a few lines about this goal:

_____

_____

_____

_____

(continued)

(continued)

What are some specific objectives or milestones that will help you reach that goal? These are specific things you need to reach your goal. Skimming over the preceding lists can provide ideas. Examples include identifying companies in a geographic area that are family-friendly; finding people who have insight into the culture of, and possible opportunities at, certain family-friendly companies; and getting to know five people this week who work in midsized pharmaceutical companies. Write your objectives in the following space:

_____

_____

_____

_____

Who can help you reach your goals and objectives? Include categories of people who might be able to help you move closer to your goals. For example, the person with a goal of developing new business in the pharmaceutical industry might need to connect with scientists or people in companies that make the equipment used in pharmaceutical labs. The family-oriented job seeker might want to connect with people who congregate in online parenting forums.

_____

_____

_____

_____

Developing a Full-Service Network

As you start to think about how you're going to use social networking to reach the goals you've identified, first consider what you're already doing in the way of traditional networking and think about the quality and quantity of your network itself. Consider these questions:

- How large and strong is your network? How many of those people do you have solid business relationships with, as opposed to having nothing more than contact names in a database—people you barely know?

- How well rounded is your network? Are your contacts spread across industries and organizations, or clustered in one organization you've worked for or within one industry or professional field?

- How geographically dispersed is your network? Are there certain locations where you could benefit from knowing more people?

- What roles do the people in your network fulfill? Are they mostly referral sources of business or primarily coworkers and former work colleagues? Are they more personal contacts than professional?

To make sure that you have someone to turn to for every need that might arise as you strive toward your professional and business goals, consider how well rounded your network is. A good model for this is the "STARS" system, developed by career consultant Michelle Tullier and described in detail in her book *Networking for Job Search and Career Success* (JIST Publishing). She defines a well-balanced network as one that includes relationships with people who can play the following roles in your career or business development:

- **S**trategists: The people who help you plot a course toward your goals. They give advice, feedback, and coaching to direct you down the right path.

- **T**argets: The people most closely linked to your career or business goals—the people you've set your sights on reaching, such as prospective employers, customers, or clients.

- **A**llied forces: The professionals who provide expertise to strengthen your networking efforts and brand expression. They might be image consultants, website designers, career coaches, communications consultants, and more.

- **R**ole models: The mentors or sages who serve as role models for your business or career and who can offer advice and wisdom.

- **S**upporters: The people who provide emotional support and cheer you along the path to reaching your goals.

Do you need more STARS in your network? If so, social networking might be the answer to developing not just a larger network, but a more "full-service" one.

 QUOTE

The past 25 years of working around the globe allowed me to have an important international network, but many of those relationships went cold or died, simply due to the effort in maintaining them. Now with a presence online, regardless of physical location, we can share emotions, pictures, and stories, bringing much-sought-after information and intimacy into those relationships.

—Rudy Augsburger, president, Celta Consult

In this chapter, you've thought about what you want to accomplish in your career or business and have been introduced to the main ways to network online. Don't worry if you don't fully understand what some of these things are or exactly how to go about doing them. In subsequent chapters, we provide more how-to details of using each of these social networking methods.

Key Points: Chapter 3

- Having an online identity is becoming increasingly important as a way to establish your credibility and personal brand and to attract career or business opportunities.

- The first step in establishing your online identity is to google yourself and assess how strong your "digital footprint" is and whether it conveys positive information about you.

- You have three choices for dealing with negative online information about yourself: replace it with more positive content, have it removed, or wait it out and let new content appear over it.

- To communicate your personal brand online, develop a self-marketing sound bite—a brief statement that conveys who you are and what you have to offer.

- Before determining which social media you'll use for networking, it's important to identify your career or business goals so that you can choose the right avenues for reaching those goals.

CHAPTER 4

Harnessing the Power
of Social Networks

Congratulations! You've completed some of the most challenging tasks on your social networking job search journey. In chapter 3, you identified the unique attributes that shape your personal brand, scripted marketing messages, and defined your networking goals.

In this chapter, we take you beyond planning and thinking about social networking into the realm of actually doing it. Here, you learn more about the most popular of the social networks, as well as rules of engagement for networking online.

In This Chapter

- *Develop a deeper understanding of social networks and their benefits.*
- *Learn common features and functionalities of various social networks.*
- *Identify other popular sites beyond LinkedIn.*
- *Learn the rules of social networking etiquette.*

The Language of Social Networks

Let's first clarify terminology because it can get a bit confusing. You know by now that the term *social networking* refers to all the things you can do online to meet people and develop relationships, as well as to make yourself visible so that they want to meet you. Social networking can be carried out using various social media, such as LinkedIn, Twitter, and blogs.

So it might surprise you to find that a chapter on social networks isn't going to say much about Twitter and blogs. Bear with us here! Don't shoot the messenger because we didn't come up with the conventional language around all this. The term *social networks* is usually used to describe sites such as LinkedIn, Facebook, XING, and the like. So that's why this chapter is called what it's called and why it focuses on giving you an overview of the social networks without much mention of the other ways you can do social network*ing*, such as through Twitter, blogging, and so forth.

What Are Social Networks?

Social networks are huge online databases in which individuals upload information about themselves—usually referred to as a *profile*—for the purpose of networking with others online. In its broadest sense, the term *social network* includes sites that have a predominantly personal focus as well as those that are more business and professionally oriented.

QUOTE

In my first session at Right Management, the point was clearly driven home about the importance of having a robust profile on LinkedIn and building your contacts. The job I'm in right now is a direct result of that. I was contacted through LinkedIn by the HR director. LinkedIn works if you work it!

—Angie Amon

Personal networking sites focus on helping people stay in touch with friends; make new friends; reconnect with old contacts; share opinions about music, movies, and hobbies; and find dates or romance. Sites such as Facebook, MySpace, Tagged, Classmates.com, hi5, Meetup, and MyLife are among the most popular in this category.

Business or professional networking sites, on the other hand, focus on exchanging information for career opportunities, consulting assignments, new business ventures, job inquiries, expertise requests, business deals, business promotion, and more. Sites including LinkedIn, Ryze, Viadeo, Biznik, Ecademy, BrazenCareerist, FastPitch, SageSpark, and an ever-expanding list of others fall into the professional networking arena.

Not to confuse matters, but these two camps are not mutually exclusive and have become less so over the last several years. More and more, jobs are found and hiring is done on the personal networking sites. Facebook is the best example of this, and that's why you find a whole chapter devoted to Facebook in this book about social networking for job search. And reconnecting with former colleagues and classmates on the more business-oriented networking sites does (we hear) lead to social opportunities, friendly encounters, and perhaps even dates! But the business sites vary from the more personal sites in terms of information you put in your profile, search capabilities, rules of engagement, and general tone of the conversations on the sites.

The Benefits of Social Networks

All social network sites are based on the idea of six degrees of separation. In other words, it's not just the people you know, but the people your contacts know, and the people their contacts know, that can reap networking rewards. The premise is that if you reach out far enough (six degrees, according to the adage), you can connect to everyone. With these sophisticated social network platforms facilitating the process, however, experts now estimate that only about four to five degrees of separation connect everyone. Regardless of the number, it is truly amazing how your network grows on these sites.

ONLY 3 DEGREES OF SEPARATION FROM MORE THAN 11 MILLION PEOPLE!

As of this writing, your author Ellen has the following network on LinkedIn:

- **First-degree network: 2,434.** These are the people she has connected to directly.

- **Second-degree network: 501,800+.** These are the people her direct (first-degree) contacts know.

- **Third-degree network: 11,052,000+.** These are the people in the first-degree networks of her second-degree contacts.

- **Total members she can contact directly or be introduced to: 11,556,300+!**

(continued)

(continued)

> When Ellen searches her network to find contacts or assistance, she is searching a database of more than 11 million people—evidence of how a network can grow exponentially when you use a social network.

By signing up on one or more of the professional networking sites, you can dramatically increase the scope and reach of your network. Thousands or perhaps millions of people globally can view your information 24/7! (Don't worry; you control how much personal data you put out there for people to see.) You can broadcast your message faster and farther than is possible with traditional networking and some of the other social networking options.

And networking interactions are easier to schedule. You don't need to be in the same place to network. You don't even have to be net-working at the same time. In other words, you can make professional connections despite time and location barriers. You can meet people on the social networks that you wouldn't be able to meet otherwise because of location, time constraints, physical limitations, or your level within your organization or professional community. If you're an introvert, social networks have the benefit of enabling you to network at your computer instead of facing the crowds at traditional networking events.

 QUOTE

In 2010, I found myself in a job search in another country. Communications were expensive and challenging. But I found that LinkedIn offered an easy, inexpensive way to conduct a global job search. The turnaround response has been great as more and more people around the world use social media sites like LinkedIn.

—Greg Hollod, PhD; environmental, health, and safety executive

There are also technological benefits. You don't need to have strong computer proficiencies to use the social networks. Basic computer and Internet skills will suffice. So if the thought of launching a blog or hosting a podcast is just too daunting, the social networks are a good option for you. Even if you plan to start a blog or get into podcasting, the social networks should still be a significant part of your online strategy.

In addition, the social networks offer more functionality, more members, and a more diverse audience than online discussion groups (such as Google groups or Yahoo! groups). In discussion groups, a smaller number of members tend to share a similar interest and don't offer the broad range of talents and interests represented on sites such as LinkedIn.

WHY PICK SOCIAL NETWORKS FOR YOUR ONLINE ENCOUNTERS?

- They're less time and labor intensive.

- You use them on your own schedule instead of having to attend meetings or events that might not be as convenient.

- They broadcast your message faster and farther.

- They give you access to a global audience 24/7.

- They help you unearth influential and hard-to-find people.

- You can get by with minimal computer skills.

- Everyone's doing it!

How Social Network Sites Work

The various professional networking sites differ from one another in significant ways, such as headquarters location (which can affect the geographic slant of the membership), location of members, size of the membership, rules for connecting, and advanced features beyond the basic posting of a profile and browsing other people's profiles. Yet all these sites have some common features:

- **Requiring membership:** You have to join the sites. Some sites are by invitation only, whereas others are open to all who find their way to the home page. But you must sign up and become a member.

- **Posting a profile:** You represent yourself on the site with a profile that you fill out. The profile provides information about your skills, work history, education, and credentials.

- **Sending and accepting invitations:** You grow your network by inviting others to join your network on the site and by accepting invitations from other people to connect to their networks.

- **Searching for contacts:** You explore the site's membership to find people. You search for people you already know but may have lost touch with. You search for people you don't know but who have something in common with you professionally or who do something or work somewhere that's of interest to you. You search by name or other criteria and reach out to the people you find to ask them to join your network. You can also request an introduction to people in their networks or start a dialogue with them to share ideas or get information and answers.

- **Joining relevant groups and subgroups:** You can dive more deeply into your networking by selecting and joining groups and/or subgroups that are of interest. Most of these groups are searchable by keyword or by the actual name of the group. Joining such groups enhances your networking efforts exponentially and makes connections with like-minded people that much easier.

 QUOTE

I am a transition specialist for the U.S. Marine Corps in Okinawa, Japan. I work with military members, veterans, and military spouses in their employment search. Through LinkedIn, I've met recruiters from large companies, gathered information on how military members should apply with their companies, and received job announcements. I continue to build connections, join groups, and add to discussions. I continue to learn and gather information, not only for my clients, but for myself as well.

—Lori Cleymans, Transition Assistance Management Program, Camp Courtney, Okinawa, Japan

The Ever-Changing Landscape of Social Networks

Providing a comprehensive list of all the business-oriented social networks is a constant challenge. New sites arrive often, older ones disappear from view, and other types of websites expand their offerings to resemble social networks.

LinkedIn, with more than 70 million members from a wide variety of backgrounds and industries, is by far the largest exclusively professional networking site and therefore is the focus of the next chapter. Facebook, because of its size (more than 500 million members) and increasing use for professional networking, also warrants its own chapter (chapter 6). But, as mentioned earlier, these are by no means the only professional networking sites.

TOP PROFESSIONAL SOCIAL NETWORKS

We're calling these top sites based on their popularity, membership size, and broad range of features. These sites were all functioning and going strong at the time of this writing. Several of them are so large and well established that they're not likely to dissolve any time soon.

- www.linkedin.com
- www.facebook.com (Primarily a personal social network but up and coming for job search and other business or professional use.)
- www.viadeo.com
- www.xing.com
- www.ecademy.com
- www.ryze.com

In fact, other large sites with diverse memberships, as well as niche sites specific to one field or industry, could be more effective and targeted for you. We encourage you to explore them so you can decide for yourself which one or ones are best for you. Following is brief information to help you select alternative or additional sites for your professional networking.

XING

Now headquartered in Hamburg, Germany, this site was previously known as Swiss-based Open BC. XING has just under nine million members and is truly a global site (now boasting a multilingual platform in 16 languages). It appears to be especially strong in Europe and Asia, but many of our U.S. contacts are enthusiastic members.

Ecademy

Headquartered in the UK, this site is a social network for business-people worldwide. It has a strong entrepreneurial focus and less of a job search focus. Ecademy combines online interaction with offline networking events in major cities. It boasts more than half a million members globally.

Ryze

Ryze was founded in California by a technology executive and investor. The name is derived from people helping each other rise up through quality networking. It now has 500,000 members in more than 200 countries. The site hosts special networks for organizations to help members interact with each other, as well as offline meetings in many major cities.

Viadeo

Founded in France in 2003, this was initially a private networking venue. Now it's a public site for business networking, with over 30 million members and one million joining each month. It's international in scope, with users networking in seven languages and more to be added soon. Viadeo allows searches out to four levels (compared to LinkedIn's three levels).

QUOTE

XING is widely spread in the Germanic regions such as Austria, Germany, and Switzerland. Viadeo is rarely used in Switzerland but most popular in France. LinkedIn is more international, geared toward the native English-speaking countries.

—Sonja Robinson, career management consultant, Right Management in Zurich

Social Network Protocol

Whether you are networking on LinkedIn, Facebook, Viadeo, or other sites, the written and unwritten rules of behavior are much the same. The tips provided in this section will help you get the most from your networking activities and keep you in the good graces of other members.

Do

- **Create a complete profile on each site.** Make yourself appealing online. Make sure that your professional image on these business networking sites isn't tarnished by radically different portrayals of your personality on some of the personal networking sites. Consistency in your profile, site to site, is also important, so ensure the same level of detail and quality regardless of the site it's on. If you can't keep your profile up-to-date on multiple sites, it's better to stick with just one site (or just one personal and one professional).

- **Grow your network.** Whether you subscribe to the "bigger is better" theory or are more comfortable with the "close and personal" strategies for growing your network, you need a reasonable number of connections to make good things happen. How you define reasonable depends on your field and your needs, but for many people, a reasonable size of an online network might be at least 50 to 150 people.

- **Facilitate introductions.** As part of a large online network, you should help other people connect. You can recommend them if you know them and are comfortable doing so. Or just say "for your consideration" if you don't know them well. The old theory about "my reputation is on the line" when making introductions is, in our opinion, just that—old! Networking introductions are much more fluid online.

- **Remember your manners.** Treat people virtually as you would in face-to-face gatherings—kindly and with respect. Don't wear out your welcome or bombard them with repeated requests for introductions to others. They are likely to drop you from their networks.

Don't

- **Be selfish.** Remember that networking is a two-way street. You need to give as well as you get, help other people, and not just be looking selfishly at how you can benefit from the interaction.

- **Have unrealistic expectations.** Don't expect something good from every connection. Just as in live networking settings, not every contact is a helpful contact. But even if you don't see yourself doing business with someone, you never know whom that person might know or how you might provide assistance to him or her or one of that person's contacts in the future.

- **Try to accomplish too much too fast.** Build rapport first. Just as you wouldn't walk up to someone at an initial meeting and immediately ask for favors, introductions, jobs, or business deals, you shouldn't do that online, either. Wait until the person knows you and has some investment in helping you connect, likely in a second or third conversation or exchange.

- **Spend all your time online and ignore offline networking strategies.** Both are important, and the need to meet people face-to-face or by phone will be a constant in your business and professional life.

 QUOTE

Social media has changed the way business is being conducted. I can interact with my clients faster and more often and have a better quality of conversation.

—Camille C. Roberts, Certified Resume Writer and Certified Federal Resume Writer

The Future of Social Networking

Certainly, social networks with a business or professional orientation are here to stay. Every site we've joined and profiled here is growing at a rapid rate as more and more people become aware of the many benefits of networking through this medium. Having 24/7 networking capabilities, access to contacts globally, and essentially the world at your fingertips is a big draw to everyone.

QUOTE

I had an amazing LinkedIn experience. I was contacted via LinkedIn by a search firm based in Australia. The search firm was looking for resources who could serve as an extension of its client, an Australian-based consulting firm. Specifically, the search was for individuals with a particular certification and facilitation capability, which I had. I was put in touch with the consulting organization and interviewed via Skype. I agreed to contract with it and serve as an extension of its organization. I then participated in a certification program that was two days in person (held in the U.S.) and two additional teach-back sessions via Skype to Australia. I have subsequently served as a facilitator of its program content with a global IT firm headquartered in the U.S. I still marvel at the ability to so easily connect and network with people from around the world! What amazing tools we have available to us now.

—Lori Addicks, learning and development consultant

The sites themselves will continue to evolve. New sites are being started all the time. Some don't make it and disappear from view. Some start out as other types of sites and then add features that move them into the social networking arena. And, there will also be ongoing crossover between the personal networking sites and the professional networking sites. (Facebook is a good example of this movement.)

MORE SITES TO CHECK OUT

Plaxo began as a personal online contact manager and calendar (kind of an Internet-based address book). Spoke describes itself as the largest online directory of business people. But both have ventured into social network territory, offering more features to find and connect with people, not just store contact information. Zoom Information is one to watch also, as it's a Plaxo competitor.

Professional networks are still a relatively new concept. Even the largest and most established sites are not that old. Most of the big ones today started in 2003 and 2004. So don't get too attached to any one site. Other options will certainly develop in the coming months and years.

Key Points: Chapter 4

- Social networks are large databases in which individuals upload information about themselves for the purpose of networking with others online.

- The term *social networks* includes those that have a predominantly personal focus as well as more business and professionally oriented sites.

- Social networks provide access to a global audience 24/7, yet they do not require advanced computer skills to use.

- To use a social network, you have to become a member of a site, post a profile, and send and accept invitations to join others' networks. You can expand your social network by searching for contacts and joining groups.

- LinkedIn is the largest of the exclusively professional sites, and Facebook is the largest of the personal networking sites. Yet there are many other social networks that you may find to be more useful.

- Rules of accepted behavior on social networks dictate that you treat others with respect, focus on building rapport as you would in face-to-face networking, and facilitate introductions for others.

- The social network landscape is changing rapidly. New sites are starting all the time, and other types of sites are migrating into the professional networking arena.

CHAPTER 5

Leveraging LinkedIn's Power

LinkedIn, a California-headquartered company, was started in 2003 and grew to more than 70 million members in its first seven years. More than 2 million new members join each month, and there is no end in sight to the rapid growth. LinkedIn is the clear front-runner of the professional networking sites. If you have time for only one social networking strategy, this should be the one! It's that important.

In our career coaching and public speaking on social networking, we issue a clear and consistent message to our clients and, now, to you: Take the time to learn all the features and functionalities of LinkedIn and build your expertise on this site first. When you are fully leveraging LinkedIn, you can begin to explore other social media. (See chapter 10 for help in developing and implementing your complete social networking strategy.)

In This Chapter
- *Understand why LinkedIn tops the social media hit list.*
- *Learn what constitutes a robust profile.*
- *Learn how to grow your network on the site.*
- *Learn to use Q&A and Status Update features.*
- *Hear about helpful LinkedIn applications.*
- *Pull it all together to fully leverage LinkedIn.*

Who's Networking on LinkedIn?

The LinkedIn audience is very diverse. Geographically, more than 200 countries are represented—this is definitely not just a U.S. fad. In terms of industry and functional skills, more than 170 industries and

every conceivable job title are represented on LinkedIn. It's diverse in terms of employment status, too. LinkedIn members are unemployed, self-employed, employed by companies of all sizes, students, and retired. It's also diverse in terms of level of position. You'll find everyone and anyone from entry-level employees to senior management. More than 400,000 CEOs are on LinkedIn. All the Fortune 500 companies have members on LinkedIn, and all the Fortune 500 are represented at director level or above. Powerful people are on this site—and a lot of regular folks, too!

TIP

If your idea of a network is your contact database, think of it this way: On LinkedIn, you have not only your own contact database, but also your connections' databases and their connections' databases!

You might have already received some invitations to join LinkedIn. If so, just accept those and that will get you started as a member. If not, go to the site (www.linkedin.com) and sign up (the following section explains how). You don't need to have an invitation to join.

Perhaps you've accepted some invitations already, but, due to time constraints or lack of understanding about the site, you never got fully up and running on it. Many people fall into this category, so you're not alone. They tell us, "I think I signed up already." That might have been months or even years ago. Then someone or something (perhaps job loss) triggers their desire to start working the site.

A LinkedIn Convert

A former client of ours, Doug P., recently contacted us by sending an invitation to connect to him and his network on LinkedIn. In his message he explained, "I am getting on board with the LinkedIn process. It has been a long time coming, but I am beginning to see the light!"

We were curious as to why it had taken him (a veteran salesperson, skilled networker, and active job seeker) a while to "link up" or in. He explained, "The principal reason was (and, in part, still is) that I don't fully understand how to take advantage of LinkedIn. It looked like another thing (like learning to add new apps to your iPhone) that I would have to struggle through. The combination of not knowing how it works, what exactly it does for me, and the time element involved with learning it (I have four small kids so not much free time) were the reasons I did not jump in right away."

He continued, "What prompted me or pushed me over the edge was an article I read in a business journal that said that more and more recruiters were using LinkedIn for reference checks and to make sure that you were who you claim to be."

Regardless of whether you are new to LinkedIn, somewhat familiar, or already to some extent on the site, now is the time to get connected or more fully connected. Connecting is not difficult. We'll walk you through all the steps you need to join and get up to speed on LinkedIn. By the end of this chapter, you will have all the information you need to leverage this critical professional networking site.

Join LinkedIn

Go to the LinkedIn website (www.linkedin.com) and move your cursor to the first field of the Join LinkedIn Today box to sign up for a LinkedIn account (see figure 5.1).

Figure 5.1: *LinkedIn opening page.*

You are asked to enter the following:

- **Your first and last name**
- **Email address:** LinkedIn allows you to enter more than one email address if you think that people might send invitations to you at different addresses, such as work and personal. You do, however, have to select one address as the primary one where you want messages sent to you from LinkedIn. Because of the lack of job security in today's market, it's a good idea to use a personal email address as your primary email on LinkedIn.

TIP

Many people who lose their jobs rush to delete their old work email from their LinkedIn profile. Leave it there! As long as LinkedIn was able to confirm it when you first signed up, people will still be able to use this email address to send you an invitation to join their network. This "old" email address remains valid because it isn't being sent through your former employer's server; it's coming to you through LinkedIn.

You may consider using more than one email address (in addition to your primary email address) for your LinkedIn account. The advantage to this is to provide contacts who know you and communicate with you through a work setting, or outside of work, to be able to use the appropriate email address to make that LinkedIn connection with you.

To edit email accounts attached to your LinkedIn account, go into Settings (top right corner of your home page), Personal Information, and then Email Addresses. From this page you can add, delete, or edit existing email accounts.

- **Password:** Enter a password to go to the next screen.
- **Status:** Choices are employed, business owner, looking for work, working independently, student.
- **Company, Job Title, Country, Zip Code:** Populate these areas.

After entering this information, select the Continue button. At this point, LinkedIn gives you the opportunity to start searching for and inviting others to your network. We recommend waiting to invite others until your profile is set up by choosing to skip these steps.

The last step in the joining process is to choose your plan level. You're given the option to select a free or paid membership on LinkedIn. Before you decide which level is right for you, test-drive LinkedIn as a free user by selecting the Choose Basic button and then following the tips we suggest in this chapter to get as much out of the site as possible. You'll then be better equipped to make a decision about upgrading to a paid membership.

Develop Your Profile

Once you're a member, the first important step is to complete your profile. When you join LinkedIn, the site puts together a very simple profile based on the information you provide. However, we recommend that you provide comprehensive profile information, including all of your work and educational history. Your profile helps former colleagues, clients, prospects, and potential business partners find you. You want to ensure that everyone who may know you is able to connect to you on LinkedIn, so plan to spend some time on this step.

QUOTE

I use LinkedIn as my interactive Rolodex. I rarely keep business cards any longer. Rather, when I meet someone and exchange business cards, I then extend an invitation to connect on LinkedIn. I utilize the Notes feature to maintain information such as discussion topics, interests, personal information shared, follow-up action, etc. LinkedIn is an organized and efficient vehicle to communicate with business contacts, stay in touch, and keep track of their career movement.

—Jeanette Matern, career coach

LINKEDIN PROFILE TIPS

Be thoughtful and cautious about what you include in your LinkedIn profile because millions of people—including current and former bosses and colleagues—may be viewing it tomorrow!

- Be truthful and accurate. Lying is not acceptable.
- Be thorough but concise. Your profile shouldn't tell your whole life story.

(continued)

(continued)

- Make sure your spelling and grammar are up to par.
- If you aren't sure how you are coming across, ask some colleagues for suggestions.

Enhancing the Basic Information

To view your profile, choose Profile and then Edit Profile in the menu bar. Check the information that appears there to see whether any changes are needed. Select Edit after the information to go to a screen where you can change the following information:

- **Name:** You will need to enter your first and last name and also designate how you want this to appear on your profile.

- **Professional "Headline":** This is the text that appears on the line just below your name. If you entered a job title, it appears here. To make the most of this section, however, you should use appropriate keywords that indicate your areas of expertise as opposed to focusing just on a title. This is especially true if you are in job search mode. Consider including your primary skills (for example, Human Resources Generalist or Lean Manufacturing and Operations Specialist).

 TIP

Keyword searches are a popular way of finding job candidates on LinkedIn, so be sure to enter relevant keywords in your professional headline, in the Specialties section, and throughout your profile to drive traffic to your profile.

- **Country and Zip Code (Area):** Make sure this information is current.

- **Industry:** Unfortunately, you can pick only one from a comprehensive list. So select the one where you have the most experience or the one that is the focus of your current job search.

You can also add a photo to your profile by choosing Add Photo. When this feature of LinkedIn was first introduced, it caused a great deal of discussion on blogs and LinkedIn forums. Opinions ran the gamut:

"Feels too much like the personal networking sites, seems unprofessional."

"Will create discrimination issues, especially with so much hiring happening through LinkedIn." (To address this issue somewhat, LinkedIn does have an option in another section where you can choose who views your photo.)

"Helps to be able to put a face with a name!"

Keep in mind that current social media trends indicate that a complete online profile should have a recognizable avatar (which could be a photo), and your LinkedIn profile will never be considered "complete" (by LinkedIn standards) unless you have a photo included in your profile. If you do upload a photo, remember that 70 million people could be viewing your photo and are expecting to see a professional demeanor.

Finally, don't overlook the section called Public Profile. This is your unique Uniform Resource Locator (URL) that takes visitors directly to your page on LinkedIn. As you are signing up, it will appear as www.linkedin.com/pub/ followed by your name and a random combination of numbers and letters. LinkedIn allows you to edit this. Be sure to get rid of the random numbers and letters and keep some version of your name, much like you would customize a new email account. This gives you additional online presence and will further your name recognition on Web searches.

 TIP

For effective self-marketing, consider adding your LinkedIn URL to your resume, e-signature, business cards, and other marketing materials. This creates a path to your LinkedIn profile if imbedded in your electronic communication, provides your LinkedIn connections information for networking, and makes you appear LinkedIn savvy.

Highlighting Your Skills in the Summary and Specialties Sections

The Summary section is the place where you'll enter your self-marketing sound bite (developed in chapter 3). You might also have a profile or summary section at the beginning of your resume that you can use here. This section should provide readers with an overview of your skills and experience (your positioning statement or personal brand) and any networking objectives.

The Specialties section affords you a place in your profile to list your keywords, which you can pull directly from a formal keywords section of your resume, if you have one, or from the main contents of your resume. These keywords might include job titles, industry names, product names, acronyms known in your field, software programs related to your work, specific skills that set you apart from others—any words that someone doing a keyword search might use to find you. Be sure to use all variations of your keywords—full names, abbreviations, acronyms, alternate words—to increase the chance that you will be found in searches.

Adding Your Experience and Education

Basically everything you would include in your resume should be included on your LinkedIn profile. You could—but wouldn't necessarily need to—include all of your achievement bullet points from your resume or all of your job descriptions. But you do want to include all of your job titles, your employers, and the colleges and universities you have attended.

NOTE

There is now an option to upload your resume to complete your profile. It works marginally well. But you can also copy and paste your resume information there section-by-section to be sure your information goes where it is supposed to go. Whichever option you choose, be sure to spell check your content before you upload it or paste it into LinkedIn. There isn't a spell check mechanism on LinkedIn, and nobody wants a profile with typos!

Add all your work history in the Experience section to mirror the information on your resume. We recommend presenting most of your

data in narrative or paragraph form, but you can incorporate bullets as well. Completing this section fully will help others find you and will automate the process of extending invitations to former colleagues. (We tell you more about how that works later in this chapter.) If you are currently unemployed and seeking a new opportunity, you can list that as your current company: "Seeking new [insert job title or function] role." Or you can leave this blank with all work history shown as past positions. It's your choice, but we typically recommend that you be open about your present status. Some recruiters may actually search for words such as "currently," "seeking," "searching," or "exploring" in the current employment field to find candidates who could be available quickly.

In the Education section, select the state, choose an institution from a drop-down menu, and then select the dates attended. You will need to enter the dates you attended college in your profile if you want to invite former classmates to join your network through LinkedIn's automated invitation process. However, you can remove the dates later (after inviting your friends from your college days) if you don't want to make it easy for people to calculate your age (just as you might omit your graduation dates from your resume).

Providing Additional Information

The Additional Information section provides space for you to add the following:

- **Websites:** LinkedIn lets you insert links to three other websites. These would typically be to your personal website or blog, but can also be to sites about your books or other publications or to quotes about you in articles. They might also be to organizations that you have some affiliation with, such as professional associations you're a member of or a company you work for. Check your links periodically and update them if necessary. Be creative, but keep it relevant to your personal brand.

- **Twitter:** This field is where you can list your Twitter handle. If you have an active Twitter account that's a companion piece to your LinkedIn profile, it's a good idea to designate this link on your LinkedIn profile. This allows others to check you out on Twitter and provides another connection point for networking. (Chapter 7 has more information about Twitter.)

- **Interests:** This is typically a keyword list separated by commas. You can include some personal interests or hobbies as well as professional interests. This is one field in your profile where you can let your personality shine through, be a three-dimensional person, and allow people to connect with you on other levels.

- **Groups and Associations:** This can include professional associations, community organizations, nonprofits, or clubs that reflect your hobbies. Do not include anything controversial that would detract from your personal brand.

- **Honors and Awards:** This section provides you the option of adding relevant awards and honors you've received that you want to highlight in your profile.

TIP

Although setting up your profile on LinkedIn is easy, you should set aside a block of time to accomplish this task. Or you can work on it in several sessions. Doing this is well worth the investment of time, so don't get impatient. Recognize that this is a critical step.

Completing Your Profile

There are just two more sections to address in order to complete your profile (see figure 5.2). Somewhat new to LinkedIn, the Personal Information section can be populated in several ways. You have the option of adding phone, address, IM (Instant Message), birthday, and marital status. You may not want to share all this personal information considering you are likely to be using LinkedIn for primarily professional purposes, but you're given the option to add these details to give more information about you and to provide alternative ways for others to connect with you.

The Contact Settings section lists things you would like to accomplish on LinkedIn. The eight options are career opportunities, consulting offers, new ventures, job inquiries, expertise requests, business deals, reference requests, and getting back in touch. By default, all are checked. You can deselect some or simply leave them all checked. Having them all checked is usually regarded as the sign of an open networker, someone willing to interact on a variety of conversation topics.

Figure 5.2: *Example of a complete LinkedIn profile.*

To keep track of your progress as you work on your profile, you can view the LinkedIn status bar, which shows visually and by percentages how complete your profile is (see figure 5.3). Of course, your goal is to get to 100 percent, but for now, aim to make it thorough enough to present you favorably, knowing that you can add to or edit your profile in the future.

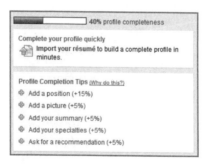

Figure 5.3: *LinkedIn's profile completion meter.*

No matter what you choose to include in your profile, LinkedIn lets you select how much of your profile data you want to make public. We recommend giving people full access to your profile, especially

if you are in an active job search. The benefits of transparency and being visible and accessible should outweigh any privacy concerns you might have.

But you might have serious privacy concerns and want to limit the public view initially. That's fine. As you evolve in social networking, you'll find your own comfort level. Just pick a starting place. You can make changes to your privacy settings at any time by choosing Profile, Edit Profile at the top of the LinkedIn home page and then choosing Edit Public Profile Settings (see figure 5.4).

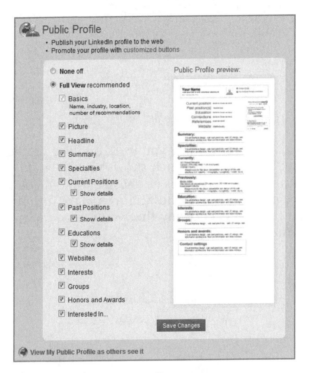

Figure 5.4: *Pay close attention to your public profile settings.*

Changing Your Profile and Privacy Settings

After entering your profile information, select Settings at the top right on your home page. This brings up the screen where you can adjust various parts of your LinkedIn profile. Here are a few settings you may want to adjust:

- **My Profile Photo (in Profile Settings):** You can control who can view your photo by selecting either Everyone, My Network, or My Connections. Unless you are concerned that viewing your photo will be problematic, having a recognizable and professional image on your profile is a good thing to warm your online image.

- **Connections Browse (in Privacy Settings):** With this option, you can choose to allow or not allow your connections to view your own connections list. We strongly recommend that you make your connections visible to others. Sharing and collaboration are the point of participating in LinkedIn. People who refuse to share their contacts risk being snubbed by other members. However, we are sensitive to the plight of people in business development roles. You may not want to publicize your contact lists that could be viewed by competitors.

- **Profile and Status Updates (in Privacy Settings):** With this setting, you can choose to notify your network when you make significant changes to your profile. You will ultimately want people to be notified when you earn a promotion, complete a degree or certification, land a new job, or launch a new business. While you are frequently tweaking your initial profile, however, we recommend turning off this feature because you don't need your contacts to be notified every time you make a change to it. Make this adjustment by selecting the "No, don't notify..." position and choosing the Save Changes button. This avoids peppering your network with updates until you are finished with your significant changes. When you are finished with your latest round of changes, you can then turn these settings to "Yes, notify...".

There are some other choices to make in this section as well. You can indicate how you wish to receive invitations, messages, notifications, and introductions, or you can simply stick with the default settings until you get a feel for the site.

Rest assured that there is a great deal of privacy and protection built into the LinkedIn process. LinkedIn is not the typical contact-management tool that allows you to collect and store phone numbers, addresses, and other data about your contacts. No one can change your information except you. No one can connect to you without your permission. And if you want to disconnect from people, you can do that easily and discreetly because a notice is *not* sent to them saying that you dropped them from your network.

Once you've completed your profile and chosen your account settings, you are ready to grow your network on LinkedIn.

Grow Your Network

Now that you have completed your LinkedIn profile, you need to connect with others. People you know are undoubtedly already on LinkedIn, but you are not connected to them until one of you sends an invitation and the other person accepts that invitation. It doesn't matter who invites whom. Once an invitation has been extended and accepted, you are both in each other's first-level network.

LinkedIn provides options to invite new contacts, existing contacts, or former colleagues and classmates to join your network through the Add Connections screen (see figure 5.5).

Figure 5.5: Add Connections screen on LinkedIn.

There are multiple ways to get to the screen to issue an invitation:

- Choose Add Connections at the top right corner of the home page.
- Choose Contacts at the top left side of the home page and then select Add Connections from the pull-down menu.

Entering from either of those points brings you to the same screen where you can invite people in four different ways.

1. Enter one or multiple email addresses to issue a single invitation or a small number of invitations.

TIP

When you are ready to start inviting others, we recommend that you scroll through the list of individuals and select those whom you'd like to connect with, versus using the Select All button. We've heard many stories of professionals new to LinkedIn who inadvertently did a mass invitation, not realizing they had used the Select All option. The potential issue here is that your mass invitation could appear to be exactly that and may not be well received as a result. This could cause your end recipients to deny your invitation, which could be damaging to your LinkedIn account. It's also a good idea to get into the habit of customizing your communications to your connections on LinkedIn to avoid this very issue.

2. Choose an option to import contacts that you already have in Outlook, AOL, Hotmail, Yahoo!, or Gmail. (You'll see the list and can simply select those you would like to invite).

3. Select the Colleagues tab at the top of the screen. LinkedIn automatically searches its entire member database to find all persons who indicate that they work or worked for any of the organizations listed in your profile. For each employer, you can view a list of names and titles (a long list, likely, if you have worked for large organizations) and check those you'd like to invite.

4. Select the Classmates tab at the top of the screen. LinkedIn automatically searches for members who attended your alma maters during the years you attended, whether you earned a degree or not. Simply check those you'd like to invite.

TIP

The LinkedIn feature that identifies past and present colleagues and classmates to facilitate sending invitations is one of the key reasons to include all your work and educational history in your profile. If you omit any of your past employers or schools from your list, LinkedIn has no way to reconnect you with people you may have worked or studied with.

With options 3 and 4, the people receiving your invitations are already members of LinkedIn. In options 1 and 2, they may or may not already be on the site. To those persons, you may want to include a brief explanation about LinkedIn in your invitation in case they aren't familiar with the site, if you are able to customize the message.

Customizing Invitations

We recommend customizing your invitation messages to remind people how they know you and approach them in a more personalized way than the standard, default LinkedIn message that says simply, "I'd like to add you to my professional network on LinkedIn." Sending that canned note is a sure sign that you didn't take the time or care enough to personalize the invitation to remind the invitees who you are and how they know you. Such a message may even be viewed as spam by some seasoned LinkedIn members.

One of our Atlanta contacts, Keith Warrick, a LinkedIn enthusiast and frequent presenter on this topic, won't accept an invitation if it's not customized. Instead he sends a message back asking why he should accept the invitation. He terms the practice of not customizing a LinkedIn invitation as the "lazy networker syndrome."

However, LinkedIn has recently made customizing an invitation message much more difficult. We mentioned two ways of arriving at the Add Connections screen. As of this writing, neither of these will permit you to send a personalized message. We understand that LinkedIn plans to reinstate the customized message option soon, and we certainly hope that's the case. Watch for changes in this area.

Meanwhile, there is still one way to customize the invitation message. If you go to the person's profile, you'll see the option at the right to Add (Name) To Your Network. Clicking on this option opens an invitation screen that provides space for you to create a message of up to 350 characters.

Through the years, we've seen some terrible invitations and some great ones. Following are some of our favorites (good ones).

Clearly an experienced and enthusiastic social networker:

> *I found your interesting profile in my network, but we are not directly connected. If you want to connect, feel free to send me an invitation. Or let me know if you run out of them, and I will send you one.*

I was also thinking that, if you are not already a member, you should consider [suggests another site]. It could be an ideal resource for you. Membership is free and takes only minutes to register. One signal of the exclusivity and caliber of the people and opportunities is the fact that [other site name] is by invitation only. You can enter through [gives link to website]. If you have further questions, do not hesitate to ask me.

Have a great day!

A clever approach in a nice, brief message:

You showed up as "someone I might know" on LinkedIn, and after viewing your profile, I think the correct expression is "someone I would LIKE to know." I would appreciate your connection and the opportunity to build our networks.

Thanks.

Good use of flattery:

I am a former student and lecturer at [college name/alma mater shared by the recipient of this invitation]. I received my MA in 2000 and recognize you as a leader in the field of education. I would be honored for you to join my growing list of contacts.

Short and sweet:

I came across your profile, noticed that we are both members of the Association of Finance Professionals, and would like to invite you to join my professional network on LinkedIn.com.

I trust that our connection will lead to a beneficial relationship for us in the future.

A nice friendly tone plus a little networking philosophy:

I have found that the only way to build real networks and networking opportunities with others is to take an active approach by contacting those whom I feel are like-minded or those who could benefit by networking with me. LinkedIn is the perfect online community in which people can connect with each other and build networks comprised of diverse people with regard to backgrounds, education, experience, and cultures.

I would like to add you to my professional network on LinkedIn and create an online relationship where we can work together and help each other.

Please accept my invitation.

Outlines what the recipient can expect from this connection:

I think you might be open to adding new connections. I would appreciate if you would join my network.

I forward messages for LinkedIn members quickly and help members when time allows. I believe giving is receiving, and that helping others is helping myself. My network is one of the largest and a proven reliable route for members. By joining my network, you can also expand your network and find more business/professional opportunities.

Looking forward to networking with you. Thank you for your time and best wishes.

From an active networker:

Are you open to adding connections?

Unfortunately, I reached the maximum number of invitations allowed by LinkedIn. So should you consider contacts beneficial, please do not hesitate to go to my LinkedIn profile [provides his LinkedIn URL] and send your invitation to [name and email address].

This last person mentions that he has exhausted his supply of invitations. You have a lifetime limit of 3,000 invitations that you can send on LinkedIn. That's probably more than enough for most of us. Typically when you reach a certain size of network, you won't have to send as many invitations. People will see you as a LinkedIn 'hub' and someone they should invite. But some of the active open networkers on the site do run out. LinkedIn has been known to issue additional invitations in increments of 500. Just in case, you should not be indiscriminate in handing out invitations.

Don't Get Your Account Frozen

Although you do want to develop a large network, it's important to issue invitations thoughtfully and cautiously. People receiving invitations to join your network choose one of three responses: Accept, Ignore, or Reply. Clicking Ignore brings up another set of options, including "I don't know_____" (LinkedIn inserts the sender's name in the blank). If just five people select "I don't know _____" when you send them invitations, your account on LinkedIn is frozen. With appeals to the LinkedIn customer service department, you will be asked to read and agree to LinkedIn's membership policies and will probably then be reinstated. But we recommend taking some preventive measures to avoid that problem.

Jason Alba, accomplished networker and author of *I'm on LinkedIn—Now What???*, suggests that you ask people outside of LinkedIn (via email or during traditional networking conversations) if they will join your LinkedIn network. When they say "yes," you can extend the invitation through LinkedIn and have confidence that your invitees will accept because you've given them a heads-up.

Jim Browning, an Atlanta sales and marketing leader who offers training on LinkedIn to job seekers and networking groups, recommends that you include a statement in your invitation: "If you do not wish to connect, please do not select the 'I Don't Know Jim' button. Instead, just ignore the invitation."

Choosing an Approach to Growing Your Network: *Quality Versus Quantity*

So much has been written about the topic of growing your network. If you read any of the blogs about LinkedIn or join an email discussion group about LinkedIn or other social networks, you are sure to get plenty of information on this topic.

What's all the fuss about? There are two seemingly opposite philosophies about how you should grow your network. The labels applied to these two approaches are typically "Quality" and "Quantity."

The *quality* side is what LinkedIn as an organization advocates. On the site itself, you'll see the admonition to "Only connect to those persons that you know and trust." One of our colleagues prefers this approach. She can't imagine having little-known acquaintances in her first-level network. She accepts invitations only from people she knows well and can recommend to others.

The *quantity* side believes that the larger the network, the better. The goal of this group is to have many contacts to increase their reach. Some LinkedIn members have more than 20,000 first-level contacts. Do they know all those people personally? Of course not! Your authors have adopted this approach to growing our own LinkedIn networks. The larger our networks, the more apt we are to have a contact that one of our clients or other contacts might need. The term for this is *promiscuous linkers*, those who will connect not only to people they know well, but also to people they know marginally well, or don't know at all! Okay, so we admit it. We are promiscuous linkers!

We take exception to the quality versus quantity labels and the inference that these two approaches are mutually exclusive. We don't agree with the idea that only people you already know well can be high-quality contacts. Neither do we believe that people with large networks have somehow jeopardized the quality of their connections. Years of networking experience—our own and our clients—have produced many examples in which close contacts may provide little networking support, whereas other people, practically strangers, render invaluable assistance. Still, knowing your first-level connections well does yield some degree of confidence that they will accept your phone calls or email and entertain your requests. That's a good thing.

Obviously, labels aside, there are solid arguments for both sides which keep the discussions going. You will probably have your own personal preference along the quantity versus quality continuum. Choose your approach based on your networking goals as well as your comfort level with the process. You can monitor the size of your network by choosing Contacts at the top of the home page and then selecting Network Statistics (see figure 5.6).

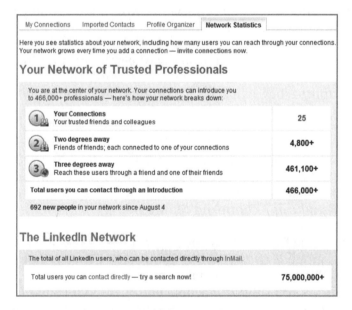

Figure 5.6: *Watch your network grow on LinkedIn!*

Give and Get Recommendations

With your network growing (at a rapid rate, we hope), you are ready to add some recommendations (see figure 5.7). Access this part of the LinkedIn site by choosing Profile at the top of the home page and then choosing Recommendations.

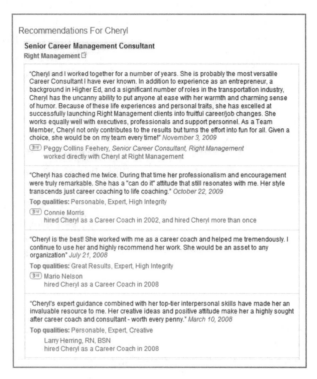

Figure 5.7: *Recommendations strengthen your profile.*

Recommendation is LinkedIn's term for a reference or endorsement. Colleagues, bosses, vendors, customers, or others can write a recommendation of your work (in connection with one of your positions listed in your profile). Some people will volunteer to write a recommendation for you or will even surprise you by sending a recommendation without your having to ask. You then approve that recommendation and make it public on your site, or not, as you wish. You can't, of course, edit what your references write, but you can try asking them to make changes if their recommendations contain errors

or aren't to your liking. The process is much like the way you would coach a boss on providing a letter of recommendation or verbal reference offline.

Whether you are employed, in job search mode, or in customer acquisition mode, asking people for a recommendation on LinkedIn is perfectly fine. Typically, this would happen as you are finalizing the more traditional offline list of references. The caveat to this approach is that endorsers need to be members of LinkedIn. They don't need to have complete profiles and be active users; just basic profile information and a free membership level will enable them to write a recommendation for you.

Don't forget that you can also write a recommendation for your references and service providers. Your name and a link to your profile page will then show up on their profile. Writing a recommendation often yields a reciprocal recommendation. In fact, when you write recommendations, the people you recommend are prompted by a message asking if they would like to reciprocate and write a recommendation for you. So if you are timid and reluctant to ask someone for a recommendation (which you really shouldn't be), this can be a more subtle approach.

TIP

A good recommendation doesn't have to be long; a short recommendation, if it has the right elements, can be very impressive. A critical aspect of a good recommendation is supportive, detailed language that highlights relevant skills and supports the expertise of the individual. It's a good idea to have a balance of "hard" skills (measurable, quantifiable, "must have" skills) and "soft" skills (qualities that are harder to measure, such as initiative and collaboration). If the person you've asked for a recommendation is not skilled at this type of writing or needs guidance, offer to write something to provide him or her with a framework of what you'd like to have covered, which he or she can use to draft the final recommendation.

Most importantly, writing a recommendation for someone else is just a nice way to help someone. Networking, as we've said in earlier chapters, is as much about helping others as benefiting yourself.

 QUOTE

My first recommendation from a former colleague was a complete surprise. I didn't know how much she appreciated my work when we were working together. That motivated me to write a few unsolicited recommendations for former colleagues whose work I appreciated. It's a great way to pay it forward!

—Connie Morris, engineer

LinkedIn recommendations, as stated above, are tied to specific positions or education listed on your profile. This is just a tad limiting. For example, we have had candidates who wanted to include other references, perhaps someone they had worked with in professional associations during their job search. If you are faced with this dilemma, you have a couple of options. You can list that volunteer activity as a position on your profile, which will enable that person to create a recommendation tied to that experience. Or the person can simply attach the recommendation to one of your positions and reference the work you did together.

Recommendations need to be genuine. Some people, in attempting to maximize their number of recommendations, misuse this feature by requesting references from people they just met at a networking event. Others will say, "I'll write one for you if you'll write one for me." Don't do that. This could put your credibility at risk, and these types of blanket references won't be considered valid. Ask only true references—former bosses, colleagues, customers, and vendors. And if you are approached to write a reference for someone you don't know well or prefer not to endorse, find a diplomatic way to say "no."

How many recommendations should you have on your profile? You definitely need some recommendations. We've heard from more than one recruiter that if a potential candidate has no recommendations, they will not look at that person's profile! At least three to six is ideal. If they are really genuine references, more is fine, too. The goal shouldn't be to amass large numbers, but rather to have solid messages about you from people who count.

If your references or people you would like to recommend haven't heard about LinkedIn or joined, you can share information about the site and social networking, which can, in turn, help their career or

assist them in growing their business. After all, networking online and offline is all about giving back, sharing information, and helping others.

Having recommendations is very impressive to recruiters and prospective customers and can even make the reference-checking process easier and quicker. Some of our candidates have arrived at interviews to see their interviewers perusing a printed version of their recommendations on LinkedIn. And in some of those instances, the company relied exclusively on those online references, requiring no further traditional reference list.

The reference checking process has changed dramatically with the advent of social networking sites. Checking your references used to be the last thing that companies did before extending an offer. Now, employers often check your references online before ever inviting you for an interview.

Bottom line, this LinkedIn step is a critical one in your social networking and career management process. Recommendations are great. Someone is willing to say nice things about you to the vast LinkedIn world! And the people who are willing to serve as references for you are a vital part of your network. Cherish and nurture those relationships!

QUOTE

In my last job transition, I used social media, particularly LinkedIn, extensively to accomplish one objective—to land my next job. However, along the way in accomplishing that objective, two other objectives became a byproduct of the first one. Those other objectives became building my network of contacts in order to discover hidden opportunities and helping others with their search efforts.

As I grew my LinkedIn network and paid it forward with job leads and introductions, the opportunities that came my way increased tremendously. As my interviews and introductions to key personnel at target companies continued, I went from social media believer to enthusiast to LinkedIn guru. I began speaking passionately about LinkedIn and how important it is as a part of everyone's job search toolkit and social media presence.

All of this was topped off with my return back to gainful employment as a consequence of the power of LinkedIn. I was contacted by a LinkedIn network connection that I had checked in with at the beginning of my search when jobs at his company had been frozen. Several months later, he checked his LinkedIn network to see if I was still available. When he found out that I was, my process to get hired was wrapped up in two weeks, and he used my LinkedIn recommendations for references!

LinkedIn is powerful, and it truly does work when one works it properly!

—Keith Warrick, business analyst

Search for Jobs

LinkedIn has become a popular place to promote and peruse positions online. Those in the know estimate that approximately half of the activity on LinkedIn is related to job search.

Recruiters and employers are choosing to advertise positions there. The cost is reasonable, considering that the LinkedIn audience is very large. LinkedIn is a place where employers and recruiters can find passive candidates (those not specifically looking for new positions) as well as active job seekers. This easy access to a huge pool of talent has made LinkedIn the most popular sourcing tool, surpassing the Internet job boards several years ago.

If you are a job hunter, not only will you find positions that recruiters and companies have posted directly on the LinkedIn site, but you can also see jobs from other sites as well. LinkedIn is an aggregator site, meaning that it pulls positions that match your criteria from other sites, including Monster, CareerBuilder, Yahoo! HotJobs, and craigslist. Not having to visit a number of sites individually can be a major timesaver for busy job hunters.

The LinkedIn search engine is similar to those on the major job boards. You can access it by going to the Jobs menu at the top of the LinkedIn home page and choosing Find Jobs. By selecting the Advanced Search tab, you can search for positions by keyword, title, function, industry, company, location, level, and date of job posting (see figure 5.8).

Figure 5.8: *Finding jobs on LinkedIn.*

QUOTE

I find that most of my clients who have worked for large companies would not trade that experience as it provided the grounding or foundation for their careers. However, one disadvantage of working for large companies is that your skills become channeled into a silo and you cannot be entrepreneurial and participate easily in areas outside of your sector. This is not the case with smaller companies that can be more flexible. The problem now becomes how one can find these firms. LinkedIn is one of the easiest and most accessible tools to use.

LinkedIn is terrific in identifying these other companies by using their advanced search feature to identify the industry, the company, the size, the location, and the individual by title. In addition, a number of recruiters are culling LinkedIn for candidates to interview with these firms. It has connected some of our "big fish" clients to some very lucrative "small ponds."

One example is a former client who had been in home building with a major 35,000-employee firm for more than 25 years. He was contacted at home by a recruiter who saw his profile on LinkedIn and wanted him to interview with the managers of a 10-year-old, small (89 employees), private firm that had three offices around the world and billions of dollars to spend. He had never heard of the firm but decided to meet them. They liked each other very, very much, and the package he was offered greatly exceeded the package he held with his former company.

Another client had formed his own consulting practice and got a call at home from a recruiter who had seen his profile on LinkedIn. He reluctantly agreed to speak with the organization, but first he wanted know the name. It turned out to be the Bill Gates Foundation, and he ended up joining the organization.

When you are in transition, you do not know where your help is coming from. So you need to be visible, and LinkedIn is one of the best means of doing this in a professional manner so that you can be noticed.

—Cheryl Robinson, senior career management consultant

As career coaches, we must point out that anytime you search and apply for jobs online, you need to go beyond the application step if you want to have much chance of success. Whether the job is posted on LinkedIn, on an online job board like Monster, or even directly on a company website, just applying online is no guarantee that your credentials will even be reviewed. You might even feel as though you are sending a message into a large, black hole.

Don't leave anything to chance. Don't sit back and hope that you will be found amidst hundreds or perhaps thousands of other candidates just through a keyword search. You need to tap into your traditional network and your online network for help. This is where LinkedIn can play a critical role.

One way LinkedIn provides the help you need is through a free tool called JobsInsider, which is part of the LinkedIn Browser Toolbar. (To get this tool, select Tools from the bottom of the LinkedIn home page and then choose to download the toolbar that corresponds to the browser you use.) When you have this tool installed and find a posted opportunity online, LinkedIn shows the name of the person who posted the opportunity and also identifies any LinkedIn contacts that you may have in that organization (see figure 5.9). This information enables you to use your LinkedIn network to secure an introduction to the organization and to help get your resume noticed. (We explain LinkedIn introductions later in this chapter.)

Figure 5.9: *LinkedIn shows you not only jobs, but also who's connected to the employers.*

Even if you aren't in job search mode, you can still benefit from the Jobs section of LinkedIn by doing competitive research. Seeing the staffing activities of your competitors can provide much information about their strategies and growth.

Research Companies

Many job seekers we meet do their company research prior to an interview by looking at the company's own website. That should certainly be part of the preparation. But information on the company website is exactly what the company wants you to see and know. It's not especially objective data. We recommend doing additional research. You can use company databases in libraries (or online via the libraries' networks). If you have corporate-sponsored career transition services, you can utilize any research tools provided by that outplacement firm. You can do a Google search to find online mentions.

And remember LinkedIn! It is an excellent source of information that you won't be able to find anywhere else.

To access company information on LinkedIn, choose More at the top of the LinkedIn home page and then select Companies. Search for a specific company, keyword, or location, and you'll find solid company data, with a twist!

You will certainly find the normal company descriptions, revenue and employee data, stock valuations, and news events in a company research report on LinkedIn. But here's the twist! You'll also find information based on the demographics of LinkedIn profiles. For example, you'll see

- People in your network who work at that company
- People who have left that company (which could yield some interesting information)
- People recently hired at the company or promoted there, as well as companies they worked for before being hired at this company
- Common titles of the company's employees on LinkedIn
- Geographic hubs with the largest employee populations
- A list of the company's employees on LinkedIn whose profiles have been viewed most often

LinkedIn has recently added an option to follow companies. This option could give you additional information on a target company in the form of regular updates that you can tailor in terms of the type of information you'd like to receive. There are two main ways to access this option. From a company overview page, select the Follow Company option in the top right corner. Or from an employee profile, click on the small box at the end of a company name and then select Follow Company.

Another option for following companies of choice is the Company Buzz application. This application provides tweets (Twitter messages) for a particular company or subject. After you download the Company Buzz application (choose More from the LinkedIn menu bar and then choose Application Directory to access it), the updates will show up on your LinkedIn home page.

Search for Contacts

One of the primary reasons to be on LinkedIn is to have access to a wide network of contacts when you need them. Keep in mind that when you search for contacts, you are searching your first-, second-, and third-level contacts. The more contacts you have, and the better connected those contacts are, the larger the database of LinkedIn members you'll be searching.

To access the screen to enter your search criteria, make sure People is selected for the search box at the top right of the LinkedIn home page and then select Advanced. This will bring up the Advanced Search screen (see figure 5.10). You can search for people there by name, keyword, company (current, past, or both), title (current, past, or both), industry, location, or school. A recently added feature also allows you to search by level of connection. In other words, you can search all LinkedIn contacts or limit your results to just your first- or second-level contacts.

The search engine on LinkedIn is very powerful. You can do simple searches, looking for matches in one field only. You can also search for data in multiple fields at one time.

Figure 5.10: The Advanced People Search option on LinkedIn.

You also can develop complex search queries in any field—name, company, title, keyword, or school—in the following ways:

- Using Boolean logic by grouping terms with AND and OR (make sure the OR and AND are in all capital letters)

- Grouping multiple search terms in parentheses

- Enclosing phrases you want to search for in double quotes

To search for multiple items in the same category checklist (such as industries), you can hold down the CTRL key and select all the items you want to search for.

Location searches are somewhat more limited. You can search all locations, the default on LinkedIn. You can search by country. Or you can search by zip code, selecting a radius from the zip code from 10 to 100 miles. If you want to look for contacts in multiple cities or states, you'll need to run several searches. As an alternative, you could list those cities or states in the keyword field. Just be aware that the results won't be as accurate. You might pull some people who previously worked or attended colleges in those locations who now live somewhere else.

When we demonstrate the power of the LinkedIn search to clients and participants in job networking groups, some of those job seekers are immediately excited about the possibilities. Others look overwhelmed and uncertain, as if to say "What does this do for me exactly?" LinkedIn gives you access to individuals in your functional area, people in your industry, people who can influence a hiring decision, people who can make introductions to decision makers or other key contacts, and hub contacts with large networks. The ability to identify contacts through LinkedIn adds a tremendous burst of power to every aspect of your job search networking.

Suppose you...

- See a job posted and don't just want to trust that your resume will be noticed by the recruiter or staffing department. You can find people at that organization who can provide advice, background information, or even a direct connection to Human Resources or the hiring manager.

- Have an interview scheduled and want some background information on your interviewers. Look up their profiles in advance to find areas of common interest and information about how their careers have progressed at that company and others.

- Aren't sure which companies utilize your particular skills, certifications, or degrees. Search for people on LinkedIn with that same background and notice where they work to build a target company list.

- Want to explore a new career. Don't just assume you know what that field is like. Find people in that career who can give you the real scope or scoop!

- Need or want to move to a new city. Find people there who can help you navigate the new landscape.

- Want to connect with people in your field to share information and strategies for career development purposes. Enter your search criteria, and you'll find plenty to choose from.

By now, you should be beginning to get the big picture. And we do mean big! Through LinkedIn, you have a built-in network of 70 million people who can direct you, advise you, consult for you, refer you, and maybe even hire you! Networking the traditional way through face-to-face connections is still a vital part of your process. But social networking on LinkedIn expands your reach tremendously.

For example, Ellen spoke recently at an Atlanta association meeting for professionals in nonprofit organizations. She explained that if they approached her via a phone call or during a face-to-face encounter asking for introductions to her connections in other nonprofits, she would probably be able to think of four to six people to contact on their behalf. However, if they did a search on LinkedIn, they would find thousands of people in her network in the Atlanta nonprofit world, some of whom she knows personally (probably more than the four to six she would recall on the spot), but also many, many others who are known to her LinkedIn contacts and their contacts. With thousands to choose from instead of only four to six, just imagine how much more focused and productive the resulting networking would be!

Connect with Others

Suppose that you've just completed a search for people (see the preceding section), and you've found a number of individuals who interest you. What do you do now? How do you contact them?

If a contact is in your first-level network, you will be able to see that person's email address in his or her LinkedIn profile and can make contact directly by sending him or her an email either outside of LinkedIn or through LinkedIn (an option on the person's profile page).

If a contact is a second- or third-level connection, you will probably not have the person's email address (unless that person has provided it somewhere in his or her profile—the sign of an "open networker"). With no email address to contact that person directly, you have several options. Go to the bottom of that person's profile, and you'll notice two choices there: Get Introduced Through a Connection or Send an InMail.

Selecting the Get Introduced Through a Connection option brings up a screen with two message fields. You are asked to write one message to the person who is your first-level contact and who will hopefully be passing along your request for an introduction. Then you are asked to write a second message to the person you are ultimately trying to reach explaining the reason for the request. There could be just one person (your first-level contact) between you and your target contact. Or there might be an additional person, your contact's first-level contact, who has the connection you need. If there is another person involved in the chain of connections, don't worry. You don't have to figure out who that is. The LinkedIn system finds the link.

Selecting the Send an InMail option enables you to send a direct communication to your intended recipient. This option circumvents the chain of introductions required in the Get Introduced option. If you have the basic or free membership on LinkedIn, you'll need to pay for each InMail. The current charge is $10 each. If you have an upgraded membership, depending on specific benefits of the membership plan you select, you will get several free InMails each month. They accumulate if you don't use them, much like rollover minutes on cell phone plans. Currently, the first upgrade earns you three InMails per month, and you can store up to nine.

TIME FOR AN UPGRADE?

The free version of LinkedIn is robust. You can do what you need to do, at least initially. But when you are actively using LinkedIn and run into the limitations of the free version, such as having only five requests for introductions, no InMails, and only 100 results on searches, you'll know that it's time to upgrade. The paid plans offer more introduction requests, InMails, and search results—how much more depends on the plan you choose. You can view these options by selecting the Settings tab and choosing Compare Account Types.

Note that LinkedIn offers job seekers the option to upgrade to a Job Seeker Premium account that provides many of the same benefits as the first-tier upgrade, plus "moves you to the top of the list" of jobs you apply for through LinkedIn. As this is a relatively new option, we can't yet offer an opinion on it. But getting priority attention for jobs posted on LinkedIn sounds promising. You can access this membership option through the Jobs tab on the LinkedIn home page, either by choosing the Job Seeker Premium option or selecting the upgrade advertisement on the side of the page.

Both methods of contacting LinkedIn members have some pros and cons. Being introduced through the chain of contacts is free, which is an important consideration if you are out of work. It's also more of a warm lead, a request presumably coming to them from others they know who have passed it along. On the other hand, there is always a chance that someone in the chain of two or three people may not forward it on, or at least not in a timely manner.

Sending an InMail is the more expedient option. You don't have to wait and wonder if others will honor your request for introduction. The downside is that it costs money, a significant expenditure if you are unemployed. But for that reason, it seems to get respect. People know that you have paid money to reach out to them, either a fee for that InMail or by having paid fees for upgraded services. Yet it's a cold contact—someone you are only indirectly connected to.

If you have time for the chain of communications, we recommend starting with the introduction approach. If you need to reach someone quickly or if the introduction process isn't working, try sending an InMail.

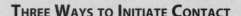

THREE WAYS TO INITIATE CONTACT

If you start feeling confused about how to communicate with people on LinkedIn (a natural reaction!), keep in mind that the process boils down to three basic choices:

- **Invitation:** Inviting others to join your network or accepting their invitations. When an invitation is accepted, the sender and the receiver become each other's first-level contacts. This is free. LinkedIn allots 3,000 invitations to each member, and invitations sent to you by others do not count against that total. There is no cost to issue or accept invitations.

- **Introduction:** Asking that your contacts introduce you to one of their first- or second-level contacts. The chain of communication goes from you, to your contact, to the target contact, or to another intermediary contact, and then to the target contact. These are also free, and with the free LinkedIn account, you have five of these to use at any time. You are credited back when the introductions are forwarded or you withdraw them, restoring you to five available.

- **InMail:** Sending an email-like communication directly to someone not in your first-level network through the LinkedIn communication channel. With the free LinkedIn account, there is currently a $10 charge for each InMail. A varying number of InMails are included with the upgraded memberships.

There is one more way to connect that, in our opinion, has advantages over either introductions or InMails: joining a LinkedIn group. If you are a member of the same group as the person you want to contact, you will likely have direct access to that person through group communications. It depends to some extent on how the group was established on LinkedIn and whether the person you need to contact through the group has agreed to receive communications from other members of the group. But in most cases, you will be able to send fellow group members a message through the group at no cost.

In our personal experience, the rate of getting through to an ultimate contact via both introductions and InMails is very high. Most people on LinkedIn are there because they acknowledge the value of professional networking and are happy to facilitate introductions and help others. But we suspect that the rate of success might be even higher in a group setting. You have already established a common bond by

being a member of the same group, a bond which may yield even higher rates of return on requests for assistance and information. (The next section has more information about groups.)

Join Groups

Groups are one of the best tools and best kept secrets on LinkedIn. There are currently more than 450,000 to choose from! There are groups for every conceivable shared interest. You'll find alumni associations, professional associations, networking groups, and many other special interest groups, including job search networking groups that might be specific to an industry, a job function, or a certain geography. Many traditional associations or groups have a LinkedIn group as well. So if you are a member of a local or national professional association, check LinkedIn. You are likely to find your fellow members already congregating there, sharing leads and discussing topics of interest.

 QUOTE

A typical mistake I see job seekers make is that they join many LinkedIn groups that are clearly marked as a community of job seekers. With LinkedIn's Network Update emails, if your job search is confidential, it soon won't be. All of your contacts—including your manager and colleagues— will see what you're up to and which groups you're joining. Joining special interest groups on LinkedIn is an excellent way to connect with people from target companies. Just be sure you're not sounding the alarm bells to your current employer.

—Ruth Winden, founder, Careers Enhanced Ltd., England

As explained in the "Connect with Others" section, one of the biggest reasons to join groups is to have an easier way to connect with other like-minded LinkedIn members. Depending on the protocols of each group, you'll most likely be able to communicate with your fellow group members via sending direct messages to individual members either through the group or from their profile pages or by posting questions or comments for group discussion and response. So it becomes a way not only to expand your network but also to bypass the need to request an introduction or send an InMail to reach others. Of course, being able to "meet" other people with similar interests on LinkedIn is a real benefit in its own right.

To explore the group landscape, choose Groups at the top of your home page. You have four options:

- **My Groups:** This tab reminds you which groups you've already joined.

- **Following:** Use this tab to monitor activity on selected groups.

- **Groups Directory:** From this tab, you can select those groups best suited to your networking objectives.

- **Create a Group:** Use this easy, intuitive process if you can't find just the right group among the 450,000.

Selecting Groups Directory brings up a search screen (see figure 5.11) where you can search by category or group type—that is, work group, professional association, alumni group, and networking group. You can also search by keywords. Again, the search engine on LinkedIn is very powerful. You can search by single words or phrases enclosed in double quotes. You can also use a Boolean search query, combining terms with AND and OR and grouping words in parentheses.

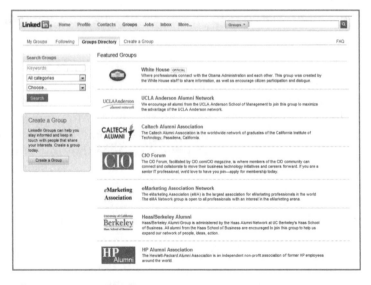

Figure 5.11: *Finding groups on LinkedIn.*

For example, if you wanted to search for groups related to nonprofits, you could enter the following search in the keyword field:

Nonprofit OR "non profit" OR philanthropy OR foundation

Notice that we used two spellings for *nonprofit* as we see that term written as both one word and two words. It's often even hyphenated as *non-profit.*

This search for groups related to nonprofits will probably yield hundreds of options. So you could narrow the choices by geography or type of nonprofit as follows:

(Nonprofit OR "non profit" OR philanthropy OR foundation) AND (Philadelphia OR Pennsylvania OR PA)

or

(Nonprofit OR "non profit" OR philanthropy OR foundation) AND (art OR museum)

You get the idea. You can be very specific or leave the options open and review a longer list to help you find and select just the right group.

The results of your searches for groups are sorted in order of number of members with the largest groups showing first on the list. When you find a group you want to join, click the Join This Group link or the group logo or title to go to a screen that gives more information about the group and provides options for you about how you want to handle your membership. For example, to reduce the time required to read daily information updates from your groups, you can opt to receive a weekly digest email message. Many groups do not require approval for membership or it's almost instantaneous. However, you may find some that require approval from a membership director.

You can join as many as 50 groups on LinkedIn, although that would be a lot to manage. While searching for a job, however, you may want to "heavy up" your engagement in groups for good reason. Companies and recruiters are now going directly to groups related to their search criteria to post openings and search for candidates. So in addition to looking at the Job Search function on LinkedIn, pay attention to the discussion and opportunities that you'll find in LinkedIn groups.

Contributing to the discussion could give you some extra visibility in the group and prompt others to engage with you. Yet you must remember the "rules of engagement" when it comes to commenting in discussion groups and other online activity. Make sure that what you're providing is valuable, relevant to who you are and how you want to be perceived (your professional brand), and not inflammatory or negative.

Ask and Answer Questions

Another amazing tool on LinkedIn is the opportunity to post a question to the network. You can ask questions to your immediate network or to the entire LinkedIn database. And you can answer questions there, too. You'll find the Answers section by choosing More at the top of the LinkedIn home page and then choosing Answers (see figure 5.12).

Imagine that you need help using a software application, advice on the best blogging platform, or recommendations of suppliers. Here is a ready network of millions of people, some of whom have undoubtedly been in your position with the same questions or concerns. Throw the question out there and see how quickly you begin to accumulate some great advice. We've tried this feature as a research tool for writing our books and had useful responses within seconds of posting our questions.

In addition to posting questions, you can answer questions posed by others, questions that are related to your area of expertise. If you are in an active job search, you will want to spread the word about your areas of expertise, ways that you can bring value to prospective employers. The Question and Answer feature on LinkedIn is a perfect place to showcase your knowledge. It's also a great way to help others, an equally important goal for networking.

Questions are grouped by topics. And there are many, many topics to choose from. For example, under the Finance and Accounting section alone, there are subgroups for Accounting, Auditing, Budgeting, Corporate Debt, Corporate Taxes, Economics, Financial Regulation, Financing, M&A, and Risk Management. You can easily find the best category for both your questions and your answers.

Figure 5.12: Show and share your knowledge in the Answers section of LinkedIn.

Questions stay posted on LinkedIn for one week, although you can withdraw them sooner if you get the answers you need before the seven days are up. At the end of the posting period, the person who asked the question chooses the best answer and ranks the respondents. If you supplied the best answer, your name will appear on that section of LinkedIn Q&A, which can go a long way toward building your reputation and credibility as an expert on that topic and as someone who provides valuable help to others.

A few people misuse the Q&A feature as an unsubtle advertising message for their business or services or just for shameless self-promotion. "Do you have a need for a...?" This is not considered to be good LinkedIn form and will usually be highlighted as spam to the LinkedIn team.

Another misuse of the Q&A section, in our opinion, is asking the philosophical types of questions, such as "What was the best advice you ever received from a mentor?" or "Who was your favorite boss and why?" These types of questions bring back awful memories from elementary school where we—probably you, too—were asked to write essays on "What I did on my summer vacation." Those essays probably served the purpose of organizing our thoughts and demonstrating our spelling and grammar skills. But in today's busy world, who has time for those types of discussions?

Do you really need some assistance? Or are you just trying to pass the time and be visible? We want to help with the former and not be a part of the latter. Give us meaty questions, such as "Can you recommend a good career coach in Toledo, Ohio?" or "Which software have you found most useful for tracking job search activity?" We can help you with those and will be glad to devote some time and ideas to be of assistance.

If you need to get more exposure or build your brand, do it in a thoughtful way by asking legitimate questions or sharing your knowledge and experience. But we recommend not engaging in the strictly self-promotional or philosophical types of Q&A. Those misuses of the Answers section are certain to create more ill will than goodwill.

A recent example of a good way to leverage Q&A was illustrated by a job seeker we were coaching who was also speaking at an upcoming professional conference. With our prompting, he asked a question of the LinkedIn network. In this question, he mentioned that he would be speaking at the conference (on such and such a date), and by the way, he wanted to customize his talk to answer critical questions of the industry—what suggestions did people have? This excellent question killed two birds with one stone—it promoted his involvement in an upcoming conference (which was great from a career management perspective) and also gave him some great feedback for the session and touch points for networking.

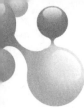

Tell What You're Working On (Network Activity Update)

Another very useful feature on LinkedIn has had several different names over the last year or two. Initially "borrowed" from Facebook, it was called "Tell What You Are Working On." Later it was called "Status Update." Most recently, it was renamed "Network Activity." Whatever the field name, you'll find an open window near the top of your home page to update others on your professional activities and achievements.

Previously 100 characters in length, and recently increased to 140 characters to accommodate tweets, it's a relatively short window. You'll need to be thoughtful and concise with the messages you post.

You choose who sees your update messages. Currently you can select your connections (your first-degree connections on LinkedIn) or everyone (your first-, second-, and third-degree connections on LinkedIn). Your update message will then appear in the Network Activity field on your contacts' home pages.

Although your updates on a more social venue might be on more personal topics, your updates here should focus on your professional news, knowledge, and objectives. You might want to let people know that you are searching for a job, that you read a good article related to your profession, attended a conference, or heard a great speaker. You can include links to articles or websites that might be helpful to members of your network.

You can also sync your LinkedIn Network Activity with your Twitter account, if desired. To do this, you can check the box next to the Twitter logo under the Network Activity field and your update will automatically show up as a tweet in your Twitter account. You can manually change this option as needed. Likewise, if you have an active Twitter account, by adding the hashtags #li or #in at the end of your tweet, you can "send" this same tweet to have it appear as a Network Update on your LinkedIn account.

TIP

How much should you communicate through your "Network Activity"? This depends on your objectives and your audience. If you are in job search mode, you may consider updating your network once a week or twice a month with some on-brand activity. Or if you are an entrepreneur, consultant, or someone who has a very active online presence, you could be "out there" communicating your activities to your network once a day with some relevant tip, article, or bit of news to share. Providing value to your network with your news as well as matching this to your audience and your objectives will ensure that your efforts are well received.

These updates get a lot of notice from people in your network. We have posted updates about our books, about interviews we've given, or speaking engagements, and those updates always draw a large number of responses. One update in particular got lots of attention. We posted a message that we had been interviewed for an article in the *Washington Post* on digital dirt. Many people in our network commented on that by sending a message back on LinkedIn or by stopping by our offices to congratulate us. The interesting thing was that no one actually saw the article. Everyone learned of our media success through the update feature on LinkedIn!

This feature offers an effective and efficient way to get the word out to a large audience. Compare that to trying to send an email to those same people! First of all, you could reach only your first-degree LinkedIn connections via email because you have email addresses only for your first-degree contacts. And think of the time involved to amass and format all of those email addresses. Fortunately, the Network Activity field saves the day!

Use Applications

LinkedIn offers a number of applications that give members and networkers new options for sharing information and connecting. As of this writing, there are 16 options for you to consider. You can keep tabs on the latest options by choosing More at the top of the home page, and then choosing Applications Directory.

Through these tools, you can

- Share presentations.
- Upload your resume, bio, or marketing document.
- Conduct polls.
- Link your blog to your profile.
- Collaborate on projects.

Here are our thoughts as to how some of these applications might be helpful for job search or career management:

- SlideShare Presentations and Google Presentation are applications that allow you to upload PowerPoint documents to your LinkedIn profile. If you've given a presentation or done some training that you'd like to share with the LinkedIn audience, try these applications.

- The Blog Link and WordPress applications allow you to sync your blog to your LinkedIn profile. You've probably already listed your blog's URL in the Website links section of your profile. With these tools, you can actually display your blog posts themselves on your profile.

- My Travel (by TripIt) lets you know where members of your network are traveling so that you can connect while you are on the road for face-to-face networking.

- Huddle Workspaces is a tool for collaboration, setting up private online workspaces for team projects with your network contacts.

- Company Buzz is a very useful application that is powered by Twitter. You can search the latest tweets related to your company or companies you are targeting for job search or business development.

- Box.net Files is an application that many of our job-seeking clients are using. With this application, you can upload Word or Excel documents (such as resumes, bios, or marketing briefs), documents that are downloadable by people viewing your profile. This can be a great way to make yourself more accessible to recruiters and prospective employers. A couple of cautions, though. If you've not publicized your phone number and address on your LinkedIn profile, be sure to take that information off the resume that you upload to the site. And if you like to tailor your resume to particular positions, posting a generic version on your profile might be confusing to employers who compare this version to a customized resume you've sent by email or uploaded to their company websites.

QUOTE

Out of the blue, I received a phone call from a corporate recruiter who had found my profile on LinkedIn. One of the things he liked was that I had attached my resume using the Box.net application. I have now been invited to a face-to-face interview, which I hope will lead to an offer.

—Mark Winn, information technology infrastructure manager

- Reading List by Amazon is a great way to promote books you are reading and enjoying to members of your network. (We hope this book makes your list!)

- Polls (by LinkedIn) is a tool for doing surveys. Some of the options on this application cost money, though. So read the fine print!

- Tweets allows you to access the tweets of those Twitter members (tweeps) you are already following, without having to go into Twitter. These updates show up on your LinkedIn home page.

At the time of this writing, there are other applications that may be worth checking out, depending on your background and self-marketing objectives, including Portfolio Display for displaying creative works on your profile, SAP Community Bio for SAP specialists to showcase their expertise, and others.

TIP

Geoff Peterson, managing principal of RecruitChute and a recruiting leader, recommends job seekers leverage all social and professional networks, post samples of their work by using applications such as SlideShare, and consider blogging to showcase their expertise.

From the very beginning, LinkedIn was a rich site filled with many tools to enhance the social networking experience. By adding these applications, LinkedIn has added additional value, ways to connect, share data, and do business.

Make LinkedIn a Key Part of Your Networking Strategy

Be forewarned that things change rapidly on LinkedIn. The LinkedIn software development and product development teams are constantly dreaming up and implementing new features and layouts on the site. Don't be surprised if you log in some day to find things looking a bit different from some of our screen shots and descriptions here. If there is anything guaranteed in social networking, it's change and lots of it. But don't worry. The steps we've provided in this chapter have prepared you to get full value from this site and to be able to negotiate the ongoing changes to the LinkedIn landscape.

We can't say enough good things about LinkedIn and emphasize enough the role that it should play in your professional life. As you might imagine, we know a lot of career coaches, job search clients, recruiters, and social media experts. We've conferred with hundreds of them to gather the latest opinions, experiences, and advice in preparation for writing this book. You can read their comments throughout this book and in Appendix B. To a person, they all agree with our assessment: LinkedIn is critical for professional networking and is the most important tool in your social networking toolbelt. Make LinkedIn your first priority. Learn to fully leverage this site. Then move on to other social media tools covered elsewhere in this book.

Many of our job search clients wait until they are in job search mode to get on board with LinkedIn. That's not what we would recommend. But if that's your situation, it's okay. Maybe you've neglected your networking while you've been hard at work and involved with personal and family activities. Now you find yourself in career transition without a large network of supporters to help you with the process. Don't despair. The reality is that you can grow a professional network very quickly using LinkedIn (and other social networking tools, too). Jump on board now!

LinkedIn is also the perfect vehicle to help your colleagues, classmates, and new contacts. Sharing your information and expertise, facilitating introductions for others, or just offering encouragement goes a long way toward building a bond and developing valued professional relationships. Paying it forward and helping others should be a priority for each of us every day.

And don't stop utilizing this tool when you land that next job! Networking online is a productive and time-efficient way to network. You can connect with people wherever you are, whenever you can find the time. And you can reach millions of people in all fields and geographic locations around the globe. Whatever information, resource, or assistance you need, you'll find it on LinkedIn. And with a little planning and time management, it fits easily into a busy working professional's life.

KNOW THE RULES!

Take time to actually read the LinkedIn User Agreement. We know, user agreements can be boring. But the LinkedIn User Agreement outlines important rules for interaction and provides a code of conduct. Knowing and playing by the rules can keep you on good terms with other members and the LinkedIn team.

In the current business world, most people change jobs every few years, whether by choice or as a result of corporate changes. Having a ready network to help you through these planned or unplanned transitions should be at the top of your "to-do" list!

Key Points: Chapter 5

- Join LinkedIn. It's easy and free at the basic level.
- Develop a complete LinkedIn profile to help others find you.
- Grow your network to increase your networking reach.
- Get and give recommendations on LinkedIn to support and enhance your credibility and expertise.
- Search for jobs on LinkedIn. LinkedIn aggregates jobs from LinkedIn and other sites.
- Research companies on LinkedIn to find relevant information and contacts, all in one place.
- Use the LinkedIn Search feature to find contacts in target companies.

- Join groups to find others with common interests/backgrounds.
- Ask and answer questions on LinkedIn to showcase your expertise.
- Provide updates through LinkedIn to promote your brand.
- Try the applications to demonstrate your LinkedIn savvy.
- Make LinkedIn a key part of your networking strategy. It provides a way to help others, enhances your effectiveness, and speeds your success!

CHAPTER 6

Using Facebook for Professional Purposes

You might be surprised to find that a site known primarily for personal social networking is included in a book on job search, career management, and other professional pursuits. A few years ago, you would not have found us recommending Facebook for those purposes. But the site has changed in terms of its demographics and the way people are using the site, so our advice has evolved as well.

When we wrote the first edition of this book in 2008, we were beginning to see some blending and blurring of the lines between the strictly professional LinkedIn and the predominantly personal sites such as Facebook. That movement continues today and the lines are even more blurred. LinkedIn has loosened up a bit, adding photos, a status update field, and applications that enhance the collaborative nature of the site. Likewise, Facebook has added features to encourage businesses and other professional organizations to build a presence on the site.

As you develop a social networking strategy, we suggest giving Facebook serious consideration. To be candid, many of our job search clients question that advice. They don't think of Facebook as a serious site. Many still view it as a college-age networking platform, or they may already be on Facebook for personal networking with family and friends and can't imagine how to use it for professional purposes. Can Facebook be a valuable tool for job search and professional networking and should it be used as one? Our answer is yes, absolutely!

Who's on Facebook?

Facebook, like LinkedIn, is a California-headquartered company. It was founded in 2004. Initially, membership was open only to college students. In 2006, it was opened to anyone over 13 years of age with an email address. Since then, Facebook has grown rapidly to become the world's largest social network, with more than 500 million active networkers (compare that to LinkedIn's 70 million networkers).

With a large audience to connect with and draw from, Facebook is a great option for professional networking. And the fact that many of your "friends" on Facebook are truly your friends in real life (IRL) means that they will care about your professional status and want to help.

QUOTE

The line between Facebook for socializing and LinkedIn for networking has blurred, as has the line between socializing and networking in general. I consider my social activities to be a form of networking since people want to do business with people they like or have had positive experiences with. Facebook is now being used to find leads in companies or for contract jobs, to post jobs or contract positions, and also to advertise businesses and services. Sometimes it's easier to source a candidate through your personal network and hire a friend of a friend than it is to sort through hundreds of resumes of complete strangers.

—Amanda Gettler, talent management consultant, Right Management

The demographics of Facebook are changing dramatically. It's not just for teens and twenty-somethings anymore. In fact, the fastest-growing age group on Facebook is the over-55 segment! This older population may be driving some of the younger networkers away. One of our clients told us recently that his college-age sons have stopped using Facebook because of all those "old people" on it.

Facebook also has added applications and features to draw more of the business crowd. Through setting up Facebook pages and groups, organizations can build a presence on the site. They are now flocking to Facebook in droves to attract talent, communicate with customers, and promote their brands.

The Facebook Dilemma: Business or Personal?

You've no doubt heard horror stories of people who lose out on being hired for a new job or even get fired from jobs because their boss or a recruiter saw a photo of them on Facebook drunk and wild at a party or read a status update that was negative about their employers, their job, or something equally damaging. You might not make a habit of wearing the proverbial lampshade at parties or putting your foot in your mouth, but you do need to think about your image or personal brand and how your Facebook activity reflects on the professional side of you.

Facebook still has a more social feel than sites such as LinkedIn, and your friends and colleagues might be using Facebook for purely personal networking (and maybe you are, too, if you're already on the site). Therefore, it can be more challenging to keep a purely professional focus when you use Facebook or more difficult to have your personal Facebook network see you as a professional colleague rather than as a friend.

So the first step in using Facebook is not, as you might expect, setting up a membership and profile and inviting people to join your network. The first step is to determine how and why you're going to use it or whether you're going to use it at all. If you decide to use Facebook, you have three choices: use it just for connecting with family and friends, use it only for professional networking, or walk the fine line between professional and personal.

 QUOTE

I moved to San Diego after being in Atlanta for almost two years and wanted to align my career coaching and resume writing business with other local career management and/or outplacement firms. Upon my arrival in San Diego, I was invited through Facebook to a networking lunch-and-learn sponsored by an outplacement, management consulting, and recruiting firm. After multiple interviews and meetings, I was selected to be a senior consultant with that firm—and it all started on Facebook!

—Janet Andrews, M.A., strategic career consultant, resume writer, and executive coach

Sticking with Strictly Personal Networking

If you use Facebook only for personal networking, then you might choose to post vacation photos or pictures of the kids. You might fill out the marital status, religious views, and political views section of your profile. And you might post frequent status updates that are related to your nonwork life (although do your family and friends really want to know what you had for breakfast or that you're waiting in line at the post office?!).

If you are using Facebook for personal purposes only, do not link any of your other social media accounts to Facebook. Also, keep your Facebook privacy settings set on the strictest levels so that only friends and family in your network can view your information on the site, and recruiters, prospective or current employers, and other professional colleagues cannot access your pages unless you choose to treat them as friends and let them into your network.

Using Facebook for Professional Networking Only

Perhaps you have no interest in using Facebook for personal networking. Maybe you have no time to load photos and tell people what you ate for lunch or what your favorite movies are. You might prefer to keep up with family and friends the old-fashioned way by picking up the phone, catching up over lunch, or sending email or letters.

Or maybe you do network with friends and family in more contemporary ways. Perhaps you have a personal or family blog, visible only to select personal contacts. Maybe you load your photos to a site such

as Shutterfly (www.shutterfly.com), Kodak Gallery (www.kodakgallery.com), or Flickr (www.flickr.com). In those cases, you don't necessarily need to add Facebook to the mix of ways you interact with people.

That leaves using Facebook for strictly professional reasons. In that case, you would treat this social network the way you would LinkedIn or any other such site. From your profile information to the status updates you give, you can establish your brand and position yourself as an accomplished person in your field who deserves to be hired, promoted, or contracted for products or services.

Walking the Fine Personal-Professional Line

Not sure you want to limit yourself to strictly personal or professional use of Facebook? That's fine. We can work with that.

One option is to set up two different profiles on Facebook: a personal one and a professional one. Allow only friends and family into the network for your personal profile and adjust the privacy settings so that only they can view all your stuff. Then set up a separate profile using a slight variation of your name (perhaps your full name rather than a nickname) and allow former and current coworkers, recruiters, prospective employers, and any other professional contacts into this network. And make sure that all of your information—profile data, pictures (if any), status updates, and the like—is reflective of who you are as a professional.

But what if you don't want to deal with two separate profiles? Or maybe you already use Facebook actively for personal networking but now find yourself in job search mode and want to leverage your already-amassed Facebook personal network for professional gain. In that case, you need to be prepared to make a transition. You don't have to hide who you are personally, but you do need to scrutinize and scrub your profile.

Go through all the information about you, all your photos, any silly applications and games you might use, and delete or remove ones that could reflect negatively on you in the workplace. And make sure that your status updates are related to your work and your talents (avoiding revealing any confidential or proprietary information from your current or past employers).

TIP

If you end up installing an application on Facebook, watch for a pop-up notice or fine print that asks whether you want news of your having installed this application, or an icon of it, to appear on your profile. Make sure nothing ends up on your profile that reflects negatively on your brand.

We spoke with several of our favorite career and personal branding coaches about their use of Facebook and they offered some interesting and different perspectives. Miriam Salpeter (Keppie Careers) is an advocate of keeping her personal and professional lives separate and distinct on Facebook. To support this, she's developed a Fan page for her professional contacts. When professional contacts she does not know personally or clients want to "friend" Miriam, she invites them to join the Keppie Careers page. This separation helps drive her professional fan base while keeping her personal profile on Facebook separate. She also recommends keeping a close eye on privacy settings because Facebook often makes adjustments that impact what other people may access in a profile without users knowing. Attending to these settings reduces the chance that private information will become public.

Walter Akana (Threshold Consulting) has a blended approach to his Facebook page, which is both personal and professional. He controls potential issues by adjusting his privacy settings.

TIP

In Facebook you have the ability to create distinct lists to categorize your friends, such as coworkers, relatives, college friends, and so on. The advantage of doing this is that when you customize your privacy settings you're able to adjust the way you message, allow for viewing of photos, and so on with these groups of people that match the way you want to communicate with that particular group. To get started with creating a list, click the Friends link on the left-hand side of your profile and then click the Create a List button on the Friends page.

There is no one right way to manage your Facebook profile. In order to determine how best to set up and maintain your profile, you need to assess your objectives for being on the site.

Should You Set Up a Fan Page for Yourself?

If you're considering setting up a Fan page, complete this checklist to determine whether this is a good approach for you. Check the statements that apply to you:

❏ You would like to keep your personal and professional profiles separate on Facebook.

❏ You have a business (consulting, freelancing, or other enterprise) that you want to promote.

❏ You want to reach a broad audience and build a following.

❏ You have time to keep your audience involved with frequent outgoing communication and updates.

If you checked all of the above, then setting up a Fan page could be an excellent approach on Facebook. One of the benefits to a Fan page is that it separates your personal and professional profiles on Facebook. You'll also have the ability to reach out to and communicate with an infinite number of "fans" and reach a broad audience. When fans of your page choose to "like" your content, this will be shared via their news feed, so this spreads your Fan page content virally. Maintaining a Fan page does take work, so make sure this fits into your overall self-marketing and business objectives. You will need to post/respond to/moderate comments and provide updates to keep your fans engaged and to continue to build a following.

If you'd like to get more information about setting up and maintaining a Fan page, you can go to the Help section on Facebook or you can use the following links to begin the process and get support:

- www.facebook.com/pages/create.php
- www.facebook.com/FanpageHelpCenter

Joining Facebook

Now that you know your options regarding the personal-professional dilemma of Facebook, let's walk through the mechanics of the site. Facebook has similar features and functions to other social networks such as LinkedIn, MySpace, XING, Plaxo, and others. The screens may look a bit different from one to another, but you can accomplish much the same things on all of these sites. You start by joining the site and building a profile.

Unlike LinkedIn where you choose between a free or paid account when you join, all accounts on Facebook are currently free, even company pages. So there's no decision to make here, at least for now.

To join Facebook, go to www.facebook.com and register there. Registration includes providing your name, email address, password, gender, and date of birth (see figure 6.1).

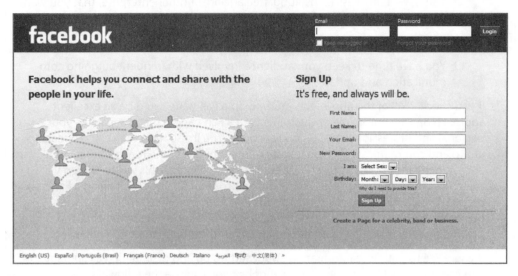

Figure 6.1: *Facebook registration screen.*

The next step is to create your profile. Note that because this is a book on career-oriented or business-oriented social networking, we describe the profile steps in terms of using the site for professional purposes with minimal personal information. Facebook is easy to use and intuitive. With LinkedIn fresh in your mind from chapter 5, you will be able to navigate this social networking site easily.

Creating a Professional Profile

Even before you enter your profile information (and throughout the profile process), Facebook will suggest that you find friends. You'll see the message, "Many of your friends may already be here. Searching your email account is the fastest way to find your friends on Facebook." Reject or skip these requests for now if you prefer to enter your data first.

There is a reassuring note on every page that Facebook will not store your password. That is probably encouraging news to a new Facebook user, given some recent articles and blog posts about Facebook's privacy policies. We tell you more about that later.

The profile fields on Facebook are quite different from those on LinkedIn. The Basic Information data fields include Current City, Hometown, Sex (that is male or female!), Birthday, Interested In (choices are women or men), and Looking For (choices are friendship, dating, a relationship, networking). You can pick more than one option! Just think. With one step, you can make your Facebook profile a one-stop shopping service for all of those critical life connections! We're just kidding, of course. This is where you start to present yourself professionally. Leave your birthday out, don't specify whether you're interested in men or women, and say that you're looking for networking.

Basic Facebook Safety Tips

You can take some simple steps on Facebook to prevent being spammed, protect your privacy, and avoid being contacted by someone who is not a welcome connection:

- Change your password frequently and be watchful of sharing this with anyone.

- Limit the personal information you include on your profile (for example, you probably don't want to include your phone number or birth year).

- Remove your connection to friends who post strange links.

- Avoid chatting with people you are not familiar with.

The next fields are Political Views and Religious Views—not exactly what most people need to be talking about in professional circles, especially not if you're a job seeker. Leave these fields blank (unless you happen to be applying for a political or religious job where these views would be relevant).

The Bio field is where you can be really professional. You may upload a short bio or copy the summary portion of your resume or other

short biographical note. In the Favorite Quotations field, consider posting some quotes related to your line of work or to work-related qualities.

To add a profile picture, you can upload a photo you already have on your computer or take one with your webcam. Keep in mind that it's acceptable for your Facebook headshot to show a little more personality than profile pictures you might post on some of the other professional networking sites, such as LinkedIn. However, don't put up a profile photo of a pet, child (or you as a child), or you with someone else. This is your profile, not your friend's/spouse's/partner's, child's, or pet's profile!

After this comes the Relationship Status field. Choices are single, in a relationship, engaged, married, it's complicated, in an open relationship, and widowed. Be careful here. This information isn't a prospective employer's business. It's your choice as to whether you want to indicate your status as this could be perceived in a positive or negative light. Your best bet may be to leave this field blank.

You also can enter a family member's name and email address, and Facebook will send an invitation to him or her to become your friend on Facebook and to confirm your family request. But again, for professional purposes, you may want to leave this field blank.

The Likes and Interests section of the profile allows you to enter data about your activities, interests, and favorite music, books, movies, and TV shows. You may want to leave most of this blank, but if you do enter some preferences, choose carefully. They don't all have to be business-oriented—it's great to show that you are a balanced, well-rounded person with interests outside of work. But do avoid anything that could be seen as controversial in the professional circles in which you travel.

 TIP

Don't have an incomplete or inconsistent profile. Make sure you've taken advantage of the option to share preferred information with your connections and that your Facebook image is consistent with your other online profiles.

In the Education and Work History sections you are able to post professional information, current employer, employment history, and educational background. Here's where you provide more details about your college major and degrees. Then you can add multiple employers, positions, cities, dates, and brief job descriptions.

In the Contact Information section, you can list your email address, IM screen names, mobile phone and land line numbers, address, neighborhood name, zip code, and website. Use your judgment about what you want to share, both from a logistical standpoint of how you'd want employers or other business contacts to reach you and from a security standpoint. Even though you can keep your information visible only to your network, you may not want to take any chances when it comes to revealing exactly where you live.

That's it! You have now completed your profile (see figure 6.2)!

Figure 6.2: *Diane's public Facebook profile.*

Understanding Privacy and Facebook

Facebook has been the brunt of many negative comments regarding privacy. As we are writing this book, QuitFacebook, QuitFacebook Day, and Facebook Protest are pages on the site. There is also a website, quitfacebookday.com, along with discussions on Twitter. Facebook is attempting to address these concerns with new security infrastructure. It has posted a how-to video on the site to instruct users about security settings and options.

It's understandable that technology problems and security issues would result from so much growth in so short a span of time. Certainly, everyone needs to find his or her own comfort level and achieve an appropriate balance between privacy settings and public networking. But just remember that as a job seeker, you need to stay visible and accessible in cyberspace. Don't be the leader of the QuitFacebook movement just as you are beginning to make connections and reap the benefits!

After you set up your profile, you are next reminded to "visit your privacy settings to control who can see the information on your profile."

You can control

- Who sees your photo and who can post to your wall.
- Who can contact you on Facebook and see your contact information and email.
- Whether your friends, tags, and connections display on your profile.
- What information is available to Facebook-enhanced applications and websites.
- Who can see your search result on Facebook and in search engines.
- Who can interact with you on Facebook.

To access the privacy settings, click Account in the top right of your Facebook home page and choose Privacy Settings from the drop-down list. Then choose Customize Settings. You can choose who has permission or can view your information. Your choices are Everyone,

Friends of Friends, Friends Only, and Customize. You can then choose what, with whom, and how you share information.

TIP

Because Facebook (like all social media) changes often, it's a good idea to monitor your privacy settings on Facebook on a regular basis and adjust them as necessary to support your objectives.

To make sure your image doesn't get tarnished with too much transparency on your Facebook profile, you should take the following actions:

- Prevent tagged photos of you that may be unprofessional. (Friends in your network can "tag" or label you in photos of you posted on the site. You'll get a notice that you've been tagged, so you can always untag yourself.)

- Scour the postings other people have put on your wall for any that are embarrassing to you or could be misunderstood taken out of context.

- Control who is posting to your wall. If you have a few very active friends who routinely populate your wall with irrelevant or unprofessional comments or links, you can adjust this by hiding or blocking their posts on your wall.

To access the latest information on Facebook privacy settings, click the Privacy link at the very bottom of your Facebook page.

TIP

For additional information on adjusting your Facebook privacy settings, consult this great and detailed post at Nick O'Neill's AllFacebook.com blog: www. allfacebook.com/2009/12/facebook-privacy-new/.

Building Your Network of "Friends"

A LinkedIn network is made of connections. On Facebook, your network is made of friends. Building your network on Facebook is basically a two-step process: searching for friends and then contacting them to ask them to be part of your network.

Searching for Friends

To start adding friends to your network, click on Friends on the left side of your home page. On this screen, you can list your email address and let Facebook search for your contacts who are already on the site.

You can also look at some suggestions, people that Facebook thinks you might know. How does it do that? It's a little bit of magic, a little bit of mystery, and a lot of clever programming to go through places you've worked and studied to find people from those networks, as well as looking through the networks of friends you already have to see if some of them could be mutual friends. It's a hit-or-miss process, but you might find that Facebook turns up some actual friends or old acquaintances you'd like to reconnect with.

You can also search for people by name and find people that you IM. (Facebook can import contacts from AOL, ICQ Chat, Windows Live Messenger, or Skype.)

When it comes to searching your network for connections to a particular company, Facebook suffers by comparison with LinkedIn. Yet Facebook has people search capabilities that work, especially when you are looking for someone by name. And as you build your social network in Facebook, your contacts' employment information is typically quite public. You'll likely have a "friend" who can help you make the connection. But the search engine is not quite as sophisticated as that on LinkedIn for identifying new contacts with specific companies, certain titles, in particular locations, or with certain keywords or for doing complex searches using Boolean logic.

Near the bottom of the Friends screen is the Search for People tool where you can enter a person's name or email address. When you enter something in the text box, you will be taken to another screen where you can further refine your search by location, school, or workplace (see figure 6.3). Facebook also provides links to groups of people that you might want to search, such as alumni from your college graduating class or coworkers at your current employer, based on information you entered on your profile.

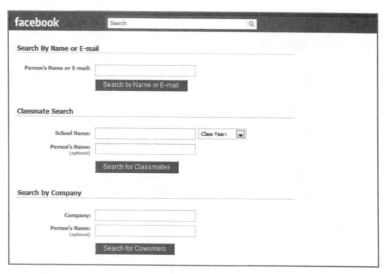

Figure 6.3: *Searching for people on Facebook.*

Searches we've done have worked well, assuming that everyone has entered his or her professional information. If your Facebook search turns up good matches, stick with those and get in touch through Facebook. If you need the more robust search power of LinkedIn, do your search for contacts there. Remember that if the resulting contacts are a part of your LinkedIn network, you can approach them through that site via a LinkedIn introduction. If they are outside of your three levels of connection on LinkedIn, before sending a LinkedIn InMail (which costs money), search for them on Facebook. If they are there, you can approach them with no fees. They might actually spend more time on Facebook than on LinkedIn, which means they might see your message sooner. Plus they might be in a friendlier mood there instead of the "all business" mentality of LinkedIn.

TIP

You may want to add a recruiter or two as friends. They could potentially post job openings through their status updates.

Contacting Friends

Once you've found a person you want to connect with, it's easy to make the connection on Facebook. You can send a message to anyone you find through a search. The person doesn't have to be a friend or a friend of a friend to be accessible to you. You can message nearly everyone, and there is no limit to how many messages you can send. This is quite a contrast to LinkedIn, which limits invitations and requests for introduction and charges fees for InMail messages.

When you see a thumbnail profile photo and recognize that you have the correct person, you can either send him or her only a message or make a friend request with the option to send a personal message explaining the reason for connecting. To send a message, click the person's thumbnail photo to open his or her profile. Then choose the Send a Message option below the full-size photo. (See chapter 5 for ideas on how to word networking messages to people you don't know.)

When you find a person you want to add to your network, click Add as Friend on his or her profile to open a box where you can enter a personal message and send a friend request (see figure 6.4). You can also choose to add this person to any friend lists you have created. The person will then have to accept your request in order to become part of your network.

 TIP

Although you can have up to 5,000 friends on Facebook, you shouldn't get overly zealous in adding a multitude of friends. Focus on the quality of these connections, not the quantity.

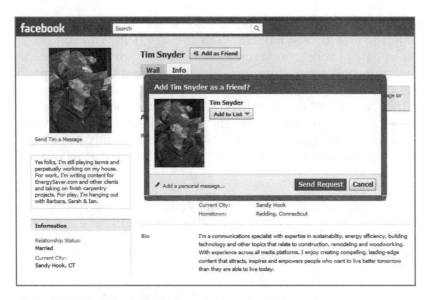

Figure 6.4: Adding a friend on Facebook.

Communicating with Your Network

To keep your network updated on what you are working on, you can either "Write something about yourself" under the profile picture, or you can post an update in the "What's on your mind?" field. The former (write something about yourself) is visible only when someone visits your profile page. The latter is broadcast to the audience you have specified in your settings—everyone, friends only, friends of friends, and so on. If you are using Facebook for job search and career management, make sure you are posting a professional update.

QUOTE

Many people tend to overlook Facebook as a professional networking tool. They think of it as social only, where Facebook had its roots. But the face of Facebook is changing and has moved much more toward professional networking. But whether you connect to professional colleagues there or not, your friends and family can be an important part of your professional network, too. Often job leads and business opportunities come from close friends and relatives. So I recommend sharing with your Facebook friends not just what you did on the weekend, but also what you do or want to do for work.

—Carol Williams, international MBA, French and German

You also can ask questions anytime of a large audience on Facebook by entering it in the "What's on your mind?" field. You can post a status update (a short message) or create a wall post (often used when you want to post a lengthier message or include a link to an article or site). Depending on the settings you've chosen, your messages will be seen by your friends only, or friends plus friends of friends, or everyone on the site. Although there isn't the structure of the Q&A section on LinkedIn to categorize the question, you'll probably get a high rate of response because of the more personal nature of relationships on Facebook.

Keep these general tips in mind when communicating through Facebook or any other social networking platform:

- Be subtle! Blatantly asking for a job or for customers for your business could be a real turn-off.

- Respond quickly to messages and posts and to any online missteps.

- Individualize and customize your direct communications to others to avoid being perceived as spamming your network.

- Make sure that your online messaging supports you and your professional and personal brand.

GETTING AND GIVING RECOMMENDATIONS ON FACEBOOK

You can handle references on Facebook in a couple of ways. You can add the application Testimonials and ask your professional contacts and employers to be references for you. You can also link your Facebook account to your LinkedIn account, if you have already compiled a number of recommendations there. We would recommend the latter (assuming you are keeping your Facebook network purely professional or at least carefully scrubbed of controversial, unprofessional data). No need to trouble your references by asking them to promote you on two different social networking sites. You can link your Facebook page to your LinkedIn account in a couple of ways. You can share your LinkedIn URL in your Facebook bio, or you can share the URL to your LinkedIn account in the Website field of the Contact Information part of your profile if you don't have another site listed there.

Searching for Jobs

Although there isn't a Facebook job board as there is on LinkedIn, there are still jobs on Facebook. Both CareerBuilder, a major Internet job board, and SimplyHired, an Internet aggregator site (it pulls job leads that match your criteria from multiple sites), have pages on Facebook (see figure 6.5). From those pages, you can click on links to find helpful advice, tools, and job leads.

Figure 6.5: CareerBuilder's page on Facebook.

RESEARCHING COMPANIES ON FACEBOOK

Facebook doesn't have a company research database like the one on LinkedIn. But a simple search for a company will bring up that company's Fan page (if it has one) plus lists of "friends" who work there.

You can also post a status update or send inbox (private) messages asking people in your network if they know anything about particular organizations you're researching.

Joining Groups

Just as on LinkedIn, many jobs are now being posted in the discussions of Facebook groups. So it pays to join appropriate groups. There are tens of thousands of groups on Facebook. You can certainly find plenty of groups that match your professional interests and your personal interests, too. Just make sure that any personal groups don't

etract from your brand image. And make sure also that you have a
ood balance between professional and personal groups—not all fun
tuff!

Once you are a member of a group and depending on the group
administrator's settings, you can find and contact members of the
group as well as create wall posts (links, photos, articles, comments,
questions, and so on). You can share your status there if you are
in job search, but make sure your requests for help are balanced by
offers of help. Other group members can then "like," comment on,
add additional related links, etc.—all public to that group. You can do
all the things in the group that you could do on a person's wall page.
And you can select some members of the group to invite to be your
friends.

Using Career-Focused Applications

Facebook has 77,000 applications to choose from, and those are just
the approved ones. There are many others that are being used by a
small number of members and therefore don't appear in the Facebook
Applications Directory. Many are games or silly activities and not
appropriate for job search and career management. So choose wisely
to make sure that your time spent on Facebook will be productive for
your career objectives.

To access applications, click the Applications link on the left side of
your home page and then click the Applications Directory link. Here
is a list of applications that could be helpful for your job search and
career management:

- EasyCV adds a mini version of your resume to your Facebook profile.

- MeetingWave helps you move social networking to live networking meetings.

- Inside Job connects you to industry leaders at your target companies, helping you find just the right contact.

- Work With Us (by Jobvite) displays jobs. You can review postings,
  see where friends work (if you don't already know), and send
  jobvites to your contacts—a nice way to pay it forward and help
  others!

- Jobs Indeed is an application powered by Indeed.com, another aggregator search engine.

- The Job Search powered by MonsterTRAK application helps students and new graduates search for internships, part-time jobs, and entry-level jobs.

- The Jobster Career Network application offers job alerts, career advice, and job search capability.

As you check out applications, Facebook lets you know if any of your Facebook friends are using those applications—a great vehicle to check their usefulness before investing valuable job search or career management time.

TIP

If you install an application on Facebook, double-check your profile to make sure this does not cause an unexpected news bit to show up on your profile. This is not necessarily a given for all applications; but a little extra vigilance on your part could save you from something unrelated to you or your brand populating your profile.

Making Facebook a Key Part of Your Networking Strategy

We hope you're convinced that Facebook is a viable option for professional networking. But as we close out this chapter, we need to issue a word of warning. Don't let the casual nature of the conversation on Facebook cause you to drop your guard.

Prospective employers and recruiters may be viewing your profile on Facebook and monitoring your activity there (depending on your privacy settings and who you let into your network). Make sure that your communications remain professional and present a consistent image across all sites. It's not good to have a very professional image on LinkedIn and a party-hearty image on Facebook (unless you plan to keep your Facebook purely personal with airtight privacy controls). Keep it businesslike. Think before you post. Don't let the ease of the site and the relaxed nature of the relationships there result in bad judgment that could cost you opportunities and career advancement for years to come.

QUOTE

If LinkedIn is about no-nonsense business information and networking to communicate your strengths and your value, Facebook is a way to inject more of your personality into your brand while still communicating other on-brand messages.

—Walter Akana, personal branding and online identity strategist

After publishing the first edition of this book, Ellen recalls lecturing her young adult son who at the time had fewer than 30 LinkedIn connections. "You've got to be more active on LinkedIn! Not having a robust LinkedIn profile is like committing career suicide," she told him. As a sales professional, he was already a Facebook enthusiast with many friends online and offline. Those friendships have always been a major part of his business networking, either as customers themselves or as bridge contacts to new friends.

Within a day of concluding her motherly career coach lecture, she received a Facebook invitation from her son to join the member group "Use LinkedIn...Stop Career Suicide" and their immediate "Cocktails Curbing Career Suicide!" event, with a two-dollar special on LINK-DRINK shooters. She was immediately reminded of why she and her husband had shipped him off to boarding school years before. Talk about moving online contacts offline! That event was the start of a face-to-face networking group called "Careers and Beers."

Ellen is pleased to say that her son now has a healthy network on LinkedIn in addition to his large number of Facebook friends. But he still prefers Facebook. And as Facebook has morphed more toward professional networking, she has to concede that he was right. Facebook fits his style, and it may be a great option for you, too.

> ### FACEBOOK'S PROFESSIONAL NETWORKING ADVANTAGES
>
> Facebook offers the following benefits in professional networking:
>
> - Easy to search for people and contact them freely
> - Unlimited friend requests
> - Less formal
> - Less time-consuming
> - No tie required
> - Cool to catch up with friends from the old days
> - A hybrid of social and professional
> - Profiles are easy to set up
> - It's fun!

We can't argue with this site's popularity. You can't stop this social media machine any more than you can stop time! And who would want to?

Key Points: Chapter 6

- Facebook has evolved from a purely social networking site to a site that is also useful for professional networking.

- Carefully consider how you're going to use Facebook: for strictly personal networking, strictly professional, or a combination of the two.

- Facebook is free and easy to join.

- As with all social networks, make sure you develop a complete Facebook profile so that people can find you and learn about your background and credentials.

- Take time to adjust your privacy settings to match your objectives for using the site and audit your Facebook profile routinely to make sure that your online brand isn't being tarnished by others' posts on your wall.

- Facebook's people search feature is not as robust as that of LinkedIn, but its advantage is that once you find people, you don't have to be connected to them already to send them a message.

- Post status updates that are relevant to your professional goals and personal brand.

- Join relevant groups that match your professional and personal interests to expand your networking reach and connect with others.

- Many Facebook applications have been developed to help with job search and other career management tasks.

CHAPTER 7

Building a Following with Microblogging and Twitter

What's all this fuss about Twitter and microblogging? Is it worth your time? Is it right for you? If so, what are the benefits? To tweet or not to tweet, that is the question.

Microblogging is a smaller, fragmented version of a traditional blog. The content can contain text, links to video, or pictures and can be internal and proprietary within an organization or group or external and open, like Twitter. Companies including IBM have been using microblogs to share knowledge and resources, recruit, collaborate, and add a personal touch to a professional environment.

This chapter focuses on the largest open forum for microblogging, Twitter. Just as with other forms of social networking, Twitter is an excellent vehicle to build your visibility, get information, and connect with others. In this chapter, we shed light on what makes the site unique and how it can provide a return on your investment of time. We demystify Twitter by providing you with an understanding of how it works, how to get started, and how to be a good Twitter "citizen."

In This Chapter

- *Understand what Twitter is and what it can do for you.*
- *Develop a Twitter profile.*
- *Learn how to tweet.*
- *Build relationships and make connections.*
- *Learn insider tips for job seekers.*
- *Get introduced to Twitter "Dos" and "Don'ts."*
- *Benefit from advanced tips for using Twitter.*

What Is Twitter?

According to personal branding and online identity strategist Walter Akana, Twitter is like "Facebook on crack…it takes Facebook's status update function and strips away everything else." Indeed, Twitter has put its own twist on the "What's on your mind?" function and allows you and others to post information and interact with each other in 140 characters or fewer.

These short posts that are used to communicate in Twitter are called *tweets*. They are shorter than a traditional text message and are communicated, by most users, in real time. Tweets are archived on the Web and are searchable on Google and other search engines. More recently, Google and Bing have even started to display activity for users in real time on search results. If you follow Twitter conversations, you are following an ongoing stream of Twitter information that is diverse, dynamic, and rapid-fire in terms of frequency. This is not merely noise. In fact, Twitter has achieved such significance that the Library of Congress will be archiving tweets, beginning back when Twitter started in 2006, capturing tweets "of note" and important information about our culture and way of life.

Twitter is all about communicating and gaining visibility with others of similar interests. As you can on LinkedIn and Facebook, you can interact and build relationships with others on Twitter, starting by "following" others and reading their tweets. If you find value, you can continue to follow them. Likewise, you will find that others can choose to follow you and read your tweets.

Twitter is distinct in several ways from some of the other popular social networks, such as LinkedIn and Facebook. LinkedIn users must follow built-in rules regarding engaging and connecting with others, which can sometimes take a long time. Facebook users who want to connect need to "friend" someone and wait for a response to their friend request. Unlike the formal, forced etiquette, and sometimes drawn-out time frame it takes to connect on LinkedIn and Facebook, connecting via Twitter is casual, informal, and immediate. Think of Twitter as a party or networking event where you can come as you are and everyone is invited.

QUOTE

A producer from CNN contacted me one morning, wanting to interview one of our authors in a segment about job hunting via Twitter. I had just an hour or two to find job seekers who had landed via Twitter, or the opportunity would fizzle. Immediately, I turned to my network on Twitter and Facebook for help. Within a few minutes, I had found successful job seekers who had one thing in common: They wouldn't have known about the job they landed without the help of social media. These opportunities weren't listed on any job board or in a classified ad. They were announced in fewer than 140 characters. And candidates were able to instantaneously access a specific individual to express their interest in the job—something that's much harder to accomplish when relying on traditional job search methods.

—Selena Dehne, publicist, JIST Publishing

Benefits of Twitter

Twitter had approximately 90 million visitors worldwide as of May 2010. This number is not a true measure of active users of Twitter, but even still, this reflects a large volume of people checking out Twitter activity. Whether you are looking for a job; want to stay on top of your career; or need to develop business as an entrepreneur, salesperson, or recruiter, you may find Twitter to be a beneficial part of your social networking repertoire.

Twitter is a great vehicle to

- Share relevant information with others who share common interests.

- Get and give feedback and enjoy quick turnaround with both.

- Communicate in short, concise bursts (if expansive writing is not your thing, you're going to like tweeting!).

- Learn about current and emerging trends.

- Access news of the moment.

- Connect with others who may not be accessible through other mechanisms.

- Increase your network and networking reach.

- Reinforce and communicate your professional brand to a large audience.

- Gain the inside advantage by accessing job postings, leads, and information that may be hidden otherwise.

QUOTE

I cross-post my blog entries on Twitter, my company's Facebook page, and sometimes on my LinkedIn profile. I use Twitter to provide snippets of job search advice to build credibility and name recognition. Job seekers can similarly use social media to market themselves as experts in their own field.

—Laurie Berenson, CPRW, president and owner, Sterling Career Concepts, LLC

Your Kind of "Tweeps"

Another compelling reason to get onboard with using Twitter is the vast array of people who routinely use it to communicate with others. Here is a starter list of Twitter users (*tweeps*) you might want to meet...

- Subject matter and industry experts

- Career coaches

- Recruiters

- Hiring managers and hiring decision makers

- C-level leaders

- Prospects, clients, referrals, business partners, vendors

- Journalists

- Politicians

- Celebrities

- Public relations professionals

The possibilities are endless, so you can add your own preferred target contacts to this list, based on the types of people you need to know or the kinds of information you need for your career or business goals.

Twitter is, for the most part, self-policed. If you're on Twitter strictly to sell, you've missed the opportunity to build productive relationships in which you provide value to other Twitter users. Even though Twitter is casual in nature, it's still important to be polite and focus on building relationships.

JOB SEEKER ALERT

Recruiters and employers like to do keyword searches on Twitter to look for candidates. This is made easier for them by the fact that tweets are indexed by search engines such as Google and others. So if you're tweeting, you're likely to be visible to the people who could hire you. On the flip side, companies and hiring managers like to use Twitter to build their brand and build a following, so they are visible to you, as well.

Get Started

One of the most important things to remember about Twitter as you're getting started is that you can scale your use of it in a way that makes sense for you and your objectives. Twitter users we surveyed have varying amounts of time they spend on Twitter on any given day, from 10 to 15 minutes to several hours or more. Like many of the social networking sites we've already covered in earlier chapters, Twitter may take you more time initially to get set up than it will take to use regularly.

Set Your Objectives

To make your launch into using Twitter as effective as possible, answer these questions:

- Who is your target audience? Who you are trying to reach?

- What themes do you want to tweet about? (Having more than one theme gives you the opportunity to broaden your appeal and make your tweets more interesting and engaging.)

- Are you using Twitter for professional or personal use or both? How will these objectives direct your messaging?

- What do want to accomplish?

- What makes you unique? (Refer to chapter 3 and appendix A for additional resources to help you answer this question.)

- Which keywords will play a recurring role in your messaging and profile description?

TIP

To make sure you're well equipped to start tweeting, check out the Twitter landscape to see what is already being tweeted. This will give you a better feel for existing conversations and how you want to add your voice to the Twitterverse.

TWITTER SPEAK

To get started on Twitter, you'll need to know some basics of Twitter vocabulary. This vocabulary includes terms related to the site as well as acronyms you'll use to communicate in your tweets. When you have only 140 characters in which to express yourself, you can imagine how helpful acronyms can be!

What's listed here is only a starter vocabulary. For more information, there are several resources in appendix A, or you can use http://twictionary.pbworks.com/.

- **DM:** Direct, private message you send to another tweep. The recipient of the DM must be a follower of yours.

- **F2F:** Face-to-face.

- **Handle:** A Twitter user name that shows up in tweets and as a self-identifier prefaced with the @ symbol. For instance, Diane's Twitter handle is @dicrompton.

- **Hashtags:** The # symbol places tweets in categories and makes this content searchable. For example, you can key in #healthcare in Twitter to search for tweets focused on health care.

- **IMHO:** In my humble opinion.

- **LMK:** Let me know.

- **NP:** No problem.

- **PRT:** PRT is the polite form of asking other tweeps to consider RTing a tweet.

- **RT:** RT is to repeat another's tweet.

- **Tweeps:** Twitter users.

- **Tweet stream:** The ongoing, continuous flow of collective tweets.

- **Tweetup:** An in-person gathering of tweeps that is organized through Twitter.

- **Twesumes:** Resumes using social media tools.

- **Twitterviews:** Interviews using social media tools.

- **YMMV:** Your mileage may vary, meaning that your experience may be different from mine.

Develop Your Profile

If you don't already have a Twitter account, visit www.twitter.com to sign up as a new user. To create an account, you have to provide a full name, a user name, a password, and an email address.

Your Twitter user name (called your Twitter *handle*) requires some careful thought. This is how your name will appear in tweets, replies, or direct messages (your handle is typically preceded by the @ sign, as in @dicrompton). So if your Twitter handle is unusually long, this chews up space when others tweet about you. Also, you want your name to be recognizable as you. If you pick something obscure, others may not make the connection. Because of this, using some of the characters of your name or your business name makes sense for your user name.

TIP

In order to create an effective Web-based "loop" for your various electronic profiles, make sure you add your professional Twitter handle to business cards, resumes, your e-signature, and other self-marketing material.

To establish yourself as an active Twitter member, you'll need to set up a profile (see figure 7.1). Your Twitter profile is the "landing page" that other tweeps will see when they search for you, want to check you out, and, you hope, connect with you. So it's important to fill it out completely because you have only one chance to make a great first impression.

Figure 7.1: *Diane's Twitter profile.*

From your home page, choose Settings and then Profile to enter the information for your profile:

- **Picture:** This is an important part of your Twitter profile. It's considered good practice to include a headshot or appropriate avatar; it warms your Twitter image and supports your brand.

- **Name:** This is what appears on the side of your Twitter profile above your location. You can make this longer than your user name/handle and include spaces. Entering your complete first and last name here makes it easier for people to find you on Twitter.

- **Location:** List the area where you live and work.

- **Web:** Enter a site of your choice, such as your blog or LinkedIn URL.

- **Bio:** You get a total of 160 characters for your bio. This means that you'll need to be very succinct in your description to fit important details. Include important keywords that relate to your areas of expertise, experience, and personal brand. Similar to other social networking sites such as LinkedIn, Twitter is searchable by Google and other search engines. You can increase connections and hits to your profile by adding keywords that are important to your target audience.

Make sure there is uniformity between your Twitter profile and various online profiles as you could be cross-referenced on these. Keep your profile updated and complete, and make sure all the details, including your profile picture and background, are consistent with your personal brand.

TIP

To give your profile personality and to support your brand, customize your Twitter page. You can do this with designs available on Twitter or select from a variety of outside programs (for example, Photoshop and PowerPoint). Choose Settings from the menu bar and then Design to see your options.

Go Tweet!

Before you start following anyone else, start to create some buzz by tweeting. To do this, go to your Twitter home page, type your tweet in the What's Happening? field, and select the Tweet button (see figure 7.2). The idea is to have a bit of a Twitter stream for others to check out when you start to follow other Twitter users. As you begin following others, they will determine whether they want to follow you back. If you don't have an active Twitter account and tweet stream, this could throw up a red flag that you may might not be worthy of a connection.

Figure 7.2: A sample tweet.

Initially, consider tweeting about 15 to 20 times per week to start to become more visible. As you build your number of tweets, consider ways to add more depth and breadth. This will be directed by the interests of your audience, your brand, and your objectives.

TIP

It's easy to get enthusiastic with tweeting, but too much of a good thing (more than 20 tweets a day) may not add to your bottom line results and could wear out your welcome with your audience.

Learn the Art of the Tweet

Starting to tweet and condensing your language into sound bites is a little challenging initially if you are used to communicating in larger blocks. Realize that you have 140 characters to grab interest, convey a message, and engage others.

TIP

Don't go over the 140-character limit for your tweets. This is like continuing a conversation on the phone after someone has already hung up—that person is not going to get the full message you were trying to communicate.

Tweet about topics you are interested in and knowledgeable/passionate about. To get started, consider tweeting about the following:

- Events related to your field

- Industry trends

- The type of work and job you are targeting (if you are currently looking for a job)

- Something interesting you read, be it a book or a blog post, related to your professional area of expertise (just make sure to include a shortened link)

- A recent accomplishment

- Resources that have been helpful to you

- Thanking people for their efforts

- Your interests and "on brand" activities (for example, "volunteering to manage a project, love leading a team toward a common goal")

- Work-related stories that support your professional brand

- New skills or information you have learned

- Request for advice and information (you can preface your tweets with "looking for" or "need help with")

If you include a link to a website and want to shorten it to reserve more of the 140 characters of the message, you can use a URL shortener like bit.ly (http://bit.ly/) or TinyURL (http://tinyurl.com/). These free sites allow you to copy and paste the original link into an electronic field that will automatically generate a unique, shortened version of the URL for you to copy and paste into your What's Happening update field on Twitter (see figure 7.3).

Figure 7.3: *Shorten URLs using bit.ly.*

Including hashtags (#) with related keywords at the end of a tweet can make the tweet more searchable and can serve as an interest "magnet" to encourage reader traffic. But don't overdo it. Even though hashtags increase the searchability of your tweets, they can give the appearance of inappropriateness or even cluelessness if you overuse them.

THINK BEFORE YOU TWEET

The great thing about Twitter is that your tweets can go viral and spread quickly to lots of people—that's also the bad thing about Twitter. Tweets are a public record, an information stream that can be picked up by Google and other search engines. Because of this, you'll want to make sure that your tweets are messages that are okay to live on as a permanent cybertrail created by you.

You can delete tweets if you've made an error or change your mind about something you've posted. However, because your tweets are part of the public realm and may already be archived, it's not a good practice to tweet and then delete if you can avoid it.

To avoid any tweeting mistakes, follow these guidelines:

- Don't share information of a proprietary or inflammatory nature on Twitter (or on any other social networking sites).

- Don't share the same content on multiple Twitter accounts. Otherwise, your followers might get redundant tweets.

- Don't send a private message publicly. This might offend the intended recipient. Plus the public message could be misunderstood and taken out of context. Use DM instead.

- If you've landed a new job, don't announce it until you absolutely know this is going to happen (when your offer is finalized).

Pay It Forward with Retweeting

A great way to build goodwill, kindle a relationship, and share engaging information is through retweeting someone else's article, blog post, or tweet. Retweeting is like viral marketing of a particular message.

 TIP

Take the opportunity to retweet your Twitter followers when it's appropriate by linking to their blog posts and endorsing their online messages.

When you find something you would like to share through retweeting, check to see whether there is a retweet widget at the top or the bottom of the blog post or article. By clicking on this widget, the tweet will self-populate in your Twitter status update field, where you can leave it as is or customize it before sharing.

If no widget is available, you can manually copy and paste the URL for the post in order to shorten it, if needed, as we described earlier. You can then edit the tweet if desired. If you use tools like TweetDeck, Hootsuite, or SocialOomph, you can also shorten a long URL. (The section "Use Advanced Twitter Features and Applications" has more information on these Twitter tools and others.)

TIP

If you have the good fortune to have someone else retweet your tweet, it's considered good form to reply to that person (using "@person's Twitter name") to say thank you. Public thank-you tweets build goodwill. If that person is already following you, you can make this reply a more private communication through a direct message (DM).

Search for People and Information in the Twitterverse

There are many ways to find other people who are on Twitter. The most basic is to click on the Find People tab in Twitter to search by name, Twitter name, category, Twitter URL, or keywords.

TIP

Use the Company search function on LinkedIn (see chapter 5) to get information on particular companies and identify key contacts. You can then search for these same contacts to follow on Twitter.

You can also search by keywords for your industry and areas of expertise. In addition, using hashtags to precede a word or phrase and entering this into the search field (for example, "#environmental") will yield Twitter accounts where the owner has tweeted about a topic of interest to you, allowing you to decide whether to follow that person.

TIP

To monitor Twitter for tweetups and other local events, use a hashtag and your location to categorize your search.

If you need to further define your search, try Twitter's Advanced Search feature by going to http://search.twitter.com/advanced. You can include specific phrasing, words, or hashtags; exclude words; find tweets from, to, or about a certain person; and search by location or date and even language. The following sections describe other search techniques for Twitter.

Several sites are available to help you search for information on Twitter. One such site is Listorious (www.listorious.com). This powerful and comprehensive search site provides a quick and easy vehicle to conduct a number of searches on Twitter including "most followed," "top listed," and many other searches (see figure 7.4).

Figure 7.4: *Find people on Twitter using Listorious.*

You can also do a Google search in combination with hashtags, which will enable you to use many variations on a theme and still get a good yield on your search. For instance, to find career coaches using Google for your search, you could enter "twitter: #career coaches." This would bring up coaches on Twitter and lists for coaches, tweets from coaches, and so on.

Follow and Be Followed

A big part of the attraction with Twitter is the ability to quickly and directly connect with people who interest you by following them. You may decide to follow an industry leader, a person with particular expertise, a topic or event, an association, or a variety of people or things of interest to you.

TIP

If you're actively seeking a job, follow recruiters, hiring managers, thought leaders in target companies, and their respective Twitter and career lists. By all means, reply to recruiters who have positions you are interested in, but don't expect them to jump through hoops on your behalf just because you expressed interest.

You can easily opt to follow someone by going to that person's Twitter profile and clicking the Follow icon under his or her name field. Or you can do this through other Twitter tools such as TweetDeck, many of which give you the option of customizing and streamlining various Twitter functions.

As you begin to look for others to connect with on Twitter, you'll need to decide whether you want to follow others with similar interests or "auto follow" anyone that follows you. There are valid arguments to support both of these practices. You'll need to decide which approach works best for your overall networking and self-marketing strategy.

TIP

To grow your list of people to follow, you may consider taking advantage of a Twitter practice called "FollowFriday." This practice was started by tweep Micah Baldwin in 2009 to suggest people to follow on Fridays. These tweets are populated with recommended Twitter handles of people to follow. If you'd like to explore this further, go to: http://search.twitter.com and enter #followfriday. Have fun!

Our advice is to grow your network slowly and thoughtfully. You don't want to give the appearance of being a "spam" Twitter user who follows a lot of people, but has few following back.

GOOD PEOPLE FOR JOB SEEKERS TO FOLLOW

To begin following experts and access sites on Twitter that could be good resources for your job search, use the following lists as a starting point:

- Job-Hunt.org's list of "The 101 Best Twitter Job Search/ Career Experts Plus 6" at http://www.job-hunt.org/job-search-news/2009/06/30/the-101-best-job-searchcareer-twitter-accounts-plus-6/

- Career Rocketeer's list of "150+ Experts on Twitter All Job Seekers Must Follow" at http://bit.ly/aptKJQ

- Applicant.com's "30 Profiles (And Sites) Every Job Seeker on Twitter Should Follow" at http://bit.ly/dlxwqY

- Job-Hunt.org's Employers Recruiting list on Listorious at http://bit.ly/cfHtXl

QUOTE

I entered the job market at a difficult time. I learned from the experts that using all the technology tools at your disposal is important. On Twitter, I started out by following target companies and the people and firms they followed. Then I joined the conversations and began developing relationships. I learned what forums and conferences like-minded people were attending, went to a few, and furthered my connections. One of the conference trips led to the role I have today.

Many of my Twitter relationships have become LinkedIn contacts as well as ongoing business relationships. Twitter is real time and valuable for interacting on many work-related topics.

When I joined my new firm, these newly learned skills were very relevant and useful. I recently tweeted our global conference!

—Debbie Brown, senior sales executive

Develop a Following

Spend a bit of time on Twitter each day. Ideally, spend 10 to 15 minutes, two to three times spaced out over the day. Staying active on Twitter keeps you "front and center" with recruiters and hiring managers who routinely use tools that alert them to searches of their name and their company name. You can't expect to build a following if you are a "sometime" user of Twitter.

Monitor your Twitter account regularly to make sure you don't miss time-sensitive messages. Follow up with messages you receive within 48 hours. Otherwise, it could appear that you don't take the relationships seriously. If you want to make sure you don't miss any DMs or mentions, you can also sync your Twitter account to smart devices including iPhone, BlackBerry, and others. There are several choices of apps, or Twitter clients, to use, including Tweetie and TwitterFon (iPhone applications) and Twitterberry (BlackBerry application).

USING TWITTER EFFECTIVELY

Walter Akana, personal branding and online identity strategist, offers these practical suggestions for using Twitter effectively:

- **Listen:** Regularly read the tweets of people who are relevant (to you and your brand, your areas of expertise) to see what they "discuss" on Twitter.

- **Share:** Tell the world what you are interested in. Tell other tweeps you like their comments. Keep this activity "on brand." If you find something interesting, create a link and share it by tweeting or retweeting.

- **Engage:** Interact with people online. You can begin a relationship with the brief snippets of interaction on Twitter and form the basis for more extensive interactions in other media—this is networking at its best.

It's also important to link Twitter to your other social networking sites. If you have a blog, your Twitter presence and tweets can be a major driver to build traffic for your blog. Make sure you include links to your blog in your Twitter profile, in your comments on others' blogs, and in your other online activities. Several bloggers we surveyed confirmed that their Twitter activity has exponentially increased traffic to their blogs.

QUOTE

Three years ago, I forcefully advocated that everybody blog, that a blog was an entry point to establishing your online expertise and thought leadership. Today I forcefully advocate that everybody use Twitter. It is a truly dynamic way to network, meet people, establish a presence. It reflects the way that more and more people build community online. But be strategic and mindful about who you fan, friend, follow, and connect to. Social media is dynamic and increasingly more integrated. My blog is my content. Twitter is my tool for amplification. And Facebook is the forum for discussion.

—Dan Greenfield, principal, Bernaise Source Media

LinkedIn also provides the function of syncing to your Twitter account. You may not want all your tweets to automatically get posted to LinkedIn or vice versa. You can control this on Twitter by manually adding either #in or #li to tag your tweets to "go live" on LinkedIn. Also, there may be opportunities when you comment on a blog or article to imbed your Twitter URL so that this leads back to your Twitter profile. Test out your link to make sure it works and directs people back to your account.

Whenever you can, take advantage of the opportunity to move an online connection offline or even make new connections via face-to-face Tweetups. Watch for news of these via Twitter and discussion groups.

Twitter-Related Job Resources

Check out these resources for job-related tweets:

- **http://twitter.com/JobAngels:** Site that provides advice, job postings, and guidance for job seekers.

- **http://twittjobsearch.com/:** Browse for tweeted job openings.

- **http://nearbytweets.com/:** Source jobs in your geographic area.

- **http://twithire.com/:** Job board.

- **http://tweetmyjobs.com/:** Tweeted job postings.

- **http://Twitter.com/microjobs:** Connects people to jobs; jobs are noted by hashtags at end of tweets.

- **http://twitter.com/jobshouts:** Social search engine for jobs, job seekers, and employers.

- **http://twitter.com/linkup:** Jobs on company websites.

Understand the Value of Lists

Twitter has evolved a great deal in the last year. In the past, having a large number of followers meant you were worth your "Twitter salt," but now things have changed. Twitter users can create lists of their favorite people to follow and categorize (for example, Job Experts, Career Coaches, and Local Contacts). Checking out someone's list will give you a good idea of who that person likes to follow (see figure 7.5). If a person is following thought leaders and people you think are relevant, this may impact your interest in connecting with that person.

Also, getting on someone's Twitter list is considered an honor worthy of thanks and appreciation, because this can elevate your rank on Twitter. So as you're deciding who to engage and connect with, lists can take on greater importance. In fact, if you find a useful list, you may choose to follow the list itself, which will cause individuals on the list to show up in your tweet stream. Lists are located in the sidebar of a Twitter profile and can be designated as "public" or "private" by the Twitter account holder.

Figure 7.5: *Lists are great way to find people to follow.*

TIP

Thank people who add you to one of their publicly posted lists. Being added to a list is considered an honor by Twitter standards, and thanking the person who listed you is a nice courtesy.

Use Advanced Twitter Features and Applications

We've gone through a lot of recommendations to help you get as much as possible out of using Twitter. As you get up and running, this section points to useful Twitter features and applications that can enhance your Twitter experience:

- To separate personal from professional Twitter profiles or to meet different objectives, you can create multiple Twitter accounts, each with different handles (user names). However, maintaining multiple accounts can be time-consuming.

- To gauge optimal tweet time to better reach your preferred audience, use programs such as Twitalyzer or Twittergrader.

- To track your tweets, you can set up an RSS feed for your Twitter account. To do this, select the RSS Feed widget in your sidebar to subscribe to this feed and get a running record of your tweets.

- Consider setting up an advanced tweeting plan to manage your time and tweets more efficiently (see following worksheet).

- Increase your follower quotient by sharing your lists with Listorious.com.

- Make it easier for others to follow your Twitter lists through using TweepML.com.

- To streamline (for future reference) and share your favorite searches, save them in the sidebar of your Twitter profile.

- Stay abreast of new applications that can help you manage Twitter and get the most out of it. A good resource for this type of information is http://oneforty.com/.

- Don't try to listen to every Twitter conversation. Consider using aggregator tools like TweetDeck to better manage Twitter traffic.

Do You Need a Tweet Plan?

What is a tweet plan and how do you know if you need one? To see whether you're a good candidate for a tweet plan, check the following statements to see whether they apply to you:

- ❏ I feel as if Twitter is running my life.

- ❏ I would like to have a more organized approach to tweeting.

- ❏ I'm not sure if Twitter is giving me a good return on my investment of time.

- ❏ I'm not confident Twitter is contributing to my self-marketing objectives.

If you checked any of these statements, you may benefit from a tweet plan. Some of the primary benefits to using a tweet plan include

- Streamlining the process of tweeting

- Saving you time

- Building consistency into your tweet content and messaging

- Reinforcing your branding

There are a variety of tools out there to help you manage your tweets. Some of the popular choices include the following:

- HootSuite (http://hootsuite.com/)

- SocialOomph (www.socialoomph.com/)

- TweetDeck (www.tweetdeck.com/)

These tools allow you to organize the Twitter stream in a way that makes sense for you. They are comprehensive and offer a variety of ways to manage your use of Twitter including scheduling tweets, tracking keywords, retweeting, and more.

The *Social Media Examiner* online magazine (www.Socialmediaexaminer.com) has a relevant and detailed article about setting up a tweet plan called "8 Simple Steps to Growing a Quality Twitter Following," which is available at http://bit.ly/beScE6.

TWITTER CHAT

Another way to leverage Twitter is to participate in Twitter chat. These live chats are categorized by specific hashtags according to topic. If you'd like to explore further, check out the Twitter Chat Schedule, which is a Google spreadsheet of scheduled chats, at http://ow.ly/2qkV6 to determine your level of interest in participating.

Chats can be an excellent way to get information on a particular topic (and gain expertise), connect with other like-minded people, and showcase your knowledge. Especially if you are a consultant, freelancer, or a small business owner, this is a great way to get some useful tips and build community with others.

Make sure to pay attention to the rules of engagement for participating in Twitter chat, including using appropriate hashtags to "code" your tweets, checking in advance for rules for participation in a particular chat, and not showing up late and interrupting. The benefits after a chat can be worthwhile, too. You can follow individuals involved in the chat and start to build relationships with these people. If you'd like more details regarding this, Lisa Barone has written an excellent post about this subject that is available at http://ow.ly/2q8TR. Go forth and enjoy the banter!

Make Twitter a Key Part of Your Networking Strategy

It's easy to feel intimidated when starting to use a new social media tool like Twitter, but the potential rewards are worth the effort it takes to get involved. Just remember that even though Twitter is casual in nature, be aware of and use the same etiquette you would in face-to-face interactions.

QUOTE

Just get started. The best way to join the community is to sign up, listen, and share. You will be able to grow your network and enhance your reputation, which can lead to exciting opportunities you would not otherwise have. If you don't get involved, you will never know what you are missing!

—Miriam Salpeter, job search and social media strategist

Key Points: Chapter 7

- Twitter rounds out a self-marketing and career management strategy. Know your self-marketing objectives and develop your Twitter strategy in keeping with these objectives.

- Twitter is most effectively leveraged in combination with other popular social networking tools including LinkedIn, Facebook, blogs, and others.

- Developing and maintaining a relevant and complete profile is important.

- Tweet with objectives in mind. Commit to a realistic level of involvement to get a good return on your investment of time.

- When you choose who to follow, focus on building relationships and making productive connections.

- Utilize good networking principles with regard to etiquette and expectations.

- Investigate using Twitter-related applications to become more efficient in your use of Twitter.

CHAPTER 8

Building Your Brand
in the Blogosphere

In chapter 1 you learned a bit about blogging, both having your own and commenting on other people's blogs. Not sure it's right for you? Neither was Dan Greenfield, a new media expert and former vice president of EarthLink. "I was reluctant at first to blog," Dan told us, "unsure if I had enough to say and afraid I would say the wrong thing, but deciding to blog was one of the best decisions that I have ever made professionally. My blog has been invaluable, giving me insights into my profession, helping me make contacts, and leading to speaking opportunities."

We'd like you to reap similar rewards. In this chapter, we'll help you start your own blog or learn how to say the right things on other people's blogs.

In This Chapter

- *Decide whether blogging is a good option for you.*
- *Learn to speak the language of blogging like a native.*
- *Comment on others' blogs without putting your foot in your mouth.*
- *Start your own blog in a few easy steps.*

The Basics of Blogging

If you're new to blogging, the process and technology might seem somewhat mystifying. In fact, blogs are quite simple. A blog is just a website like any other website, except that the content is more

dynamic and interactive. All blogging software is designed to support this interactive nature, and it is easy to add and change content in a blog. You don't necessarily need to be a technology buff and certainly not expert in HTML coding.

Blogs Are Dynamic

Unlike a traditional website, in which content is written and uploaded to the site and then essentially just sits there until updates are needed, a blog contains frequently updated content that makes it more like a diary or journal. That's where the word *blog* comes from; it's derived from *Web log*. Content is often posted daily or a few times a week or at least much more frequently than on most websites.

Blogs Are Interactive

The other factor, and perhaps the most important one, that distinguishes a blog from a regular website is that most blogs allow input from readers. They generate conversation. You, as the owner or author of a blog, post your thoughts on your blog that other people can read. Blogging technology then allows your readers to comment, reply, rebut, expand on, or otherwise make known their thoughts and opinions about what you've said. Blogs are therefore an excellent networking tool because they not only allow you to express your personal brand through your writing, but also to build community.

SAME FEATURES BUT DIFFERENT DNA

Blogs might sound a lot like discussion groups or online bulletin/message boards, but blogs reflect more the singular voice and brand of the person or persons who "own" the blog. The blog owner is the principal author who sets the tone for the discussion, poses the discussion topics, and manages the content of the site. Discussion groups tend to be more free-for-alls. Anyone interested in a particular topic can post questions, answers, or comments at any time. Although a discussion group usually does have a moderator who might introduce a topic or approve comments before they go live on the site, that moderator is not the main voice of the group.

Wiki is software that allows ordinary people to edit a website quickly and easily, even when that site is not registered to them. The term *wiki* refers not only to the technology, but also to a website that is collaborative. Wikipedia, the amazingly comprehensive and free online encyclopedia, is one of the most widely known and largest of the wikis. Wikis differ from blogs in that they are not so much conversational as they are informational. Wikis are more like knowledge databases in which readers can share their knowledge by adding their own content to a site. Blogs, which also can be informative and informational, are more about expressing opinions and sharing experiences to start a dialogue.

Blogs Can Be Beneficial

Blogging can be a part of just about everyone's networking efforts. If you are an entrepreneur, such as an independent consultant or freelancer, having your own blog gives you a vehicle for advertising your expertise to the world (without it looking like, or having the cost of, real advertising). If you're a job seeker, you can show off your credentials and knowledge through your posts in the hope that employers or recruiters are reading. Geoff Peterson, recruiting leader, sourcing consultant, speaker, and trainer (gpeterson@generallead.com), suggests that job seekers create a blog as an integral part of their online presence and use this as a way to further brand themselves.

NOTE

Networking is about building relationships and helping others, not simply helping yourself with a job or business opportunity. Similarly, blogging is about building relationships and sharing your knowledge and ideas with others by discussing subjects you are truly passionate about; it's not just about furthering your career. Ultimately, it's all about the conversations, not just you and your needs.

Commenting on other people's blogs is so easy that everyone should consider doing it—plus, it's free! Submitting comments to blogs, particularly those that get a fair amount of traffic, can skyrocket your search engine hits, enabling you to have more of a presence online.

Regardless of your situation or particular goals, blogging can do the following:

- Increase your visibility and credibility.
- Build and reinforce your personal brand (who you are).
- Provide a mechanism for expressing yourself and reaching an audience.
- Establish yourself as a thought leader.
- Build community with other like-minded individuals.
- Demonstrate your technical acumen.
- Help you secure jobs or clients by making you more visible and prominent.
- Enlarge your personal and professional network.
- Enable you to become a published author online.

BLOGGING FOR BUSINESS DEVELOPMENT

Louise Fletcher, founder of Blue Sky Resumes and Career Hub, finds that her blog (www.blueskyresumes.com/blog) gives her direct access to clients so that she doesn't have to pay referral fees. More than 90 percent of her business comes from the Web. In addition, she has been able to establish her own voice through her blog and has built credibility as a career coaching professional.

Clearly, there are plenty of reasons to blog, so let's get started (or bump you up a notch if you've already ventured a short way into the blogosphere). First, we define some of the lingo of blogging. Then we take you step-by-step through starting a blog or commenting on others' blogs.

The Language of Blogging Defined

When you start reading blogs, you'll run across many unfamiliar terms (see figure 8.1). Here's a quick glossary of the most important ones:

- **Archives:** Older posts stored on a blog by date that readers can access and review.

- **Blogosphere:** The term for all blogs collectively. The world of blogs. The Web-based community in which all blogs exist and are connected.

- **Blogroll:** A listing of other blogs that are favorites of the author(s) or are being promoted for some reason. Often, these are related to the point of view or personal brand of the blog's author(s).

- **Categories:** Stored posts organized by content area. Ideally, categories serve as an "information architecture" that helps readers navigate the blog.

- **Comments:** Comments are the content that readers of a blog post to the site. Comments are what give blogs their conversational nature. They are replies to posts. Comments can show off readers' knowledge and expertise (but, of course, should do so in a humble, not boastful or self-serving way).

- **Links:** A virtual connection to another blog or website. Content that is hyperlinked to another site can be clicked on to take the user directly to that site, or to specific content on that site, such as an article, a post on another blog, or a bio. This is one of the big ways that the Web possesses interconnectivity and forms a blogosphere, not just isolated, standalone sites or blogs. *Note:* The link might also be to a different post within the same blog—a link to the blogger's earlier writings. Links are highly prized, especially in-bound links to your blog from other sites. The more in-bound links you generate, the more credibility you have in the blogosphere and the higher your level of authority.

- **Permalinks:** A permanent link to a blog post, even after the post has moved from the blog's front page and into the archives.

- **Posts:** The articles or entries that make up blogs. Posts typically reflect the distinctive voice or perspective of the author. Often editorial in tone, they can be written in a conversational or personal manner as well. Some posts contain facts and links to other sites.

- **RSS (feeds):** Really Simple Syndication (RSS) is a Web application, otherwise known as an *aggregator,* that compiles specific information on the Web (summarized or in its entirety) and pushes this to a single location for ready access to the person who has subscribed to a site. It is a way to track updates to other blogs of interest without having to visit each one individually.

- **Sidebar:** The side column or columns on a blog that can contain categories, bios of the author(s), lists of services, photos, recommended books or other resources, favorite blogs (in a blogroll), and archives.

- **Tags:** The keywords associated with specific blog posts. They allow for indexing by search engines.

- **Trackbacks:** An acknowledging link a blogger uses to let another blogger know that he or she has referenced specific content. The receiving blog will typically display a list of other blogs that link to the content.

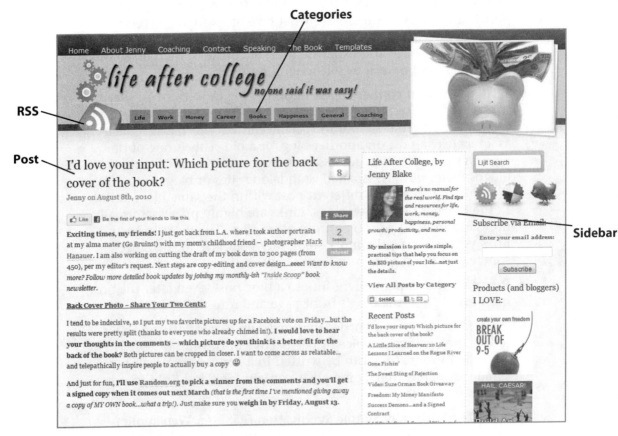

Figure 8.1: *Anatomy of a blog.*

Deciding Whether to Blog or Just Comment

Think back to chapter 3's discussion of your digital footprint. Do you have negative or irrelevant digital dirt that you need to wash over? Commenting on blogs or having your own blog can give you search engine hits that help to bury the content you want to hide. Or if you don't have much of an online presence at all, blogging is one of the best ways to have Google and other search engines come up with matches for your name.

TIP

If your preference is to share your thoughts without inviting discussion, blogging may not be for you. A traditional website on which you post content but readers cannot comment, other than to send you an email privately, might be the better choice for you.

Also, think about the goals you identified in chapter 3. How might blogging help you reach those goals?

- Are you a business owner seeking greater reach to target customers?

- Are you a subject-matter expert in your profession wanting to share your expertise, both to enhance your credibility and stature and to help others in your field?

- Are you a job seeker hoping to attract employers and recruiters so that you don't have to chase them down?

- Are you a recruiter who wants to get into conversations with potential candidates to "test" them before throwing them in the ring for job opportunities?

- Are you a happily employed person who simply wants to connect with others in your field to increase your knowledge and your network?

Both having a blog and commenting on other blogs can help in all those situations. So the decision might come down to four key factors:

- Your writing skill and interest in writing
- A passion for your subject matter

- Time available to commit to blogging
- Level of comfort with being the focus of attention

The Writing Factor

If you don't consider writing to be a top skill of yours, you might be better off commenting on others' blogs than having the pressure and spotlight on you as author of your own blog.

TIP

If you really want to have a blog but hate to write or don't do it very well, you can consider having a blog that consists mostly of podcasts (audio files you record) or video clips rather than written content. Also, you might consider microblogging on a site such as Twitter as a more time-effective option that will still give you a good return on investment.

The Passion Factor

If you lack a genuine passion for the topics you write about, your blog is not likely to be a success. It won't be seen as useful and engaging to your readers, and it won't have longevity. Both you and your readers will grow tired of it. It might also be seen as self-serving. Posting any old content without passion and true interest behind it often signals that you are using the blog only as a means of getting a job or advancing your career.

QUOTE

I love people and I love training, coaching, and building programs—I have all these things in my "dream job" with Google. I started my blog as a means of self-expression. Since that time, it has evolved into a medium where I can share my passion for coaching and training, inspiring people, building community, and meeting others. It reflects what I want in life and work.

—Jenny Blake, blogger of "Life After College" (www.lifeaftercollege.org/) and career program development manager for Google

The Time Factor

Having your own blog takes more time than commenting on others' blogs. With your own blog, there's an expectation that you will keep it fresh and dynamic with frequent posts. Ideally, you should write daily. Regular readers typically expect that you write at least a couple or few times a week—four to six times per month is about the minimum you can get by with. Any less and you risk losing readers.

The You Factor

If promoting your personal brand and advancing your professional agenda are paramount, having your own blog might be the best way to go. Your own blog gives you a platform for your opinions and for expressing who you are and what you have to offer. Sure, your readers are able to showcase themselves and their ideas in their comments, but it's still your show. You call the shots.

If, on the other hand, you just need to expand the reach of your network and connect with as many people as possible, with as little time commitment as possible, in order to advance your career, job search, business, or other endeavor, commenting on other people's blogs or selecting another social networking vehicle might be a better fit for you.

IT DOESN'T HAVE TO BE AN EITHER/OR SITUATION

Having your own blog doesn't mean you can't also comment on other people's blogs. In fact, commenting on other blogs and including a link back to your blog will help generate more traffic for you.

Commenting on OPBs (Other People's Blogs)

Start-up entrepreneurs and seasoned businesspeople are well acquainted with the concept of *OPM*, or "other people's money." They borrow money from others to start a business without having to put up their own cash or to supplement their own money, or they get other people to invest money as partners in a business venture. Commenting on other people's blogs (*OPBs*) is not all that different of a process.

By commenting on OPBs, you can establish yourself as an expert, increase your visibility, and connect with others (the social networking version of fame and fortune) without the expense and time commitment of setting up and maintaining your own blog. If you like that idea, we suggest following a few simple steps to become an expert OPB commenter.

Step 1: Scope Out the Blogging Landscape

Start by reading other blogs to get ideas of what seems to work and not work, and what you like and don't like, when it comes to blog content. Don't comment just yet. Just peruse and browse. Get a feel for what is discussed and what types of comments are being made.

As you surf the Net for blogs, make note of the ones you like the most and that are most relevant to your goals or professional style and areas of expertise. These will be your "blogs of choice"—ones that you'll revisit often, subscribe to, and eventually start commenting on. After you've reviewed a selection of blogs (over the course of minutes, hours, or days—whatever it takes for you to get a good feel for them), you should start to feel comfortable with the flow of this type of information exchange and be ready to write your own comments.

 TIP

To save time in identifying and keeping up with your blogs of choice, set up a Google alert at www.google.com/alerts. Google will search the Web regularly and email you alerts of new blog posts that match your interests. You can also enter in the search field for Google such terms as "blogs: health care" to identify blogs that contain health care in their descriptive title.

In addition, you can use an RSS (Really Simple Syndication) reader. Yahoo!, Google, and Bloglines.com can help you do this. With RSS, you select your preferred blogs and save them to be pulled up in a "reader" format. You can then quickly scan for updates to these blogs and choose to read part or all of a posting.

Step 2: Write a Comment

You might be chomping at the bit to write and submit a comment. How hard can it be, after all? But keep in mind that your comment on a blog becomes a permanent, archived record on that particular blog and might show up for a long time in keyword searches of your name. Because of this, take time to make sure that your comment is something you can be proud of and not cringe at if you see it come back to haunt you when your name is googled.

Write a first draft of your comment offline and then step back and ask yourself the following questions about it:

- Am I providing useful insight and input or just saying something obvious or mundane?

- Does the comment showcase my subject matter knowledge?

- Is the comment respectful and on-topic?

- Have I used language that is understandable to the readers of this blog?

- Is the comment thought-provoking and an expression of my opinions but not so controversial that it could offend others or mar my reputation?

- Is my comment consistent with the way I would like to be perceived by people in my field or other fields?

- Does my comment support my brand—who I am, my style?

- Is my comment free of grammar or spelling errors and written in a clear, concise way?

After questioning yourself about your comment to see whether it passes muster, edit the comment as necessary and then review it one last time. You're now ready to submit it.

Step 3: Submit Your Comment

To submit your comment, go to the blog that you want to comment on and look for a navigation button labeled Comment or Post a Comment or something to that effect. (The exact wording and location of the command will vary from blog to blog.)

Click there, and you'll see a place to paste your comment. (You can also type a comment directly into the space provided, but you can easily review and edit it thoroughly offline in your word processing program and then paste it in the blog.) Make sure you leave the URL of your blog as part of the comment to drive traffic back to your blog. Or link to your LinkedIn profile, Twitter, Facebook, or other online profile as a way for others to learn more about you.

After you've pasted your comment, you'll see a button to click to submit it. Reread your comment one more time to make sure nothing was messed up in the pasting; then go ahead and pull the trigger to submit!

TYPICAL COMMENT RESTRICTIONS THAT MIGHT TRIP YOU UP

Some blogs limit the length of comments. This limit is typically expressed in number of characters, such as "maximum 3,000 characters." So be prepared to cut out some text if you have to, although typically the space provided is ample for getting your point across in a thorough but concise manner.

You also might find that you have to register with a site or be approved by the blog owner or administrator before you can submit a comment or before your comment will go live. Some blogs are moderated, meaning that the blog owner will review your comment before deciding to post it. Just be sure to follow the rules of the blog, and you should have no trouble getting your comments published and your voice heard.

Some blogs will ask you to type in letters or numbers (CAPTCHA) before they will post your comment. This is called *word verification*, and many bloggers use this tool to keep "spambots" from posting ads as comments.

In addition to, or instead of, submitting a public comment on a blog, you can also email the blog author directly. This will not add to your online visibility, but it can be a way of building a relationship with the blog author as you express your views. Email addresses are not always provided on the blog site, but if they are, sending an email message can be a great way to let the author know that you particularly enjoyed a post and want to communicate directly about it. Or you might send an email message if you worry that your comment

 © JIST Publishing

might be controversial, misunderstood, or taken the wrong way by the readership of the blog and want to communicate one-on-one with the author instead of posting it, to be on the safe side. You might also email the author if your comment is of a personal, private nature that you don't mind sharing with one person but would rather the whole cyberworld not see.

TIP

Check whether the blog author has another online presence as this could give you an alternate or additional way to connect and engage with this person. For example, a Twitter account or LinkedIn profile could provide you with a different aspect of this blogger's brand and information stream.

You can take the same approach with people who comment on the blog, in cases in which they choose to let their email addresses be published below their comments. Emailing them encourages more of a relationship-building approach to networking than the slightly more detached process of commenting publicly.

Dos and Don'ts for Commenting on OPBs

Keep these tips in mind while posting comments:

- **Do** keep your facts straight and strive for accuracy if you are writing an informational type of comment.

- **Do** make your comments relevant to the particular posting you're responding to and to the nature of the blog in general.

- **Do** make your comments a clear expression of your professional identity.

- **Don't** just comment on a blog as a vehicle for linking to your own blog or selling something. Make your comments genuine and useful to others.

- **Don't** make inflammatory comments unless you are prepared for a backlash. Be respectful, even if you are disagreeing.

- **Don't** post anything you don't want quoted, printed, or reproduced forever. Your comment will go on your permanent record!

Starting Your Own Blog

Do you prefer to be the one who starts the conversation? Do you want to showcase yourself as a leader in your field or expert on a particular topic? Having your own blog might be the answer for you. Starting one is surprisingly quick and easy. However, as we've warned you before, maintaining a blog to keep it fresh and interesting does take a serious time commitment.

Follow these steps for creating a blog:

1. Get the "lay of the land" with other bloggers in your field of expertise.

2. Choose a name for the blog.

3. Select your blog platform or host.

4. Register a domain name (sometimes this step is part of step 2).

5. Generate content to populate your site.

6. Decide and learn how to manage comments.

7. Go live!

We walk you through the basics of each of these steps in the following sections. Keep in mind, however, that exact steps will vary depending on the blog host that you choose to use and the design and layout of your blog. Entire books are written only on blogging, so these are just the basics to help you start. The steps outlined in this chapter are designed to get you up and running with a blog quickly.

Step 1: Get to Know Your Blog "Neighbors"

Do a search for other bloggers in your field of expertise and start to engage them, comment on their blogs, and build a sense of community. This will fuel your future referrals from this network and also give you a more educated sense of topics to cover. You can set up a Google search for these relevant blogs and also crawl Twitter for like-minded experts and opinion leaders.

Step 2: Choose a Name

Like a book, movie, football team, or newborn, a blog needs a name. The name you choose should convey your blog's topic focus and use terminology that will sound relevant to your target audience. It should also reflect who you are.

If creativity and innovative thinking are your hallmarks, for example, feel free to get clever with your blog's name. Dan Greenfield named his blog "Bernaise Source" (www.bernaisesource.com/blog) after Edward Bernays, considered to be the "father" of modern public relations. And, of course, there's the fun play on words with bearnaise sauce, the classic French steak sauce. Egg yolks, butter, tarragon, and shallots have nothing to do with Dan's expertise in media and PR, but the association of Bernays and bearnaise makes for a memorable blog name!

Other blog names clearly reflect the values and mission of the authors. Guy Kawasaki's "How to Change the World: A practical blog for impractical people" (http://blog.guykawasaki.com/) and Lance Weatherby's "Force of Good" (http://forceofgood.typepad.com/) are good examples of this.

Before deciding on your own blog's name, test its uniqueness and searchability by typing it into a search engine (Google, Bing, and so on) as a keyword or keyword phrase, both with and without quotation marks around it. If nothing relevant comes up, or not many matches come up, you may have hit on a fairly unique name. You might also use your own first and last name for the blog name if they are unique.

TIP

Make sure to choose names that are in the public domain and that do not include copyrighted or trademarked materials. Ask a lawyer to help if you're in doubt.

Whatever name you choose, be sure to decide on it after careful consideration. Don't rush into a name you might end up not being happy with.

Step 3: Choose a Blog Platform

Your blogging software or platform is the technology that runs your blog. It's where your blog resides online. You can choose from hosted and nonhosted options. Some of these are free; others come with a modest fee. We point out specific hosted and nonhosted options later in this step, but we can tell you now that most beginning bloggers choose the hosted option.

When you use a hosted service, you don't have to buy and install software or have the blog reside on your own server. Hosted services are simple vehicles for blogging, ideal for people who aren't computer gurus. Nonhosted options, on the other hand, offer more complete control over your site, more flexibility, and more design options. For example, a company would probably want to host its own site on its own server for confidentiality's sake. Or a technology expert might want to design the layout and develop his or her own site from scratch.

If you're not looking to become a professional blogger or to make a living off your blog (although you never know where your blog might lead you), a hosted service is your best bet. Nevertheless, we offer more detailed explanations of both hosted and nonhosted options next, as well as examples of both types of service providers, so that you can make your own decision about which is right for you.

Hosted Services

Hosted blog platforms are the easiest on both your wallet and your technical abilities. With a hosting service, you don't have to install any software. You simply access everything you need on the host's website. The host provides easy-to-use text editors to help you create your posts without any special technical knowledge. It also provides templates for the layout and design of your blogging site so you don't have to be a graphic artist. The process is so simple, in fact, that you can have a blog up and running in just minutes with a hosted service.

The main disadvantage of a hosted service is that you have limited control over the look and functionality of your site. Although most

hosted services offer plenty of nice design templates to choose from, you are limited to the colors, graphics, and page layouts they offer. This is typically an insignificant tradeoff, however, considering the ease and cost-effectiveness of this option.

In appendix A, you'll find a complete listing of blog hosting resources, but here we've provided a quick overview of a few of the most popular ones:

- **Blogger:** Blogger (www.blogger.com) is a free service that requires little to no technical expertise. You do have to use some HTML to modify some of the templates or use some of the sidebar features, but generally the service is easy to use and great for a first-time blogger.

HTML

HTML stands for *HyperText Markup Language*. It's the language used to make Web content appear a certain way. When using HTML, you write in English (or any other language of your choice) as usual, but you use special coding (called tags or labels) to indicate the graphic aspects of your text, such as italic or bold. Most sites requiring you to use HTML will offer a simple tutorial on it. Or you can find lots of free HTML tutorials by doing a Google search with the keywords "HTML tutorial."

- **TypePad:** TypePad (www.typepad.com) requires very little to no technical expertise but does offer some fairly sophisticated options, such as a good menu of sidebar add-ons. It also has a built-in mechanism for tracking your blog's visitors, or "traffic." TypePad does have a cost, ranging from just a few dollars to double digits per month. Yearly discounts are available. With the higher-priced service levels, you get more flexibility with your design template and other upgraded features. TypePad is a good choice if you are at the beginner stage now but expect to be blogging long term and want your blog service to grow with you (see figure 8.2).

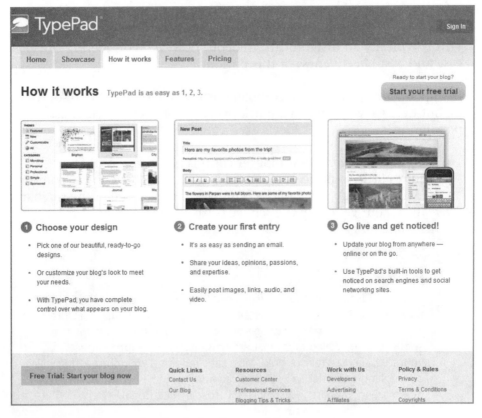

Figure 8.2: TypePad is a good option for hosting your blog.

- **WordPress:** WordPress (http://wordpress.com/) is free, or
  you can pay a modest fee for some premium design options.
  WordPress is quite user-friendly (see figure 8.3), but it's not as
  simple as Blogger. Having some technical knowledge is helpful
  if you want to use the more advanced features to move beyond
  beginner stage. The growing community of WordPress users provides opportunities to develop WordPress skills including local
  WordCamp events (http://central.wordcamp.org). One neat feature of WordPress is that it also offers a nonhosted option, which
  could come in handy if you decide to switch to a standalone blog
  in the future.

TIP

At the time of this publication, WordPress and Blog Link (which supports TypePad, Blogger, and other blog platforms) are part of the roster of applications available for LinkedIn users, providing a mechanism to synchronize your blog posts with your LinkedIn profile.

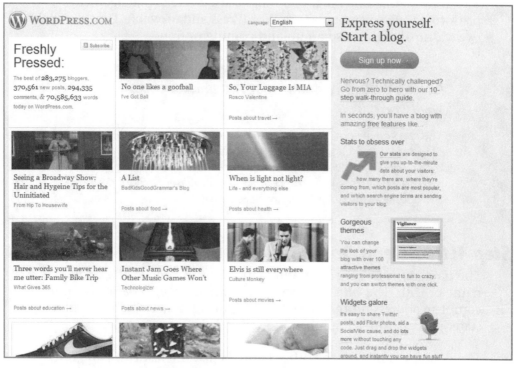

Figure 8.3: WordPress is another good option for hosting your blog.

Nonhosted Services

Nonhosted services, also called *standalone* or *server-side* platforms, give you much more design and functionality flexibility.

To go this route, you must secure a domain name as described later in step 4. Then you'll subscribe to a hosting service and download a content management system. Note that sometimes these two steps are one and the same. The blog hosting service can often register your

domain name, or if you already registered a domain name, you can go back to that same registrar and see whether it offers blog hosting services. Buyer beware, though, as the registrar will try to sell you all sorts of services and packages, but that doesn't necessarily make it the best source for blogging hosting!

To have a standalone blog, you must use a content management platform. The most popular are WordPress and Movable Type. Drupal (www.drupal.org) is also an up-and-coming option.

Can I Switch My Blog Host After Launching My Blog?

You can switch your blog platform, but not without the potential loss of some of your readership and some of your archived posts and comments. When you switch blog software, readers who have bookmarked any of your posts will lose them. So it's best to research your options thoroughly at the outset and not have to switch.

Step 4: Register a Domain Name (Optional)

The name of your blog may or may not be the same as the domain name or URL. The *URL,* or *Uniform Resource Locator,* is basically your complete address on the Web. It's like putting a street address, city, state, plus apartment number and zip code on an envelope.

The domain name, on the other hand, is just the last two parts of the URL, such as "dicrompton@yoursocialmediastrategist.com." The domain name is kind of like the name of an apartment building without the actual street address, city, state, and zip code.

If you select a hosted option, using such software as TypePad, WordPress, and Blogger, you do not have to register a domain name because you'll get domain name and URL as part of the blog hosting service. You may, however, secure a domain name anyway, if you prefer, and have it pointed to and serve as the URL for your blog (see the Ask Dave Taylor! article "How Do I Map My Own Domain to a TypePad Blog?" at http://bit.ly/dmG8tB for instructions).

If you decide to go the nonhosted route, you will need to register a domain name. Some popular domain registrars are www.Namecheap.com, www.GoDaddy.com, and www.Dynadot.com. On any of these sites, you can type in the name you have in mind for your blog and see if the name is available or already taken.

Pricing and options vary on these sites, so browse their fees and package offerings to select the one that works best for you. On many of these sites, if you pay for a year or more at a time, the service can cost less than $15 for a year with no fee charged for setup of your blog. If you pay monthly, you may end up with a setup fee in the low double digits plus several dollars a month for the service. Of course, add-on options are available for premium upgrades that cost more.

TIP

If you already have a website, you don't necessarily need to register a new domain name for your blog. Your blog can be part of your existing site. Or if you don't have a site but have a domain name already registered, such as your own name (for example, johndoe.com), you can use that domain name to create your blog.

Step 5: Generate Content

The needs of your audience, your goals and objectives, and your personal brand will drive your blog's content. Never lose sight of what you are trying to accomplish, whether that's a new and better job, advancement in your career at your current employer, business development and referrals, or just a sense of collegiality with your professional or business community at large.

Although you should always keep your goals in mind, you shouldn't shove them down your readers' throats. Of course, you should make sure that the time, effort, and possibly money that you put into your blog serves to move you closer to reaching your goals. Yet your personal agenda should not usurp your blog's ability to do some good for other people. There's no point in having a blog if it's just going to be an ego trip for you or be all about getting with no giving.

> ## Legal Implications for Bloggers
>
> Blog content is a potential minefield for employees. In some cases, employees are not allowed to have a blog, even if the blog's content is unrelated to the business of the employer. Better to be safe than sorry, so check your organization's guidelines before jumping into the blogging fray. And don't say anything on your blog that you wouldn't want your boss, colleagues, or customers to see! Also consider including a disclaimer on your blog that lets readers know that this is your personal blog and that it represents your own opinions, not necessarily those of your employer. Another resource to check out with additional information on this topic is the Social Networking Law Blog at www.socialnetworkinglawblog.com/.

How to Come Up with Content

The saying "content is king" is true when it comes to how important your content is for your blog to be effective. Make sure you understand the needs of your audience and have a way of speaking to these needs in an educational and informative way via your blog posts. If you have a website, think of your blog as the conversational aspect of your website.

Your first few posts may be easy. You have some things on your mind, so you know what to say and can easily write some posts. Maybe you even have lots of material in your files—essays, editorials, articles, or just thoughts and ideas you've written either for fun or for actual publication. In this case (assuming you have the legal right to reprint the content), you have plenty of content to post for days, weeks, or months to come.

But what happens when the well starts to run dry? Or what if the old stuff just isn't current enough to use? That's when you need to use some of the techniques for coming up with new material. Seasoned bloggers are always on the watch for new content. Some keep a notebook to scribble ideas as they come to mind. Others seek inspiration in things they read or observe offline and online.

Another tool to use as a supplement for content ideas is Google Trends to explore past and current Web search trends. Whatever you do to get your ideas, it's helpful to organize content for posts and comments at least several weeks in advance to save time. On many platforms or hosted services, you can create posts for automatic publication at later dates. Of course, you can't always use stockpiled content because sometimes you'll want a post to be a reaction to current events or recent news.

TIP

If you enjoy reading books related to your field and find yourself posting book reviews on your blog site, consider signing up with Amazon.com as an Amazon Affiliate. You can then put an image of the book's cover and its title on your blog site and link it to Amazon. If your blog traffic is high and your readers buy the books you link to, you can earn a small amount of money every time someone buys the book on Amazon as a result of linking to it from your site.

How Long Is Too Long?

Good content isn't necessarily long, so don't get bogged down writing lengthy entries to post. Good content can come in the form of a very short post, maybe even just a question to draw comments. Shorter posts consist of typically about 200 words or are even just a quick comment of a sentence or two plus perhaps a link to another site.

Dos and Don'ts for Blog Content

Follow these guidelines to create a blog worth reading:

- Do make your content relevant, interesting, and enlightening for your audience. Make sure your content provides value in terms of your readers' needs and "hot buttons" of interest.

- Do get your facts straight if you're providing information that needs to be objective and accurate.

- Do let your unique personality and style come through.

- Do stick to a schedule and post regularly (at least once a week initially) to keep your readership engaged and build a following.

- Do be courteous and civil toward your readers and be accessible to them.

(continued)

(continued)

- Do learn from your audience. You don't need all the answers, all the time.

- Do make your blog easy to navigate and view with streamlined functions and integrated design elements. The amount of patience new blog visitors have is small—especially if they can't see what is of interest or navigate your blog efficiently.

- Do include a bio and maybe a photo (optional) so that readers can get a better sense of who you are.

- Do double-check your grammar and spelling.

- Don't sell or pitch to readers in a heavy-handed way. And don't try to do it subtly because they'll typically see through your efforts. If you do want to promote something, be open, honest, and not pushy about it, but don't do it often.

- Don't try to be someone you're not. Be down-to-earth and genuine in your posts.

- Don't quote from or mirror the content of other blogs excessively. Be original.

- Don't reprint articles without asking for permission from the original source, and always give appropriate attribution to the source.

Step 6: Decide How You Will Manage Comments

If blogging is all about the conversation, why is there any decision to make about the comments people want to submit to your site? Believe it or not, some people actually create blogs that don't allow comments to be posted. We don't recommend that approach because it makes blogging one-sided and not a vehicle for generating the conversations that build relationships with your readers.

Even if you have no qualms about allowing—even encouraging—comments, you still have the decision to make about how you will manage them. Will you allow people to publish their comments directly and immediately to the site when they click Submit, or will you serve as a moderator, reviewing the comments privately before allowing them to go live on your site?

Moderating Comments

You can act as editor for your blog by moderating and approving comments. In this way, you can keep offensive or irrelevant content or spam off your blog and publish only positive, useful, or on-topic comments. Always review and approve comments promptly, as a courtesy to your readers and to invite additional comments in the future.

If you do choose not to publish a comment, it's good form to notify the writer as to why you made that decision. It's an opportunity to educate the writer (gently and politely) about the focus and mission of your blog. Show appreciation for his or her willingness to participate in the discussion and encourage the person to write again. Of course, if a comment is highly offensive, inflammatory, insulting, or simply wacko, it doesn't deserve any response.

Responding to Comments

Just because you've approved and published a comment (or let your readers submit their own comments directly) doesn't mean your job is done until you post your next entry. Keep the dialogue going by commenting on the comment or by creating a new post that builds on the comment. This is what makes blogs truly interactive and interesting. To keep your readership engaged, make it a practice to respond to comments within 24 hours. Make sure you respond with more than a tacit "thanks for sharing," as responding to comments is an opportunity to build conversation and engagement and even link back to an earlier, relevant post.

Streamlining This Process

Consider a feature to your blog to allow readers to subscribe to comments and receive updates via email. This is a great way to keep the conversation going. The most common way to do this is to add an RSS feed, which allows readers to subscribe to your blog via this feed to easily get the flow of new information. Your blog host or blogging software should have instructions on how to do this.

Step 7: Go Live!

So you've put some content on your site in the form of a first post, plus your bio, and perhaps some sidebars such as a list of services you offer if you have a business, list of favorite blogs, or maybe a book review or list of recommended books or websites. And you've decided how you'll manage comments. You've done all this in "practice" mode, setting up and playing around with your blog privately through your blog hosting platform before publishing it on the Web.

When you're happy with what you've done, go ahead and click the button (the exact name and location vary with the different hosts) to go live. This will make your blog visible to anyone on the Internet. Now you just have to watch for the comments to come in and keep posting new content!

Getting People to Your Blog

Just as you learned in chapter 3 about making yourself more visible online, you need to use similar techniques to make your blog prominent and drive traffic to your site. This is one kind of traffic jam you look forward to—lots of people reading and commenting on your blog regularly.

Having an active and diverse Web presence that includes active engagement on Twitter is one of the best ways to build a following for your blog. In our research for this book, we surveyed a variety of bloggers, and the consistent feedback was that Twitter can serve a pivotal role in building traffic and visibility for a blog. The ability to have your posts spread virally through retweets makes Twitter a perfect business partner to direct people to your blog. Likewise, you can have your tweets appear in the sidebar of your blog to direct people to your Twitter account and the information you are sharing via Twitter. (If you are new to Twitter, read chapter 7 to get some guidance on how to get started and how to leverage it.)

You can use other social media to create buzz and build traffic as well. Other social networks like LinkedIn, Facebook, and MySpace also provide additional "touch points" to engage your audience and can serve as pointers back to your blog.

Let all the people in your network know about your blog by emailing them the URL to announce the "grand opening." Also include the URL in your email signature block, in your bio, and in all profiles you post on social networks. If you have a separate website, you would, of course, also link that site to your blog. Also, be sure that your email address is displayed on your blog to encourage readers to contact you directly in case they're reluctant to submit a public comment. To avoid spam, spell out your email address in a way that humans will understand but "bots" (the nasty little Web "creatures" that generate spam) cannot. Example: janedoe@email.com can be written as jane-doe AT email DOT com.

SEARCH ENGINE OPTIMIZATION AND TECHNORATI

Search engine optimization (SEO) is the process of making sure that your blog will be easily found during keyword searches on Google, Bing, MSN, Yahoo!, or other search engines. (Blogs are indexed by the major search engines.)

There are also search engines specifically for blogs. Technorati, for example, is the authority on what's happening on the Web, particularly when it comes to blogs. Technorati searches for and organizes blogs. It tracks the links created when bloggers link to other blogs or comment on a blog, thus identifying the most active and relevant blogs. It indexes tens of thousands of content updates every hour, so the more active your blog is and the more you have paid attention to SEO, the more "relevant" your blog will be considered.

There are also mechanisms to analyze your blog traffic, including Google Analytics, Quantcast, and a host of others. These mechanisms help you know your peak and valley traffic patterns so you can adjust the timing and content of your posts accordingly.

You can use some additional techniques to increase your blog traffic or search engine optimization, including links, keywords, blogrolls, categories, meta keywords, and trackbacks. These techniques are described in the following sections.

To have your blog reach mainstream media, you could also register your blog on major media outlets. The process to get your blog registered with blog directories and blog search engines can be time consuming. Because of this, you may consider using a a blog syndication

network service such as Blogburst to help get you market share on a variety of news sites. Before registering your blog, you'll need to make sure it's optimized and ready for registering. A good resource to consult for tips on this process is www.wordsinarow.com/blogs.html.

Links

One way to get more play with the search engines is linking your blog to other places on the Web, such as other blogs, articles, press releases, book reviews, and more. This can also inspire other bloggers and sites to reciprocate by linking to your blog.

Also link to your own Web entries, both within your blog site and elsewhere (LinkedIn, newsletter, signature tag). You can link from your main blog page to your bio page, to your profile on social networks, and to sites of organizations you work with or for. This creates the interconnectivity that's critical to getting more visibility and meeting more people.

QUOTE

Social media has changed my life. I have hired people from meeting and getting to know them through Twitter and their blogs. You can build real relationships through social media that result in growth of your own business, finding services or products you need, and relationships that blossom into more opportunities. I have clients who have found me through LinkedIn and my comments on other people's blogs. I have been featured by bloggers in Jordan, North Carolina, and Wisconsin and had mentions in blogs in the UK and elsewhere. I now have friends literally all over the world.

—Julie Walraven, Wisconsin-based career marketing strategist, LinkedIn profile writer, and resume writer at Design Resumes

Keywords or Tags

Within your blog content, keywords—also referred to as *tags* in blogging language—play a critical role in search engine optimization. Keywords are how search engines find your blog when people do searches.

These words should occur early in your post and also in your subheads to optimize your post. In addition to keywords or key phrases in your posts, having them in your post titles and category headings can increase search engine hits.

Your choice of keywords is driven by the content of your blog and should include language that would be a standard in terms of the vocabulary of your audience. To determine keywords, keep in mind that the title of your post will become the URL in a Google search. There is not one magic list of keywords, nor is there any set of keywords that would be right for everyone's goals and focus. Keywords are simply commonsense terms that are closely connected to your field and the topics you are writing about. They might be hot buzzwords of the moment, long-standing technical terms, or just the everyday language of your business or profession.

There are arguments on both sides of the fence regarding keywords. Some bloggers write with SEO clearly in mind to maximize their search engine "hits," whereas others write as they normally would, assuming that they are generating keywords without really trying, sort of by default. Either way, it's important to note that keywords play a primary role in increasing traffic to your blog.

THE POPULARITY INDEX

Interested readers of your blog can vote for the popularity of a particular post with a keystroke by using "voting system" sites like Digg, Del.icio.us, StumbleUpon, and others. This can create a temporary spike in traffic to your blog which could cause it to be more noticed and more read. To add these interactive "buttons" to your blog, check out www.addthis.com/, a user-friendly site that allows you to make sharing your blog content easy.

Blogroll

A *blogroll* is a listing of blogs that you include as a sidebar on your own blog site. These blogs might be your top 10 favorite sites across many topics and categories. You might like them for their content, writing style, opinions expressed, or layout and design. Or they might be ones that are particularly useful as resources to supplement information you provide and topics you discuss in your posts. They can

also be blogs of colleagues, vendors, suppliers, or other people you want to support and promote. Just make sure they are likely to be useful and relevant to your readers and in sync with your personal brand.

If you say something complimentary about or link to another blog or blog post, the author of that blog might reciprocate by linking to you in his or her own blogroll, thus creating inbound and outbound links. These links help your SEO by increasing opportunities for hits when search engines crawl the Web for content. The more places your blog is mentioned on other people's blogs, the more likely it is to come up as a match.

Categories

Categories are the road map, or information architecture, to your blog and a navigation tool for your readers. By organizing your posts and other content into categories, you make it easy for readers to find information on your blog site, especially older entries. An optimum number of categories is four to six, but feel free to have fewer or more depending on the complexity of your blog and how long it's been around. Too many categories can give the appearance of trying to be a "Jack of all trades, master of none."

Categories help with search engine optimization because they act as keywords. Search engines love keywords, whether they are found in a blogroll, blog posts, or category names. So your category names are just one more way for your blog to be found.

Trackbacks

WordPress, Movable Type, and other platforms include the option to have trackbacks on your blog. These are a mechanism for multiple blog sites to communicate with each other. If a blogger writes an entry on a blog that refers to an entry found on your blog, the blogger making the post or comment can notify you with a trackback "ping." This allows you to see what's being said about your blog or specific content on your blog out in the blogosphere and can start a discussion across several blogs rather than just between authors and readers within one blog. Instructions for setting up trackbacks will be provided in the platform or host you choose to use.

> ### TAKE IT FROM AN EXPERT
>
> Check out the post written by Denise Wakeman (March 2010) on the Social Media Examiner (www.socialmediaexaminer.com/), "How to Keep Readers Coming Back to Your Blog," for additional tips on optimizing your blog.

Visual Elements

To make your blog "pop" with content, add and integrate other visual elements such as video and podcasts. Varying the way in which your readers can engage with your content through using a variety of media will make your blog more interesting and more interactive.

What Lies Ahead in the Blogosphere?

Blogging has rapidly grown in popularity and shows no signs of stopping. It's difficult to get a hard and fast number on blogs, with new blogs being created every day, although we know they number over 100 million. If microblogs and posts to other forms of social media are included, this number is closer to 400 million. Future trends for blogging include more podcasting (audio files broadcast via the Web) and vlogs (video blogs), both of which can keep readers more engaged in your blog. Audio Acrobat and YouTube are host media worth exploring as options for adding audio and video to your blog.

You might choose not to have your own blog. You might not regularly comment on other people's blogs or in any way join in on the blogging conversation for now. Nevertheless, you need to be aware of this powerful publishing medium and ready source of information. It's an immediate and interactive dialogue that can keep you informed about topics and trends. It's an exciting movement and application of technology that is shaping and will continue to shape the future of personal, professional, and organizational communications and interconnectivity. We hope you'll at least give blogging a try to see how it may enhance your social networking efforts.

Key Points: Chapter 8

- Blogging is an interactive way to connect with people online and build your visibility and credibility.

- Deciding whether to start your own blog or just comment on other people's blogs is often based on your writing ability, passion for your subject matter, available time, and comfort level with being in the spotlight.

- To start a blog, you first should research other blogs, choose a name and platform (hosted or nonhosted), and generate content on subject matter that you have knowledge and interest in.

- Maintaining your blog involves regular posting of content, responding to comments promptly, and growing your readership.

- Drive traffic to your blog through your use of other social media, particularly Twitter, and by utilizing search engine optimization (SEO) techniques such as having relevant keywords, a blogroll, and inbound and outbound links.

CHAPTER 9

Posting, Publishing, and Podcasting: More Ways to Connect Online

In the preceding chapters, we discussed the how-tos of using business-oriented social networks, microblogging, and blogging to enhance your visibility and meet more people. Because LinkedIn, Facebook, Twitter, and blogging are likely to be the primary ways you'll network online, those methods warranted their own chapters. The remaining social networking technologies are grouped together in this chapter.

Here you'll find descriptions that build on the brief introductions in chapter 1 for identity-management sites, discussion groups, online publishing, and Internet-based public speaking. You'll also learn more about how to get started today using these social networking avenues—or how to step up your efforts if you've already dabbled in them.

In This Chapter

- *Gain a deeper understanding of how the "other" social networking technologies work.*

- *Learn how to use identity-management sites, discussion groups, publishing, and public speaking to round out your social networking strategy.*

Identity-Management Sites

You already know from chapter 1 that identity-management sites such as Naymz and Ziggs are excellent ways to start developing, or improve the relevance of, your online presence. These sites help you take control of your digital footprint by allowing you to create and post a profile that gives accurate, up-to-date information about your experience, current professional activities, and goals or interests.

These services offer an interesting array of features, such as email alerts when your profile is viewed and the ability to connect with other people in the network via email, instant messaging, or live chats.

There is little to no downside to joining sites such as Naymz and Ziggs, so we recommend that everyone do so. If you're not already on them, how about joining right now? Both Naymz and Ziggs are excellent sites with similar features, so we recommend joining both. You can spend some time on each and then see whether you prefer to cancel one membership (which is easy to do) and focus on the other site. For demonstration purposes, we walk you through the steps of joining Naymz only, but the process for joining Ziggs is comparable.

You can join both Naymz and Ziggs in a matter of minutes. You might not be able to develop a fully fleshed-out profile or take advantage of all the features of the services, but you can at least put in your basic information and then come back later to further develop your presence on these sites.

Naymz

Go to www.naymz.com. If you click on the Learn More button, you'll see an option on the home page to take a tour of the site and learn the steps that are required or optional for membership. Be sure to take one or both of these steps before joining so that you get a feel for how profiles sound before you enter your own.

Step 1: Join

After becoming familiar with the site and what type of content people include in their spaces on it, you're ready to join. You'll see spaces on the home page where you enter your first and last names, email address, and a password that you create. Fill in this information and click Join.

Step 2 (Optional): Import Contacts

You then have a choice of importing your contacts from several places where you might happen to keep listings of people you know, including LinkedIn, Yahoo! Mail, MSN, AOL, Gmail, and .Mac. Importing contacts is safe because Naymz will not get in touch with these people unless you request that it send an invitation to them. It will not publish or share your list with others, either. If you prefer to skip this step, however, you may do so. You can always come back to it later.

RATING YOUR REPUTATION

To differentiate itself from the many other sites where you can post a profile, Naymz allows you to earn what it calls RepScores. When you have RepScores, visitors to your profile can be more confident that they are getting to know a reputable professional. The scores also open doors for you to connect with other reputable professionals on the site.

You earn RepScore points in the following three ways:

- **Community verification:** When you invite your contacts to join your network, you can ask some of them to act as references, giving you an endorsement to display in your profile. The more references, the more points you earn.

- **Profile completeness:** Earn RepScore points for completing all fields—or sections—of your Naymz profile and updating it periodically.

- **Identity verification:** Naymz has an alliance with Trufina (www.trufina.com), a personal information management service that verifies that you are who you say you are. You get the Trufina service free if you pay for the premium subscription to Naymz. You also earn RepScore points for doing so.

Step 3: Complete Your Profile

If you have joined LinkedIn or other social networks, and if you have scripted a self-marketing sound bite in chapter 2, you probably have plenty of biographical and profile-type data on hand to use here. In the About You section, paste your bio, including past work history and educational credentials.

Under Tags, list keywords you want associated with you—words that other people in the network or search engines could use to find you. These might be your areas of expertise, subject-matter knowledge, interests, functional roles, job titles, school names, employer names, hobbies, geographic location, and anything else that defines you.

You can also put links on your profile. These might be links to your blog, your company website, other sites that relate to your field, or anything relevant to the image you want to project.

Step 4: Select the Service Level

Your final step is to decide whether you want to have the basic, free membership or upgrade to premium level for a low monthly fee (or pay for a year at a time to receive a discount). Among the perks that come with the premium membership are a sponsored link at or near the top of the page on Google search results for your name; an advertisement-free experience when people visit your profile; and a report on each person who visits your profile, including that person's city, state, country, and how he or she found you.

When you're up and running with Naymz, don't forget to visit Ziggs to see whether you'd like to join its service as well.

Ziggs

Whereas the emphasis at Naymz is on identity management and reputation enhancement (with a hint of social networking thrown in for good measure), Ziggs (www.ziggs.com) touts itself as more of a total solution for managing not just your online brand, but also the groups of people in your world. A handy feature on Ziggs allows you to classify your contacts into categories such as work colleagues, family, charities, college friends, and more. This capability can make it easy for you to communicate or plan events with people who have various roles in your life.

MORE IDENTITY-MANAGEMENT SITES

Additional sites to consider beyond Naymz and Ziggs are Wink (www.wink.com) and QAlias (www.qalias.com). Calling itself a "people search engine," Wink lets you find people on the Web and also allows you to

manage your own online presence by having a profile on its site. Also offering an online profile, QAlias charges a modest monthly fee to host your online bio and other content about you that can help you be found more easily online.

Discussion Groups

Online discussion groups have been around for years. Internet pioneers used these groups to find and keep in touch with individuals with similar interests. In recent years, blogging has stolen much of the spotlight from discussion groups. Groups on LinkedIn serve a similar purpose—providing a forum for conversation on a topic of common interest. Yet discussion groups continue to play an important role in social networking. Let's look at the different types of discussion groups, how to join, and the advantages and disadvantages of joining.

What Exactly Is a Discussion Group?

A *discussion group* is an online application that allows groups of people to share ideas, post messages, and hold discussions. Also known as Internet forums, bulletin boards, and message boards, these Web applications can be effective networking and marketing tools. Discussion groups encourage individuals with common interests to form online communities for sharing ideas, opinions, advice, and best practices in their fields.

Discussion groups first came into being as common-interest groups, whether personal or professional. They have more recently become popular with job seekers and people trying to network with professionals in their fields. People from around the world use these online groups to share knowledge, find inspiration, and search for career opportunities. When we say professionals from "around the world," we truly mean it; you can easily find groups such as New Zealand Wellington Business Referral Club, Jobs-of-Egypt, Jobs in France, Seattle IT, Kansas Jobs, and All Bangalore Jobs. There is no limit to how far away or close to home these discussion groups can take you!

Why Use a Discussion Group and Not a Targeted Email List?

You could simply put together a list of email addresses of like-minded people and communicate with each other via email. So why communicate through a discussion group? Unlike email lists, discussion groups allow you to archive messages, view shared photos, upload a group event calendar, and even post member profiles. They give all members a place to go, kind of like communal websites.

Group members have the option of checking the group website to read posted messages or receiving an email alert whenever a new message or document is posted. Unlike online chat rooms and instant messaging—in which communication is live, or concurrent—members of discussion groups do not have to be online at the same time to communicate with each other. You can post a question or comment at any time, and other members can sign into the group and post a reply at any time. And unlike blogs where only a select person (the author or owner) can post content and approve others' comments, discussion groups allow anybody to post items to share (but some do have moderators who approve comments before posting them).

Members often post their profiles in discussion groups. These are useful tools if you are trying to network for professional purposes. As a job seeker, you might be able to find a networking contact in your target company. Recruiters also may spot potential candidates in discussion groups (assuming that they are searching in a professional/business-related discussion group).

You can also enhance your visibility in a discussion group. Being able to post and share documents is a great way to publicize an event that you are hosting or speaking at or an article that you have published. Discussion groups are a fast and free way to market yourself to thousands of people at any moment in time.

Where Can I Find Discussion Groups?

The most popular websites for discussion groups are Yahoo! and Google. These companies have made it easy (and free) to set up a discussion group within minutes. Don't have time to create your own unique group? Don't fret; thousands of existing groups are already out there on the Web. Locating them is just a matter of searching for the subject matter that interests you most.

Yahoo! boasts more than 26,000 discussion groups under its Business & Finance/Employment and Work category. It has groups dedicated to certain companies (for example, McDonald's Employees), industries, associations, and small businesses (see figure 9.1).

Figure 9.1: *Yahoo! is a top option for finding groups to join.*

Google has a total of more than 450,000 discussion groups, nearly 4,000 of which are related to employment (see figure 9.2). As with Yahoo!, these discussion groups are easy to use and free to create.

Figure 9.2: Google is another good bet for finding a group that matches your interests.

What Are the Benefits of Being a Group Member Versus Being a Moderator?

Being a moderator of a group brings much more responsibility and time commitment. A moderator is often the same person who created the group in the first place. As a moderator, you are ultimately responsible for the content and activity of the discussion group. If you decide to create your own discussion group, be prepared to spend time each day (or every couple of days, depending on your schedule and the level of activity in the group) posting thought-provoking articles and other content on the group website. Remember, messages will be in an email alert to each member, so make sure the content is relevant and interesting. Like having a blog, moderating a group means you need to draw in members by having an important discussion topic.

As a group member, on the other hand, you can be as passive or active as you choose, depending on your level of interest in the topics being discussed, your time availability, and how actively you need to be networking and getting exposure. If you are using discussion groups as part of your social networking strategy, we suggest that you stay active. Certain people choose to join discussion groups and simply sit back, relax, and read what other members post. However, to get your name recognized as an important person in your profession, you need to be out there posting articles, suggesting websites, and

publicizing relevant upcoming events. You want to be thought of as a mover and shaker in your field.

How Do You Start Your Own Discussion Group?

Starting your own group is easier than you think and takes only a few minutes. First, decide whether you are going to use a Yahoo! or Google discussion group. Next, choose the theme/topic of your group. The sky's the limit: SAP applications, ways to relocate to a city with better jobs and climate, human resource professionals in Palm Springs—whatever you're interested in. Choose which category and subcategory your group will fit into. Remember, you want to make your group easy to find (so that you will have a lot of members), so put it in the category that makes the most sense.

Choose a catchy group name and your group email address, write a brief description of the group, and voila! You have created your own unique discussion group. Following the simple directions provided by Google or Yahoo! to supplement what we've described here, you can begin posting messages and inviting new members immediately.

TIP

Don't be known as a *troll* or *gravedigger*. These are individuals who post unwanted or derogatory messages. Be sensitive to the audience and post only messages that are of value. Nobody wants to read spam, cheesy sales advertisements, or your political opinions.

Electronic Publishing

The Internet has made it possible for everyone to get published. Whether through an article, a newsletter, or an entire book, anyone with a computer and something to say can be an author. Is this networking? Sure, it is. If networking is about gaining visibility to attract people and opportunities to you, as well as connecting with people to develop mutually beneficial relationships, online publishing fits the bill. The power of the pen—or, in this case, the keyboard—to connect with other human beings is often just as strong as connecting by voice or through a handshake. The following sections present some electronic publishing options and tips for using them.

QUOTE

I played music semiprofessionally for five years with a reggae/ska/soul band, The Pinstripes (www.thepinstripes.net). As a band, the music is important, obviously, but promotional material (print, video, Web, etc.), Web presence, and visual design are crucial to attracting new listeners. Where things have greatly changed is use of social media sites like MySpace, Facebook, and countless other social media.

Most shows in the past have been promoted with a web banner/flyer, a static image listing all the bands, the venue, and other crucial information. A video format, instead, allows us to play music of the bands on the show, which is much more compelling than a static flyer.

But videos, like web banners and online flyers, are a dime a dozen. So by combining my design skills (I graduated from Ohio State University with a BS in Visual Communication Design) with skilled video production, we created promotional videos that are entertaining to watch, get the band's message out there, and stand out from the rest of the videos and promo material floating around Facebook and MySpace.

And because they [the promotional videos] are easily spreadable via Facebook and MySpace, many people unfamiliar with the band are able to see them. This is an easy and free way of reaching new listeners. Online videos of musicians have been around for years now, but I think we have done something relatively new with the format and have benefitted greatly because of it.

—Matthew Kursmark, graphic designer

E-newsletters

One popular online publishing option is to publish some type of periodical. This can be in the form of a document you email to a list of subscribers or content posted on a website. Your best option for publishing a periodical is to produce an electronic newsletter, which might come out weekly, bimonthly, monthly, or quarterly.

Just like a traditional print newsletter someone would receive in the mail, an e-newsletter usually includes a few or several short articles that are informational and/or editorial in nature, as well as perhaps

some news and announcements of events that would interest your readers.

You can go the do-it-yourself publishing route and incur no cost. This simply means that you type a message in an email and send it out to people or create a document in PDF format and email it as an attachment. The downside of this approach is that many people aren't going to want to open an attachment, either out of concern over computer viruses or because doing so is inconvenient. Sending your letter within the body of an email (rather than as an attachment) is not necessarily a better option, though, because you don't know how the layout and format might become messed up in transmission. The publication that people receive may not have the professional, polished look you intended it to have.

If you're serious about wanting to communicate with your network through an electronic newsletter, a better alternative might be to use a professional service. Numerous companies offer templates and distribution services for online newsletters. They charge a modest (often less than $20) monthly fee for the service. Constant Contact (www. constantcontact.com) is one of the best to use.

Ezines

The earliest online periodic publication was the *ezine,* a sort of online magazine. The first ezines appeared in the 1980s as articles posted on the Bulletin Board System, or BBS—a precursor to the World Wide Web. In the 1990s, ezines grew in popularity and were more likely to be distributed through email via the Web. Today ezines have some stiff competition from blogging because blogs offer interaction with readers. Nevertheless, you might come across ezines from time to time or hear the term, so just be aware of what they are.

Articles, Wikis, and Lists

If you have your own website or blog, you certainly have plenty of opportunities to write and publish content, whether it's an article, editorial, or essay. You can educate, inform, provoke thought, amuse, and show off your knowledge and writing skill with online publishing.

Articles

You don't have to have your own site or blog to write articles. Many professional associations need content to keep their sites fresh and either actively solicit articles or accept unsolicited articles from both members and nonmembers. Just be sure your topic is relevant to the readership, contributes meaningful ideas and information, reflects your brand, and is well written.

Wikis

Wikis are website pages that anyone can edit. If you've ever gone onto a website and been frustrated by content that contains factual errors or could have been written more clearly, you'll like wikis. On a wiki, you can add to, delete, or modify what's been written or introduce content on a topic that hasn't yet been written about on that site. Wikis are particularly useful for knowledge-sharing and are often collaborative, group efforts of academic, scientific, and technical professionals.

SharePoint is an example of a wiki-like document management platform that lets groups of people, usually within a large organization, manage work that they do together. SharePoint solves the problem of emailing various versions of documents back and forth and running the risk of losing track of what's what. All the versions can be maintained on SharePoint, and anyone with permission to access the folders the documents are stored in can do so at any time. It also encourages more collaboration because individuals can go into the SharePoint folders and edit each other's work, make comments, and share notes and ideas.

Lists

When we talk about lists in terms of the Internet, we can mean two different things. There is e-list technology, often called a *listserv*, which is the software used to develop or manage electronic mailing lists. Then, there is a list in the conventional sense of the word—a list of people, places, or things. In this case, though, it happens to be an electronic list.

The plain old list concept is what we're talking about here. People love lists. Been on Amazon.com lately? You can hardly pick out a book on a particular topic without bumping into a list of favorite books in that category that an ordinary reader has submitted to the site. In chapter 8, you learned that a list of favorite or recommended blogs, sometimes called a blogroll, is typical sidebar content on a blog.

Lists created by regular people help us make choices about services or products to buy and events to attend. The person responsible for the list often becomes known as a thought leader in a particular field and often as someone who helps his or her professional community.

In our metro area of Atlanta, Georgia, for example, The Ruthie List (www.ruthieslist.org) is a Yahoo! group with more than 9,000 members who are recruiters and human resources professionals. The list is free and provides members with postings of open positions and available candidates and with updates on professional meetings and other happenings in the local HR and recruiting community. By offering this list for more than 13 years, senior HR professional Ruthie Powell has established herself not only as a leader in her professional community, but also as someone who genuinely cares about helping that community.

A Word About Webfolios

Blogs have just about burst the bubble of static websites. Websites that feature one's resume or career credentials are often used as online portfolios, sometimes called *webfolios*. Many experts such as career coaches and personal branding specialists now recommend blogs as a better way to showcase your expertise and connect with people in a more interactive manner. Blogs are more in keeping with Web 2.0 trends, which made the Internet a more interactive place. Blogs provide a place to connect with others, start dialogues and conversations, and generally have a more dynamic experience.

Blogs do take a great deal of time to maintain, though, and typically aren't designed to include a lot of static content. Blogs usually do include the owner's bio, but the focus is more on the log of posts, comments, and archives of posts rather than on portfolio documents.

If blogging is not for you for any number of reasons, having a webfolio can be a relatively easy, low-maintenance way to have an online presence. Just be aware that you might risk being seen as not quite "with it" and may want to have both a blog and webfolio that link to each other.

Internet-Based Public Speaking

In chapter 1, we introduced you to the idea of public speaking as an element in your social networking repertoire. For some of you, that might have been the first time you thought of public speaking as networking. Others of you may have already experienced the value of speaking as a way to enhance your professional stature and expand your range of contacts but might not have taken your talents online. With the broad reach that technologies such as podcasting and webinars offer, public speaking online can do wonders for your networking efforts.

TIP

You don't have to be a top-of-your-field, famous personality in your area of expertise to get a speaking gig. As long as you have a high degree of knowledge in a particular area, you'll do fine. Success in public speaking comes as much from having an engaging, energetic, and friendly but authoritative speaking style, as well as solid experience, as it does from your actual knowledge level. In other words, it's what you've done and how you talk about it that counts just about as much as what you know.

Where to Find Speaking Opportunities

You can find public speaking opportunities online in much the same way you would offline opportunities. Professional and trade associations are among the most common sources.

BE HEARD ONLINE

LinkedIn has many groups that are focused on providing information on speaking opportunities that you might want to check out. Here are just a few:

- Need a Speaker, Be a Speaker
- Public Speaking Network
- Professional Speakers and Seminar Leaders

In the past, most associations have offered special talks to members primarily at national conferences and conventions or at the occasional local or regional meeting. But now many associations host ongoing series of Web-based lectures, training seminars, or other informational sessions because they are easier and cheaper. If you're a member of an association, check to see whether there are any options for you to share your expertise and experiences with the membership. Or if you're not an expert on a particular topic, you could possibly moderate a panel discussion or interview a guest speaker.

Additional sources of online speaking opportunities are educational institutions (particularly distance-learning degree programs and training institutes that offer a lot of online programming), nonprofit organizations, corporations, speakers' bureaus, and individuals who work as meeting or event planning professionals.

TIP

To find names and URLs of professional associations in various fields, use Yahoo's listings at http://dir.yahoo.com/business_and_economy/ organizations/professional/ or Weddle's Association Directory at www. weddles.com/associations/index.cfm. You can also find copies of the reference book *Gale's Encyclopedia of Associations* in many libraries. It's an excellent resource.

How Podcasts Work

A podcast is a digital audio file that allows you to record a radio-style broadcast for distribution over the Internet for playback on MP3 players and personal computers. The term *podcast* can be both a noun referring to the content being broadcast or the actual event as well as a verb, referring to the act of making the recording. Podcasts are often archived on the sites where they originated, so over time people can listen to them repeatedly.

Podcasting has made it possible for anyone to become a radio talk show host of sorts. By having your own podcast, you can broadcast commentary about topics relevant to your profession or business arena, interview other experts in your field, or create any type of audio content that will help you present yourself as a thought leader in your field. Similarly, by being a guest on someone else's podcast, you gain visibility and enhance your digital footprint.

 QUOTE

I began a series of "Innovator Interviews" with successful leaders in business on innovation, creativity, strategic thinking, and related topics and broadcast them using social media networks, including LinkedIn, Twitter, StumbleUpon, Facebook, and our blog readers and newsletter subscribers. I also empowered the innovators by giving them a copy of the MP3 file and embedded code for the Audio Acrobat player so they could put the broadcast on their blogs, too.

The result? New visit traffic to our site increased by more than 85 percent in 30 days.

—Reuben Rail, chief igniting officer, Firestarter

If you like the idea of having a blog to brand yourself as a spokesperson on particular topics and to start people talking, you'll probably love the idea of having your own podcast (unless you hate the sound of your speaking voice). Starting a podcast is quite easy. It's not as easy as being the guest who just calls in (or is called) and answers some questions, however, because it does take time and planning. But the technology piece is fairly simple. With only a computer, a high-speed Internet connection, and an inexpensive microphone (probably the one that came with your computer will do fine), you can be on the air in a matter of hours.

IF WE CAN DO IT, YOU CAN DO IT

We have been guests on two podcasts. Florida residents Andy Robinson, executive career coach, and his wife, Carrie Robinson, executive recruiter, host a weekly radio show called *The Career Success Show*. You can hear our discussion with the Robinsons at http://bit.ly/bEq9A9.

Similarly, we recorded a podcast with Krishna De, a speaker, author, and consultant in Ireland with expertise in digital marketing, brand engagement, and social media. You can hear that discussion at http://bit.ly/aUq1r8.

Both of these recorded podcasts are great examples of the global nature of social networking. We can record podcasts with hosts in the next state or another country without leaving our offices.

You simply plan what you want to say (the niche focus of your program, not just today but for the long haul), record your first broadcast, create an MP3 file of the broadcast, and post it on the Internet. Okay, you need to know a few things about each of those steps, so this task is not quite as simple as we're making it sound, but it's pretty painless.

WHERE TO GO FOR MORE ADVICE ON STARTING A PODCAST

One of the best resources for developing a podcast is the advice provided by podcasting expert Jason Van Orden at his site www.how-to-podcast-tutorial.com. He offers easy-to-follow, free advice about getting started in podcasting. Although Jason does also sell products and services through his site, including a course on professional podcasting, we have been impressed by the truly useful, detailed advice offered on his site without bombarding readers with sales pitches for the money-making products.

How Webinars Work

Another option for getting your voice heard is to conduct or be a guest presenter in a webinar, which is essentially a seminar held on the Web or through a combination of Web and telephone. Webinars are typically held live, meaning that there is a start and end time, and your audience is listening to you while you're online and on the phone, rather than in a recorded session at a later time. Some webinars are recorded and archived on a website, however, for those who cannot attend the live event.

True webinars are entirely Internet based. They use Web conferencing technology that employs Voice Over Internet Protocol (VoIP) for the presenters' voices to be conveyed computer-to-computer with no need for telephones. This audio component is complemented by a visual presentation online that typically resembles a PowerPoint slide presentation. Other webinars combine telephone conference calling for the audio portion with Web-based visual presentation.

Webinars are extremely convenient for both presenters and attendees. You can participate from anywhere that you have Internet access, and a telephone, or a working microphone and speakers if the audio portion is through VoIP. Another benefit of webinars is that they can be

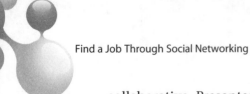

collaborative. Presenters can poll and survey the audience during the event, and attendees can ask questions, either by typing them online or speaking in a live chat.

TIP

WebEx (www.webex.com), Microsoft's Live Meeting (http://office.microsoft.com/en-us/livemeeting), and GoToMeeting (www.gotomeeting.com) are three of your best bets for Web conferencing services.

Whether through podcasting or webinars, you can make your presence known online and connect with many people, so we encourage you to consider speaking opportunities as part of your social networking strategy.

As you can see from the technologies surveyed in this chapter, there's something for everyone when it comes to networking online. Whether you prefer to write or speak, be the ringleader, or just be in the peanut gallery, you'll find a place to connect with others and build your reputation online.

Key Points: Chapter 9

- Joining identity-management sites such as Naymz and Ziggs is a great way to control your online identity.

- By joining discussion groups, you can gain visibility and forge relationships with like-minded professionals.

- Publishing e-newsletters, online articles, book reviews, and other online content is a great way to demonstrate and share your knowledge.

- Internet-based public speaking, including webinars and podcasts, establishes you as a thought leader in your field and can significantly expand the size of your network.

CHAPTER 10

Growing Your Social Networks

When we wrote the first edition of this book two years ago, we based the content largely on our own experiences in social networking, research we'd done, and consultations with some other authors and social media experts. We used a different approach to write this edition. As the ways to use online tools for networking have broadened, we wanted you to have a broader perspective on the topic. So, we connected with thousands of job seekers, recently landed job candidates, career coaches, and, yes, more authors and social media experts. You've seen some of their stories and advice in earlier chapters. Plus, we've compiled lots of success stories in Appendix B. We didn't want you to hear it just from us!

You know by now that we are passionate about social networking. We hope that has come through in our enthusiastic comments about using social media for job search and career development. You've also now heard that same passion and enthusiasm from others, too. Even those who started dabbling in social networking with some trepidation quickly became converts.

Sure, some still have concerns about privacy issues or not finding the right people just yet on their sites of choice. That's to be expected. All that means is that some folks may abandon one site, finding it doesn't fit their needs, but they aren't backing away from social networking entirely. It's working for them on many levels. We're convinced it will work for you, too!

You may be feeling a little overwhelmed right now having read chapter after chapter about the various social networking options. This chapter puts all this information in perspective.

In This Chapter

- *Make social networking a part of your job search strategy.*
- *Identify your best social networking avenues.*
- *Get over any reluctance to network online.*
- *Re-energize your job search.*
- *Look ahead to social networking trends and forecasts.*

Make a Place for Social Networking in Your Job Search

If you are a job seeker or are simply trying to manage your career while working, you should embrace social networking in a big way. Social networking shouldn't be your only method of networking. But it should be a major part of your overall networking strategy.

Networking in general is the way most people land their new jobs. ExecuNet, the executive networking organization that hosts a website listing executive-level positions as well as local face-to-face networking meetings in major markets, says:

> For 18 years of ExecuNet market research and reporting, networking and connecting with key influencers in target companies has always created more executive job opportunities than any advertisements, print or online.

In our combined 30+ years of experience coaching people through job search, that's true not only for executive-level positions, but for all other levels of jobs as well. So if networking is the most productive activity for finding a job, then it makes sense that most of your job search time needs to be spent in networking activities. That means having lots of one-on-one conversations with members of your network, meeting new people (and existing contacts) at group events, and networking online.

QUOTE

While LinkedIn, Twitter, and Facebook have become the norm for job search now, there is no substitute for building a relationship with face-to-face networking.

—Russ Hanley, financial services executive

NOT LOOKING FOR A JOB RIGHT NOW?

Remember that social networking should be a key part of your overall career management strategy. In the current world of work, it's no longer good enough to be well known within your organization. With our global marketplace and the dynamic quality of the job market, all professionals need to build a presence outside of their companies, stay current, be easy to find, and be networked.

How much social networking is enough? How much social networking is too much? We've developed a quiz to help you assess your social networking needs and build a strategy around those needs.

Ellen and Diane's Social Media Quiz

Unsure how active you should be with social networking? Take this quick yes/no quiz, and then check our recommendations below.

1. Are you currently in an active job search?

2. Might you need to start an active job search in the next 12 months?

3. Does a Google (or other search engine) search of your name turn up too few hits?

4. Does a Google (or other search engine) search of your name turn up accurate but off-brand information?

5. Does a Google (or other search engine) search of your name turn up digital dirt?

6. Are you interested in exploring a new field?

7. Do you feel your professional network is too small?

8. Does your schedule make it difficult to attend in-person networking events?

9. Do you need to stay apprised of competitors' updates and activities?

10. Do you need to stay current with news and trends in your field?

11. Does your role include business development or sales?

12. Does your role include attracting new talent to your organization?

(continued)

(continued)

13. Does your role include sourcing of products or services?

14. Do you have a business or side business to promote?

15. Do you enjoy helping and mentoring others?

Count the Yes answers.

- **1–3:** Start with LinkedIn and make sure you are fully leveraging that site (chapter 5).

- **4–6:** In addition to LinkedIn, add another social network such as Plaxo, XING, or Viadeo (chapter 4).

- **7–9:** In addition to the sites above, try using Facebook for professional networking (chapter 6).

- **10–12:** Add another social media tool such as Twitter (chapter 7).

- **13–15**: You need it all! In addition to the above, start a blog using a platform that will sync to your LinkedIn profile (chapter 8). Consider joining discussion groups, delivering webinars, creating a video, or recording a podcast (chapter 9).

Wherever you sit in terms of the social media tools you need or want to use, look for ways to integrate your social networking activities. For example, consider having your tweets update your status on LinkedIn and Facebook. Make sure that your social networking strategies are supporting each other and your career goals.

Just remember that there is no one right way or one best site. There are relationships to be made and opportunities to be found on all social media platforms.

Overcome Your Social Networking Reluctance

Still not convinced or ready to jump into the social networking fray? Maybe you fit into one of the categories of people that Joshua Waldman has blogged about. He cites three reasons that people don't use social media:

1. **I am too old (or young).** Not a good reason! The fastest growth on Facebook is in the over-55 age demographic. And some of the best-selling Twitter books have been authored by people in their 50s. It's not an age thing. It's a willingness to try new things to get different results.

   Andy Headworth, Sirona Consulting, has a compelling photo in a PowerPoint presentation entitled "How to Use Social Media to Grow Your Business." The caption is simply "Don't...." The photo shows a man in a business suit in the desert with his head completely buried in the sand. You get the message. Ignoring social networking is bad for business and for job search and career management, too.

2. **I don't like spending time in front of computers.** Not a good reason! You can control how much time you spend online. The key is to develop a social networking plan. Use social networking to build online relationships that you can move offline. At some point you do need to get off the computer and meet people face-to-face.

   In terms of time management, keep in mind that most of the time involved in social networking is up front. In other words, it takes time to build your profile and grow your network on each site. But once you are up and running on each site and in more of a "maintenance" mode, social networking does not have to be time consuming at all. Granted, we are not in a current job search, but we use our social networking contacts heavily to help a large number of our job seeker clients. And on a daily basis, we typically spend no more than 10 or 15 minutes to update our status, search for contacts for clients, and forward requests for introductions. You can accomplish so much so quickly. You'll be amazed.

   Many career coaches now believe that social networking is not only not a waste of time, but it's also more beneficial than any other tool.

3. **I am overwhelmed and don't know where to start.** We hope this book has answered these concerns. Armed with all of the information, advice, and strategies here, you can move forward with confidence.

Okay, so we admit it. If this is your first venture into social networking, having to use these new and unfamiliar tools is stressful. But they really are easy. Take it one day at a time, one social media tool at a time, and you'll soon find it working for you. You'll gain confidence quickly as you start to see the benefits!

Re-energize Your Job Search

Job search can be extremely stressful, especially if you're unemployed and need to land a new position as soon as possible, but want to take enough time to make sure it's the right position. This sort of life transition ranks right up there with the most stressful experiences in life—new marriage, divorce, death of a loved one, and moving (and some would add public speaking to that list!). Feeling down and depressed is a common reaction to this process.

We're not psychologists or licensed counselors, but we can certainly advise you to build some fun and stress-relieving activities into your weekly schedule. Being with other job seekers at networking groups can help to reassure you that you aren't alone. And draw on your friends and other professional contacts for emotional as well as job search support. Take care of yourself. And if you need some professional help to get you through this stressful time, don't hesitate to seek help from a local counselor or an employee assistance plan (EAP) that you might have as part of your benefits or severance package.

We've facilitated discussion groups to brainstorm ways to stay energized and out of the doldrums during the career transition process. We're sharing a list of ideas here that we hope will help you, too.

Take Care of Yourself

The rigors of job search can challenge even the most upbeat, energetic professional. To have the "staying power" and resilience you'll need for your search, you need to maintain your emotional, mental, and physical health:

- Take a break from your search periodically to re-energize.
- Plan some fun events that will make you feel good and build your energy and enthusiasm.

- Don't replay the negatives.

- Focus on things that are in your control; don't worry about the rest.

- Plan an activity at the end of your day that will serve as an incentive to maintain your focus and productivity.

- Realize that it's normal to go through a period of mourning for the loss of your job and allow yourself time for this. To move forward through this process, focus on next steps.

- Educate and enrich yourself: Read blogs, articles, and books.

- Use your computer to get useful information and connect with others, but use it wisely. Too much computer time can be counterproductive and isolating.

- Run each morning or pick another form of exercise you will stick with. Getting regular exercise releases endorphins and helps you get through the challenges of job search.

- Stay away from or limit your time with negative people. They can zap your energy and make it harder for you to stay positive.

- Be okay with asking others for help. Job search is humbling, even for the most qualified professionals. Allowing others to assist you could make a big difference in your emotional support.

Get Out!

There can be some real benefits to your job search by getting out and meeting others instead of staying home. Try these ideas:

- Do volunteer work.

- Help others; pay it forward. You'll end up feeling better about yourself and your value while helping someone else.

- Keep a schedule. Limit job search time to certain hours of the day, and then get out of the house.

- Go to a coffee house. Take your laptop to work among people. (We actually know someone who landed a job with a contact made at a Starbucks!)

- Go to association meetings focusing on topics of interest so that your group activities aren't all job seeker groups.

- Network with employed people, too.
- Change your environment if your home office isn't working for you.
- Meet with other job seekers in a library for study sessions.

Make the Most of the Job Search

Follow these practical tips to make your job search more effective and (dare we say it?) enjoyable:

- Let your network know that you are in transition. Informing them of your progress keeps them in the loop and gives them an opportunity to assist.
- Network without an agenda sometimes. It's productive to get together with others for reasons unrelated to job search.
- Complete a training program, get a new certification, or read materials to add to your credentials.
- Attend a conference or professional meeting.
- Remember your three greatest professional successes. Review them in your mind or reread your resume. Recall your recognition, awards, or bonuses as a way to shore up your self-confidence.
- Save encouraging emails and other messages.
- Look at old evaluations and performance reviews.
- If you don't get an offer, assume that it wasn't meant to be.
- Stay in touch with other people in transition as a reminder that you aren't alone in this process.
- Take the opportunity to enjoy this time with family and friends. Many people reflect on job search as a rare time they had to rekindle relationships.
- Remember: It's all around the corner for each of us.
- Meet with a career coach to assess search strategies.
- Don't just wait for updates from companies; follow up after interviews to determine status.
- Get up every morning as you always did for work.

- Set job search activity goals, and then reward yourself for completing tasks.
- Schedule information interviews just for data gathering.
- Reconnect with old friends.
- Find a buddy/accountability partner to do your job search with.
- Throw a party for all the people who are important to you. Let them know that you value their involvement in your life and your job search.
- Barter for services. You could save some money and this could be a "win-win" for both parties.
- Revisit with companies you removed from your target list earlier.
- Let people know you'd be available for contract or part-time work as well as full-time.
- Remember that life is about food, fun, and fellowship.

We don't expect that every single tip in these lists above will feel right to you or work for your situation. But do take some time to pick recommendations that are relevant to you and your needs and make them a regular part of your job search approach—and even more important, a regular part of your job search attitude!

Paying It Forward

Give to get, or pay it forward, is advice we just can't emphasize enough. All networking should be about helping each other, not just what you can get from the relationship.

 QUOTE

Don't be rude, don't be boring, and give to get.

—Andy Headworth, Sirona Consulting

A number of our clients, who are fully trained and up-to-speed on the latest job search techniques from their corporate-sponsored outplacement services, have started job search support groups at their churches as a way to help others and pay it forward (hat tips to Russ

Hanley, Ron DuBose, Susan Levy, Mark Clegg, and Bill Fleming). Our Atlanta friend and social networking enthusiast Keith Warrick is another great example of someone who is paying it forward. He concluded his job search successfully and now focuses on helping others who are still in job search by conducting training classes on LinkedIn and reviewing LinkedIn profiles for job seekers at a large Atlanta networking group. Keith is a firm believer that we need to facilitate the growth and development of others who pass our way.

QUOTE

More than ever today, as a job seeker, you have wonderful tools at your disposal, if you use them. Work a little bit every day on building, cultivating, nurturing, and communicating with your number one career asset…your network. Then watch the magic happen around you and to you.

—Andy Robinson, executive career coach

Consider Future Trends

This section addresses the bigger picture of social networking, the trends we are seeing in the social media landscape, and what we think the future holds. (Excuse us for a moment while we reach for the Windex to shine up our crystal ball!) Of course, we certainly don't claim to be able to predict the future, especially on the topic of social networking. Who just a few years ago could even have envisioned the concept and current popularity of Twitter except Twitter founders Jack Dorsey, Biz Stone, and Evan Williams? But we can at least discuss some of the trends and issues that are visible today and that will continue to drive growth and change in the near future.

The Growth of Social Media

First is growth. There has been explosive growth in the number of people using social networks in recent years. And the number of sites has exploded as well. *National Geographic* has even gotten into the discussion with an article and graphic in their March 2010 issue. Called "World Wide Friends," the article lists the largest social networks globally and shows graphically in which countries each is most popular. In chapter 4, we listed some of them. But any attempt at developing a comprehensive list would be out of date very quickly—not to

mention fill up too many pages in this book. We definitely expect this growth and rate of growth to continue.

Adam Ostrow of Mashable.com (a popular site that monitors trends in social networking) confirms our thinking on this topic:

> There are hundreds of millions of people on "the social web" and countless startups looking to either be the next huge social platform or to build a business by feeding into the ecosystem that the top players have created.

Homogeneity and Portability of Social Media

Ostrow points out two other important topics for discussion here: homogeneity and portability. *Homogeneity* refers to an "increasingly similar feature set, essentially the idea that you log in to a site like Facebook, Twitter, or LinkedIn and see a stream of recent activities—such as new status updates, photos, and events—from all your connections." Although the sites don't look the same, you can accomplish much the same things on all of them.

Portability means that social networking now travels with you wherever you go. Most sites have mobile applications, and users seem eager to have access wherever they are, according to a study by Nielsen. Facebook, Twitter, and YouTube all report high numbers and percentages of mobile application enthusiasts. Certainly advances in mobile phone technology have made this growth possible, and new advancements are on the forefront.

Then there is the growing trend of syncing up your sites. You can connect your Flickr, YouTube, and blog to Facebook. You can show your blog posts on your LinkedIn profile. And you can set your tweets on Twitter to automatically update your status on Facebook and LinkedIn. Whew!

Give careful thought to making these connections, however. On the one hand, these linkages can be a timesaver. One of our job search clients updates his Facebook and LinkedIn status from Twitter and is pleased with that process. But another contact stopped doing it. As a technology entrepreneur, he tweeted only about topics related to his business. It didn't take his Facebook friends long at all to tell him that they didn't really want to hear all that! So be mindful of your audiences on each of these platforms.

Managing the Flow of Information

Another issue everyone will need to deal with in the coming months and years is finding ways to manage the flow of all this information. In social networking, we constantly receive LinkedIn and Facebook updates and join in on Twitter conversations. We'll need to find helpful software applications to manage that stream. A couple of applications to watch are NutshellMail and Yoono.

In addition, you can choose how to customize your social networking activities by using tools to post blog comments back to social networks, share your location with others, and explore the ever-growing variety of mobile applications.

The increasing popularity of video is amplified by the ability to watch it on a variety of social media sites, including mobile platforms. Video sharing is taking on many forms including vlogs (video logs) and video biographies.

Organizations' Entry into Social Media

Another trend is the rapid adoption of social media strategies by companies and other organizations. Most of the Fortune 500 are now on Twitter. Companies large and small have Facebook pages. And other institutions are jumping on board now, too. Churches have Facebook pages, and schools communicate with students and parents on Facebook.

Just a few years ago, websites were putting smaller companies on a level playing field with larger players in their industry. Today, Facebook pages, company blogs, Twitter streams, and other social media tools are the new equalizers and offer opportunities for all organizations to communicate with their audience, attract and retain customers, promote their brand, engage their employees, and identify new talent for their local or global businesses.

Company attitudes toward social media are changing, too. A few years ago when we spoke at human resource meetings on social media topics, we heard a lot of questions about legal and compliance issues. Concerns about loss of employee productivity and sharing of proprietary company information seemed to dominate the question-and-answer discussions.

QUOTE

Job boards are now perceived as archaic and more for entry-level candidates. For middle management on up, these connections and leads are found through networking. Social media have helped ferment this. ADP has leveraged social media by appointing social media "ambassadors" to carry forth recruiting messages. As a result of this, they have had the best recruitment of leaders for the organization in years.

—Carrie Davis, Director of Staffing, ADP Canada

Today, there's much more acceptance and enthusiasm for social media in the workplace. According to a Manpower survey, 75 percent of employees still have no formal social media policy at work; however, things are changing quickly. And a Right Management survey confirmed that

workers are checking out prospective employers via social media tools to learn if they value and respect employees, making it critical for organizations to successfully factor social networks into their brand reputation activities.

From an organizational perspective, social media can play a positive role in productivity, collaboration, knowledge management, innovation practices, employee alignment and engagement, recruitment, reputation management, marketing/branding/PR, and even business continuity (ways for employees to communicate when other methods of communication don't work).

Companies still have a long way to go, though. As Shawn Butler, president of Relevant Social Media, points out, many organizations are still struggling to identify where the responsibility for social media lies in a company. Are they a marketing function (with responsibility for driving sales) or a PR and corporate communications function (with responsibility for driving brand image)? Shawn believes they are both. What social media have done, he says, is to "merge the two during the execution stage. Social media start as a marketing campaign, then turn into a public relations campaign, and are requiring a new blend of the two separate skill sets."

Personal Branding and Social Networking

Personal brands have become increasingly important as people have had to take full responsibility for managing their own careers. Companies no longer take responsibility for training and development. That's been obvious for a while and has become an even clearer and louder message through the economic downtown of the last couple of years. You can't rely on your company for career development and advancement. But you can take the steps needed—especially social networking—to promote your personal brand and to build strong relationships to help you with all aspects of career transition and decision making.

ExecuNet puts it this way in its *2010 Executive Job Market Intelligence Report*:

> Complacency doesn't serve the job seeker, nor does company growth and individual performance guarantee security, and the responsibility of driving a sustainable and rewarding career falls squarely on the executive. But this doesn't have to be a solo journey; the power to plan and engage in developing your career-long success rests on your ability to generate that trusted set of peers who can be your personal board of advisors on the job and whenever you are seeking a change.

Knowing and promoting your personal brand are critical today. We talked about this in chapter 3.

Nick Nanton, expert blogger whose posts are published in *Fast Company,* shares his thoughts about the importance of a personal brand:

> In the New Economy, some might say that our personal brands are increasingly important. We'd go further, saying they're all we've got left. Think about it. The Internet and technology have brought about the following changes:
>
> - Removed the barriers of information flow, allowing us to find anything we want, anytime we want it.
>
> - Made transparency a way of life, allowing the general public to piece together a story even if you aren't telling it yourself (you can't hide most things anymore if you wanted to!)
>
> - Leveled the playing field by giving everyone on Earth an instant platform to publish anything you can think of, including thoughts, muses, obsessions, hobbies, photos, videos, business ideas, invitations to social events, collaborative efforts, and more.

We've seen this technology bring about the rise of the personal brand, while we have simultaneously witnessed the downfall of the institutions that we grew up believing in.

Faith Popcorn of Brain Research (in marketing predictions for 2010) mentions the "icon toppling" too and the rising distrust of major corporations. People are looking for cultural institutions they can trust and seeking to connect with others on a deeper level.

Social Causes in Social Media

Another trend is social media for social good. Facebook is filled with discussions and messages about campaigns, causes, and issues.

QUOTE

A friend of mine has been battling breast cancer. Her daughter, a college junior, recently participated in the Relay for Life, dedicating her involvement to her "warrior mother." She set a goal to raise $100 but has now raised $1,514 by utilizing all the social media outlets. What an awesome example of the power of the message, the power of social media, and ultimately the power to transform communication into life-altering action.

—Ellen O. McCarty, president of McCarty & Co.

We could probably fill several chapters with what's ahead in social media and careers. The one thing that everyone agrees on is more change and rapid change!

Closing Thoughts

Social networking tools are just that—tools, not answers, not solutions. Don't get caught up with the technology of these sites but rather focus on the methodology and the application to your career objectives.

And you don't need to be the trendsetter. Although we immediately embraced LinkedIn and quickly saw the possibilities for job seekers, we weren't so convinced initially about Facebook and Twitter for professional networking. We jumped on to both of those sites early on to check them out. And we are certainly now believers and proponents, but we waited a bit to assess them before recommending them to our clients.

Even in the face of tough economic times, we see unprecedented career opportunities going forward. Most of our clients land jobs at least equal in scope and compensation to their old roles. Many land better jobs, ones they probably wouldn't have willingly left their old employers to seek out. In hindsight, they are often grateful to have been part of a reorganization or downsizing as that traumatic event positioned them for a better opportunity. So keep a good outlook. As ExecuNet reported recently, "Good successful leaders in today's economy are those who aren't defeated by the headlines but empowered by the hidden possibilities."

Finally, remember that social networking is still all about connecting with people. Vincent Wright, recruiter and power networker, summed it up for all of us by saying:

> These are times of important technological change. The reach and the possibilities are extraordinary....It's now easier than ever to reach hundreds, thousands, even millions of people. [Yet] there is one....little thing that we have to continue to master....how to be social to one another...how to work towards building friendships....It's NOT about the technologies. It's about human relationships.

We count all of you as our new friends and colleagues and send you our best wishes for social networking successes and rich and varied human relationships!

Key Points: Chapter 10

- Most jobs are found through networking, and social networking is a great way to build connections.

- There is no one-size-fits-all networking strategy.

- Learn from the success stories of "social networking converts" to move past any reluctance you might have to network online.

- Re-energize your job search with stress-relieving activities and new ways of networking and finding support.

- Pay it forward; always look for opportunities to give, not just get.

- Social networking is here to stay and will continue to grow and expand.

APPENDIX A

Recommended Resources

The resources listed here are intended to guide you further in your social networking efforts. Some resources have already been mentioned in chapters of this book but are listed again here, along with new ones, in one handy place for your convenience.

We've made every effort to provide up-to-date resources with staying power, but in this rapidly changing world of social networking, it is always possible that some sites may be defunct, books out of print, blogs shut down, or people out of business by the time you read this list. Many of the resources we've listed are free, but a few we've noted are fee based yet are still worth exploring.

These resources are organized into the following categories:

Assessments

Blogging

Books on Networking and Job Search

Career Advice

Discussion Groups

Domain Names and Websites

Microblogging and Twitter

Personal Branding and Identity Management

Professional Association Directories

Public Speaking, Publishing, and Podcasting

Search Engines

Social Networks and Social Media

Assessments

The websites listed here offer assessment exercises and tests, or direct you to other sites that offer them. These assessment tools can help you identify your strengths and other unique attributes that define your personal brand, as discussed in chapter 3.

The Keirsey Temperament Sorter: www.keirsey.com/personalityzone

The Myers-Briggs Type Indicator: www.mbticomplete.com (fee based)

Riley Guide: www.rileyguide.com/assess.html

The Self-Directed Search: www.self-directed-search.com (fee based)

Blogging

The following sites provide more information on blogs and blog hosting. Some are general resource sites that have blog contributors with expertise in social media; others allow sharing of blog content including video, music, and pictures.

Blogger: www.blogger.com

Movable Type: www.movabletype.com

SitePoint: www.sitepoint.com/blogs

TypePad: www.typepad.com

Vox: www.vox.com

WordPress: www.wordpress.com

These books on blogging are helpful:

Blogging for Dummies by Susannah Gardner and Shane Birley (Wiley, 2010)

Create Your Own Blog: 6 Easy Projects to Start Blogging Like a Pro by Tris Hussey (Sams Publishing, 2010)

ProBlogger: Blogging Your Way to Six-Figure Income by Darren Rowse and Chris Garrett (Wiley, 2010)

Books on Networking and Job Search

The Career Coward's Guide to Job Searching by Katy Piotrowski (JIST Publishing, 2009)

Eliminated! Now What?: Finding Your Way from Job-Loss Crisis to Career Resilience by Jean Baur (JIST Publishing, 2011)

I Found a Job!: Career Advice from Job Hunters Who Landed on Their Feet by Marcia Heroux Pounds (JIST Publishing, 2011)

Job Search Magic by Susan Britton Whitcomb (JIST Publishing, 2006)

Networking for Job Search and Career Success by Michelle Tullier (JIST Publishing, 2004)

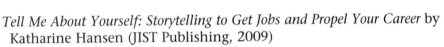

Tell Me About Yourself: Storytelling to Get Jobs and Propel Your Career by Katharine Hansen (JIST Publishing, 2009)

The Unofficial Guide to Landing a Job by Michelle Tullier (Wiley, 2005)

Career Advice

The following professional organizations include members who offer career counseling or coaching services to individuals to help with networking strategy, job search, and career management:

Career Collective: http://careercollective.net

Career Counselors Consortium: www.careercc.org

Career Directors International: www.careerdirectors.com

Career Management Alliance: www.careermanagementalliance.com

Career Success Community: www.CareerSuccessCommunity.com

Career Thought Leaders: www.careerthoughtleaders.com

National Career Development Association: www.ncda.org

Discussion Groups

Discussion groups are great places to meet like-minded people and share your opinions. In addition to these, don't forget to explore and join relevant groups on LinkedIn and Facebook.

Google: http://groups.google.com

Yahoo!: http://groups.yahoo.com

Domain Names and Websites

The following sites offer website hosting or useful information about website development, search engine optimization (SEO), or general Web trends:

BlueHost: www.bluehost.com

Brand.Build.Sell.: www.brandbuildsell.com

FatCow: www.fatcow.com

Get Page One: www.getpageone.com

GoDaddy: www.godaddy.com

iPage: www.ipage.com

Just Host: www.justhost.com

Microblogging and Twitter

These blogs and sites focus on Twitter or have some good resources and commentary about Twitter and microblogging:

Hashtags.org: www.hashtags.org/

Just Tweet It: http://justtweetit.com/

TweetDeck: http://tweetdeck.com/

TweetMeme: http://tweetmeme.com

Tagalus: http://tagal.us/

Tweet Hacking: http://tweethacking.com

Twellow: www.twellow.com

Twibs: http://twibs.com

The Twitter List Directory: http://mashable.com/twitterlists/

Twitdom: http://twitdom.com

These books can help you dive deeper into Twitter:

The Twitter Book by Tim O'Reilly and Sarah Milstein (O'Reilly Media, 2009)

Twitter for Dummies by Laura Fitton, Michael Gruen, and Leslie Poston (Wiley, 2010)

The Twitter Job Search Guide: Find a Job and Advance Your Career in Just 15 Minutes a Day by Susan Britton Whitcomb, Chandlee Bryan, and Deb Dib (JIST Publishing, 2010)

Twitter Power 2.0: How to Dominate Your Market One Tweet at a Time by Joel Comm (Wiley, 2010)

Personal Branding and Identity Management

The following sites will help you establish or manage your online identity and develop your personal brand:

15secondpitch.com: www.15secondpitch.com/new/

Intelius people search: http://search.intelius.com/

Naymz: www.naymz.com

QAlias: www.qalias.com

Reach Branding Club: www.reachbrandingclub.com

ReputationDefender: www.reputationdefender.com

Squidoo: www.squidoo.com

videoBIO: www.videobio.com

Wink: www.wink.com

Ziggs: www.ziggs.com

A good book on this topic is *Career Distinction* by William Arruda and Kirsten Dixson (Wiley, 2007).

Professional Association Directories

To find names and URLs of professional associations in various fields, check out the following:

Encyclopedia of Associations published by Gale Research Company (reference book available in many libraries)

Weddle's Association Directory: http://www.weddles.com/associations/index.cfm

Yahoo!: http://dir.yahoo.com/business_and_economy/organizations/professional

Public Speaking, Publishing, and Podcasting

These sites will help you get your written message published and your spoken words broadcast to enhance your online visibility:

Amazon book reviews: www.amazon.com

Constant Contact: www.constantcontact.com

GotoMeeting: www.gotomeeting.com

How to Podcast: www.how-to-podcast-tutorial.com

Microsoft's Live Meeting: http://office.microsoft.com/en-us/live-meeting/

TelSpan: www.telspan.com

WebEx: www.webex.com

Wikipedia: www.wikipedia.org

Search Engines

The following are portals for searching the Web:

About: www.about.com

AlltheWeb: www.alltheweb.com

Alltop: http://alltop.com

AltaVista: www.altavista.com

Ask: www.ask.com

Bing: www.bing.com

ChaCha: www.chacha.com

Dogpile: www.dogpile.com

GigaBlast: www.gigablast.com

Google: www.google.com

Google Alert: www.google.com/alerts

MSN: www.msn.com

SearchEngineWatch.com: www.searchenginewatch.com

Technorati: www.technorati.com

Yahoo!: www.yahoo.com

Social Networks and Social Media

Use one or more of the following social networking sites to develop mutually beneficial professional relationships:

Biznik: www.biznik.com

BrazenCareerist: www.brazencareerist.com

Bright Circles: www.brightcircles.com

Ecademy: www.ecademy.com

ExecuNet: www.execunet.com

Facebook: www.facebook.com

Fast Pitch: http://fastpitchnetworking.com

Go BIG Network: www.gobignetwork.com

LinkedIn: www.linkedin.com

Network 2 Connect: www.network2connect.com

Networking for Professionals: www.networkingforprofessionals.com

Plaxo: www.plaxo.com

Ryze: www.ryze.com

SageSpark: www.sagespark.com

Spoke: www.spoke.com

Viadeo: www.viadeo.com

XING: www.xing.com

This site helps you learn more about Facebook:

All Facebook: www.allfacebook.com

These sites help you learn more about LinkedIn:

The LinkedIn Blog: http://blog.linkedin.com

OpenNetworker: www.opennetworker.com

These sites help you learn more about social networking and social media in general as well as some technology trends:

MakeUseOf: www.makeuseof.com

Mashable: www.mashable.com

Social Media Examiner: www.socialmediaexaminer.com

Social Media Guide: http://thesocialmediaguide.com.au

Social Media Sonar: http://socialmediasonar.com/

Social Media Today: www.socialmediatoday.com/

TechCrunch: www.techcrunch.com

We recommend these books on social networks:

Get Connected: The Social Networking Toolkit for Business by Starr Hall and Chadd Rosenberg (Entrepreneur Press, 2009)

The Social Media Bible by Lon Safko and David K. Brake (Wiley, 2009)

Social Media Marketing for Dummies by Shiv Singh (Wiley, 2009)

Social Media Strategies for Professionals and Their Firms: The Guide to Establishing Credibility and Accelerating Relationships by Michelle Golden (Wiley, 2010)

Social Networking Spaces: From Facebook to Twitter and Everything In Between by Todd Kelsey (APress, 2010)

APPENDIX B

Social Networking Success Stories

Alison Allen, instructional designer:

I read *Seven Days to Online Networking* [the first edition of this book] and began building my profile and network. I joined appropriate groups and one day noticed a request in one of the groups for consultants to work on a short-term project. One of my LinkedIn contacts had previously worked for the company, and she allowed me to mention her name. Following some emails and an interview, I was offered project work, which has continued beyond their original request!

Dulin W. Clark, Ph.D., associate director, MBA Career and Executive Coaching, Smeal College of Business, The Pennsylvania State University:

In our MBA program, we utilize LinkedIn on a regular basis for generating job and internship leads. We conduct a seminar on the utilization of social media sites in job search. Penn State University has an expansive alumni base, making tools such as LinkedIn critical for identifying and locating alumni who might share similar backgrounds and occupational interests. MBA students are able to showcase their experiences much like a "turbo-charged" resume and connect with recruiters and hiring managers who may be interested in their backgrounds and accomplishments. Some MBA students make a point to join discussion groups so they can delve into business issues that demonstrate their content knowledge. One ambitious MBA student with an interest in Renewable Energy joined three associations specific to new energy trends and started his own blog. He appears to have generated a great deal of traffic through his LinkedIn page and has made numerous contacts through his efforts.

Trudy Cox, business executive/management consultant:

Right after I finished my Executive MBA, I was promoted by American Express and relocated, first to Canada and then back to the U.S.

Unfortunately, due to these moves, I lost many of the ties I'd forged with my MBA classmates. Thanks to LinkedIn, I learned of a reunion where I reconnected with this very important network of colleagues—presidents of companies, corporate executives, consultants, and successful entrepreneurs.

Susan G:

I have just accepted a new position that I found using LinkedIn! Without a doubt, LinkedIn has been an essential tool in my job search. I became aware of the opening when it was posted on one of my groups' job boards. I would say 99 percent of the realistic open positions I have found have been through LinkedIn by using the Find a Job tab, by reconnecting with former associates, or by being forwarded positions by my connections on LinkedIn. Not to mention what a great tool it is to research companies and people at prospective companies. As an older employee (50+), it is essential to keep up with technology and use the tools available!

Scott Kelly, senior executive for a technology infrastructure practice:

I'm the poster boy for the mantra of "networking, networking, networking." I already had relationships in one of my target companies (and now new employer!). Several of those contacts suggested people "you need to call NOW." One of them was someone I knew by reputation only. I reached out to him on LinkedIn, and his response was nearly instantaneous, accompanied by a telephone meeting invitation where he said that "lots of folks here have said I need to get in touch with you." That came at a time when I really needed to hear that kind of a message, so it was very gratifying. Multiple interviews later, I received an offer. And it all began with a LinkedIn invite.

Beth Benatti Kennedy, career and leadership coach, Benatti Training & Development:

Most of my clients use LinkedIn, and the success is unbelievable! One client wanted to relocate from Boston to San Francisco. She came up with her dream list of companies there. Then she did a search on LinkedIn and found a recruiter for her top company. She contacted the recruiter; and in less than three weeks, they flew her to San Francisco for her interview. She landed the job! LinkedIn is no longer optional. It is a key ingredient to a successful, focused job search.

Barbara Limmer, consulting campaign director, Stewart, Cooper, & Coon:

I've had two clients get interviews and ultimately get jobs directly through their LinkedIn connections. In both cases, they submitted their resumes online in response to job postings, and received no response. They then searched their networks on LinkedIn to identify contacts at the companies and reached out to these contacts, who then got their resumes in front of the right people. They were called for interviews and ultimately received and accepted offers. If it wasn't for their networking through LinkedIn, they don't believe their resumes would have ever been noticed.

Tom Oder, Worldwide Editing:

Social media helped me retain a client. The client, a team of chiropractors who have trained 250 other chiropractors globally, wanted to add social media to their marketing mix. Working with a web designer and social media consultant, I set up and maintained a Facebook Fan page and Twitter site for the client. A surprise wasn't that the site proved popular, but the ways in which students wanted to use the sites. Almost immediately they requested seminar schedules and speaker information be posted on the sites as well as directions to the seminar locations. In addition to using social media for information of value, I suggested to the chiropractors that they initiate interactive exchanges with patients and prospective patients. For example, I suggested they post short and simple questions such as, "Back or neck?" or "Where does it hurt?" to start conversations.

Hamid Rouchdi, head of network and communication services development with leading aerospace firm:

LinkedIn was my only social networking tool, but I used it to advertise a new business as well as to conduct an international job search. I was able to tap into former colleagues and classmates worldwide to get recommendations and make connections. I was contacted by headhunters in Europe. It was a very effective means of communicating my skills and personal brand and a very easy way to network.

Sherri Segari, candidate marketing consultant, Stewart, Cooper, & Coon:

A friend posted a Facebook status update expressing that she was tired and depressed due to a six-month job search with no results. Almost immediately, one of her friends responded that her company needed to

fill a position and requested that she send in her resume. Her friend put in a good word for her. Two interviews later, she was hired. Six months this girl went day in, day out looking for work, and this one Facebook post changed everything.

Ed Springer, technical support engineer:

I applied online for two positions with a major company headquartered in Atlanta. I didn't have any connections there. So I searched LinkedIn and noticed two employees I worked with almost 20 years ago. One hand delivered my resume, and the second knew the hiring manager, which led to a face-to-face interview. Although the job was offered to an internal employee, it made for a smooth introduction. Now the hiring manager has called me to ask if I would be interested in a contract-to-hire position. Yes!

Index

A

achievements
- in self-marketing sound bites, 51–52
- update messages on LinkedIn, 120–121

advice
- soliciting, 21
- websites, 243

aggregator Web sites, 22

applications
- Facebook, 146–147
- LinkedIn, 121–123
- Twitter, 171–173

archives, 178

articles online, 218

assessment websites, 241–242

B

background checks, unofficial, 23

benefits of social networking, 3–9
- for business development, 25–29
- for job seekers, 20–25
- for people content with their jobs, 30–34.
  - *See also* non–job seekers

benefits of social networks, 69–71

Blog Link, 122

Blogger, 191

blogosphere, 179

blogrolls, 179, 203–204

blogs, 11–12, 176. *See also* microblogs
- adding links to LinkedIn, 87
- attracting clients/customers, 29
- benefits, 177–178
- building traffic, 200–205
  - with Twitter, 169
- commenting, 183–187
  - versus blogging, 181–183
- creating, 188–200
- features, 175–177
- future of, 205
- protocols/legality, 196
- vocabulary, 178–180
- websites, 242
- writing content, 195–198

Box.net Files, 122–123

brand
- communicating, 26
- future of social networking, 238–239
- online identity, 36–37, 43–48
- personal branding resources, 244–245

business development
- benefits of social networking, 25–29
- blogging for, 178
- LinkedIn updates, 121
- as networking goal, 62–63
- researching competitors, 106

business networking sites, 68–69, 72–74
- Facebook, business versus personal, 128–133

business partners, finding, 27

C

candidates, passive, 33

career advancement, 33

career advice websites, 243

career decisions, collecting information for, 32

career management as networking goal, 60–62

categories on blogs, 179, 204

chats, Twitter, 173

clients
- attracting, 26, 29
- finding, 28

collaborations, finding partners for, 27

comments on blogs, 179, 182–187

companies and social media, 236–237. *See also* employers

Company Buzz, 122

competitors, finding information about, 27–28

contact information, keeping up to date, 32

contacts
- finding, 4–5
- searching for on LinkedIn to follow on Twitter, 164–165

credibility, building, 8, 28
customers
    attracting, 26, 29
    finding, 28

D

demographics
    Facebook, 128–129
    LinkedIn, 79–81
digital dirt, 40–43
    blogging to cover, 181
digital trails, leaving, 25
disabilities, building relationships before revealing, 8
discussion groups, 15–16, 211–215
    websites, 243
domain names
    for blogs, 194–195
    websites, 243

E

EasyCV, 146
Ecademy, 73–74
electronic publishing, 215–219
elevator speeches. *See* self-marketing sound bites
email lists (targeted) versus discussion groups, 212
employers
    being visible to, 22–23
    finding specific people within targeted organizations, 21–22
    finding targets, 21
    researching, 106–107, 145
e-newsletters, 216–217
entrepreneurs
    benefits of social networking, 25–29
    LinkedIn updates, 121
    networking goals, 62–63
    researching competitors, 106
expertise
    asking/answering questions in LinkedIn, 117–119
    in self-marketing sound bites, 50
    showcasing, 32
    Twitter lists, 170–171
ezines, 217

F

Facebook, 73, 77
    advantages, 149
    applications, 146–147
    business versus personal networking site, 128–133
    comparing to Twitter, 152–153
    demographics, 128–129
    history, 127–128
    job search, 145
    joining, 133–134
    keeping up with, 147–148
    network of friends
        contacting, 141–143
        joining groups, 145–146
        searching for, 139–140
    privacy, 135, 138–139
    profile, 134–137
    recommendations, 144
    researching companies, 145
    update messages, 143–144
    website about, 246
fees, avoiding, 27–28
followings, building on Twitter, 168–169
freelancers
    benefits of social networking, 25–29
    LinkedIn updates, 121
    networking goals, 62–63
frozen accounts on LinkedIn, 96–97
full-service networks, 64–66

G

goals for networking, 57–64
Google
    googling self, 38–40
    searching for blogs, 184
Google discussion groups, 213–214
Google Presentation, 122
gravediggers (discussion groups), 215
groups, joining
    on Facebook, 145–146
    on LinkedIn, 114–117
growth of social media, 234–235

H

handles (Twitter), 157
health, maintaining during job search, 230–231
homogeneity of social networking, 235
hosted blog platforms, 190–193
HTML (HyperText Markup Language), 191
Huddle Workspaces, 122

I

identity-management sites, 14–15, 208–211, 244–245
information
    gathering, 21
        on Twitter, 165
    managing flow, 236
Inside Job, 146
investors, finding sources, 29
invitations to LinkedIn, 92–98

J

job boards versus social networking, 58
job search
    benefits of social networking, 20–25
    connecting with remote contacts, 111–114
    with Facebook, 145
    following people on Twitter, 166–167
    including social networking in, 226–228
    job-related tweets resources, 170
    with LinkedIn, 103–106
    as networking goal, 58–60
    re-energizing, 230–234
    researching companies, 106–107, 145
    resource books, 242–243
    searching for contacts, 108–110
    self-marketing sound bites, 54–55
    update messages on LinkedIn, 120–121
Jobs Indeed, 147
Jobster Career Network, 147

K

keywords
    in blogs, 180, 202–203
    in tweets, 162
knowledge
    asking/answering questions in LinkedIn, 117–119
    sharing, 33–34

L

legalities of blogs, 196
LinkedIn, 73–74
    applications, 121–123
    asking/answering questions, 117–119
    comparing to Twitter, 152–153
    demographics, 79–81
    frozen accounts, 96–97
    history, 79
    job search with, 103–106
    joining, 81–83
    keeping up with, 124–125
    network of contacts
        contacting if remote, 111–114
        inviting first-level connections, 92–98
        joining groups, 114–117
        searching for, 108–110
    profile, 83–91
    public speakng opportunities, 220
    recommendations, 99–144
    recruiter use of, 24
    researching companies, 106–107
    searching for contacts to follow on Twitter, 164–165
    syncing with Twitter, 169
    update messages, 120–121
    upgrades, 112
    websites about, 247
links to and from blogs, 179, 202
lists
    blogrolls, 203–204
    job search people to follow on Twitter, 167
    publishing online, 218–219
    targeted email lists versus discussion groups, 212
    on Twitter, 170–171
listservs, 218

M

MeetingWave, 146
microblogging websites, 244
microblogs, 12–13, 151. *See also* Twitter
moderators of discussion groups, 214–215
MonsterTRAK, 147
My Travel (TripIt), 122

N

names for blogs, 189
Naymz, 208–210
networking goals, 57–64
networking, resource books, 242–243
networking (traditional)
    maintaining networks, 30–32
    starting relationships online, 7
    versus social networking, 2–3
nonhosted blog platforms, 193–194
non–job seekers
    benefits of social networking for people
      content with their jobs, 30–34
    including social networking in career man-
      agement, 227
    keeping up with LinkedIn, 124–125
    LinkedIn updates, 121
    overcoming reluctance toward social net-
      working, 228–230
    paying it forward, 233
    researching competitors, 106
    self-marketing sound bites, 53, 55–56

O

online identity, 36–37
    assessing, 39–40
    defining brand through, 43–48
    digital dirt, 40–43
    searching for self, 37–38
    self-marketing sound bites, 48–56
online presence, 5–6
online public speaking, 17, 220–224
    websites, 245
online publishing, 16–17, 215–219
    websites, 245
OPBs (other people's blogs), 183

P

passive candidates, 33
paying it forward, 233
    retweeting, 163–164
permalinks to and from blogs, 179
personal branding. *See* brand
personal networking sites, 68–69
    Facebook, business versus personal, 128–133
personal qualities in self-marketing sound bites, 50

Plaxo, 77
podcasts, 221–223
    websites, 245
Polls (LinkedIn), 123
portability of social networking, 235
Portfolio Display, 123
posts on blogs, 179
privacy issues, 8
    on Facebook, 135, 138–139
    on LinkedIn, 62, 88–91
professional associations, 221
    directories, 245
professional networking sites. *See* business net-
    working sites
professional social networking. *See* social networks
profiles, 68
    developing on Facebook, 134–137
    developing on LinkedIn, 83–91
    developing on Twitter, 157–159
promiscuous linkers on LinkedIn, 97
protocols
    blog comments, 187
    blogs, 196
    LinkedIn, 125
    on social networks, 75–76
    Twitter, 155, 162–163
public speaking online, 17, 220–224
    websites, 245
publishing online, 16–17, 215–219
    websites, 245

Q–R

QAlias, 210–211
quality versus quantity networking on LinkedIn,
    97–98
Reading List (Amazon), 123
recommendations
    Facebook, 144
    LinkedIn, 99–103, 144
recruiters
    being visible to, 22–23
    use of LinkedIn, 24
re-energizing job search, 230–234
referrals, generating, 28
relationships, 3
    building with blog authors, 186–187
    ongoing support through job search, 25

retweeting, 163–164
screening people, 7
ReputationDefender, 43
retweeting, 163–164
RSS (Really Simple Syndication) feeds, 179
Ryze, 73–74

S

sales, strategic selling, 29
salespeople
benefits of social networking, 25–29
networking goals, 62–63
SAP Community Bio, 123
screening before relationship building, 7
search engines, 245–246
search engine optimization (SEO), 201–202
websites, 243
searching for self with, 38
searching
for blogs, 184
for self with search engines, 38
Twitter, 164–165
security issues, 8
self
blogging versus commenting, 183
searching for online, 37–38
self-marketing sound bites, 43–44
developing, 48–56
on LinkedIn, 86
server-side blog platforms, 193–194
sidebars on blogs, 180
SimplyHired Web site, 22
skills
in self-marketing sound bites, 49–50
showcasing, 32
writing, blogging versus commenting, 182
SlideShare Presentations, 122
social causes, 239
social networking
benefits. *See* benefits of social networking
definition, 2–3
future trends, 234–239
including in job search, 226–228
increases, 19
managing information flow, 236
overcoming reluctance toward, 228–230

success stories, 247–250
types, 9–17
versus social networks, 67–68
websites, 246–247
social networks, 10–11, 68. *See also* Facebook;
LinkedIn
benefits, 69–71
future, 76–77
major professional sites, 72–74
protocols, 75–76
resource books, 247
site features, 71–72
versus social networking, 67–68
spam issues, 8
Spoke, 77
standalone blog platforms, 193–194
STARS (strategists, targets, allied forces, role
models, supporters) system, 64–65
strategic selling, 29
support
ongoing through job search, 25
retweeting, 163–164

T

tags in blogs, 180, 202–203
targeted email lists versus discussion groups, 212
technical skills, showing off, 8
third-party services, down side of social networking, 27–28
time
blogging versus commenting, 183
limiting online, 8–9
managing online, 56
trackbacks on blogs, 180, 204
trends
keeping up with, 28
future of social networking, 234–239
trolls (discussion groups), 215
tweeps
following, 166–167
types, 154–155
tweet plans, 172–173
tweets, 152
job-related resources, 170
retweeting, 163–164
tweeting, 159–162

Tweets application, 123
tweetups, searching for, 164
Twitter, 152
   accessing tweets through LinkedIn, 122–123
   adding handle to LinkedIn, 87
   advanced features, 171–173
   attracting clients/customers, 29
   benefits, 153–154
   building a following, 168–169
   comparing to LinkedIn and Facebook, 152–153
   following people, 166–167
   job-related tweets resources, 170
   lists, 170–171
   objectives for using, 155–156
   profile, 157–159
   protocols, 155, 162–163
   resources about, 244
   retweeting, 163–164
   searching, 164–165
   tweeting, 159–162
   types of users, 154–155
   update messages on LinkedIn, 120
   vocabulary, 156–157
TypePad, 191–192

U–V

URLs (Uniform Resource Locators) for blogs, 194–195
value contributions in self-marketing sound bites, 53
venture capital, finding sources, 29
Viadeo, 73–74
visibility, increasing, 32

W

wants statements in self-marketing sound bites, 53
webfolios, 219
webinars, 223–224

websites
   adding links to LinkedIn, 87
   assessments, 241–242
   authors' favorite blogs, 12
   blog popularity voting, 203
   blogging, 242
   career advice, 243
   discussion groups, 212–214, 243
   domain names, 243
   hosted blog platforms, 191–193
   identity-management, 14–15, 208–211, 244–245
   job-related tweets resources, 170
   microblogging, 244
   personal branding, 244–245
   podcasts, 222, 245
   professional associations, 221, 245
   search engines, 245–246
   social networking, 246–247
   Twitter, 244
   Web conferencing services, 224
   wikis, 218
wikis, 177, 218
Wink, 210–211
WordPress, 122, 192–193
Work With Us (Jobvite), 146
worksheets
   Ellen and Diane's Social Media Quiz, 227–228
   Job Seeker's Sound Bite Template, 54
   What Have You Done for Us Lately?, 52
   Your Social Networking Goals, 63–64

X–Z

XING, 73–74
Yahoo! discussion groups, 213
YOYO (You're On Your Own), 6–7
Ziggs, 208, 210
Zoom Information, 77